LIFE AND LETTERS OF GEORGE JACOB HOLY(McCABE

Publisher's Note

The book descriptions we ask book-sellers to display prominently warn that this is an historic book with numerous typos, missing text or index and is not illustrated.

We scanned this book using character recognition software that includes an automated spell check. Our software is 99 percent accurate if the book is in good condition. However, we do understand that even one percent can be a very annoying number of typos! And sometimes all or part of a page is missing from our copy of a book. Or the paper may be so discolored from age that you can no longer read the type. Please accept our sincere apologies.

After we re-typeset and design a book, the page numbers change so the old index and table of contents no longer work. Therefore, we usually remove them.

Our books sell so few copies that you would have to pay hundreds of dollars to cover the cost of proof reading and fixing the typos, missing text and index. Therefore, whenever possible, we let our customers download a free copy of the original typo-free scanned book. Simply enter the barcode number from the back cover of the paperback in the Free Book form at www.general-books. net. You may also qualify for a free trial membership in our book club to download up to four books for free. Simply enter the barcode number from the back cover onto the membership form on the same page. The book club entitles you to select from more than a million books at no additional charge. Simply enter the title or subject onto the search form to find the books.

If you have any questions, could you please be so kind as to consult our Frequently Asked Questions page at www. general-books.net/faqs.cfm? You are also welcome to contact us there.

General Books LLC™, Memphis, USA, 2012. ISBN: 9780217232074.

※- ※- ※- ※- ※- ※- ※- ※-

LIFE AND LETTERS OF GEORGE JACOB HOLYOAKE CHAPTER I EARLY YEARS George Jacob Holyoake was born on April 13th, / £ 1 7 1817, and died on January 22nd, 1906. Between those & two dates lies one of the most adventurous and profitable stretches of social development that the world has ever traversed, and its story is in many respects the story of Holyoake. He became an "agitator," and his figure is discovered at all times somewhere in the van of nearly every progressist movement, to use his phrase, of his stirring age.

He has himself described a few of the more patent symptoms of social agitation that alarmed England in the very year of his birth, but he does not seem to have observed that he was brought into a world so fretful in its misery that its rulers had withdrawn its most sacred civic right. The Habeas Corpus Act had been suspended a few weeks before his birth. For nearly a generation the bond of patriotic feeling had held rich and poor together in a common hatred of the French. When that bond was undone, by the fall of Napoleon, they fell wide apart. In the north, troops of famished workers, their haggard faces lit by a desperate anger, walked the streets and lanes with a laconic " Bread or Vol. 1. B

Blood" on their rough banners. In the south, noblemen and statesmen recalled over their wine the stories that had been told them by fugitives from France in 1789. At a very early age Holyoake came to accept, and he never abandoned, the Owenite principle that "a man's character is made for him, not by him." There was much to be said for it as a theory of his own character of agitator.

Looking back from the heights of our comparative peace and prosperity today, we can easily understand the melancholy situation into which England had fallen at that time. Hardly had men hauled down the gay bunting, that had covered the land like a holiday-coat after Waterloo, when the industrial rebound set in; and on the suffering ranks of the workers was thrown a further army of disbanded soldiers and sailors and makers of war-material. Men had time and cause enough to think of England, and brood over the changes that had for some time been undoing the old order of industry. The enclosure of the commons—more than six million acres were enclosed during the reign of George III—and the concentration of agrarian capital had unseated the cheerful yeoman, and turned him into a sullen peasant. The home-industries, by which the mother and daughter had so long eked out the scanty wage of the father, were unable to compete with the diabolical engines of the mills. Indeed, these same engines were invading the country, and the use of agricultural machinery was making strong arms idle and strong hearts bitter. Wheat ran up (in 1816) from 52J. *6d.* to 103J. In their bare, overcrowded cottages they were dragging out a joyless existence on a thin diet of the coarsest bread and turnips and potatoes.

When they set out in hope for the new manufacturing centres, they found pale and infuriated groups of workers cursing the new conditions of industry. Philosophers were talking with enthusiasm of their beneficent yoking of the great wild forces of nature in the service of humanity. It had brought strange fortune to most of them. Employers had noticed that a child could, with sufficiently vigilant supervision, control the tamed energies of the machine; and children were plentiful. A crude system of poor-relief had encouraged the multiplication of infants, in wedlock and out of it. Poor-law guardians had large numbers of orphans, or reputed orphans, on their hands, and soon the tumbrils rolled northward in all haste with their loads of timid, wideeyed children for the mills. Stunted, worn, ill-fed boys and girls of eight years—often enough of seven, and sometimes six—were handed over to the manager. By working them fourteen hours a day (in most cases), herding them like sheep, and feeding them like pigs— but less abundantly, as their fat was not marketable— one could make much money. The natives were compelled to offer their own children. Their wage was one penny a day, and they brought down the parent's wage to a shilling. A family could live, and meet its patriotic share in the new national debt of 860,000,000, on less than ten shillings a week. In cellars without windows— for windows were taxed—and without drains, where doctor must pick his way warily to the bed of the feverpatient, two or three families could keep each other warm of a winter's night

So England was lit up at night by burning ricks, and gangs of black-faced men broke into the mills and wrecked the machinery and scattered the cloth along the lanes, and troops of dragoons coursed in every direction. The townjails were full of Luddites: the countryjails with men who had tried to snare a rabbit for their starving familieSr A grim, lean, cadaverous-tinted people looked with wild glare on the stately mansions of the old gentry and the flashing palaces of the new rich. Sons of cotton-spinners and squires met on the moors in broad daylight for exercise in cavalry manoeuvres and swinging of sabres. It was rumoured that their place was taken at night by ghostly bands with pikes and scythes. Land-owners sat uneasily in the London clubs, and looked out for the latest coaches from the north. From Manchester came, a month before Holyoake's birth, the thrilling story of the March of the Blanketeers. Three hundred half-starved men had set out to march on London, with blankets rolled up on their backs and "long knives"—long enough to cut their barley-bread with—hidden about their ragged persons: twenty of them had pushed through the screen of cavalry as far as Leek. "The March of the

Marseillais," nobles feverishly whispered. From the Midlands came the news of "the Derbyshire Insurrection ": which was happily stamped out by eighteen dragoons. Other insurrections were reported from other parts: generally by Governmentagents, who found them profitable.

The Government concluded that at least there was ground enough for a revolution in the state of the country. In March (1817) the Habeas Corpus Act was suspended, and His Majesty's officers were empowered to imprison any subject they thought fit, without a trial. The village-orators of the Hampden clubs restrained their sparkling flow. Even sturdy Cobbett fled to America, and for a time one missed the sight of the farm or factory-workers gathering in the barn or the public-house by candle-light round some literate youth who read out to them the sonorous appeals of the *Weekly Register,* which they had pooled their farthings to purchase. All cowered before "a tyranny not exceeded by any of the monarchs of the Holy Alliance." The dull-felt simmering and the occasional bubble alone told the temper of the nation.

Into this seething world was Holyoake born, two years after Waterloo and two years before Peterloo. He has written so fully, and with such charm, about the scene of his early years that there is little more to be told, and certainly no pleasanter way of telling it. His parents lived above the too common level of privation, but close enough to it—indeed they soon sank quite to it—to make him feel very early the need of agitators. His earliest recollections were of a quiet, well-ordered, and happy home. It was the first house in an almost rural little street (Inge St.) that is now in the heart of the dark blot on the map that stands for modern Birmingham. St. Martin's spire rose above the trees close by, and the green fields of Warwickshire spread almost to the door. In a few years he would hear the place ring with the roar of heated crowds and the dread clatter of cavalry, but as yet it had the drowsy stillness of an old-time village. A few

doors away lived a wartwitch, a keen-eyed old lady, who peeped out between green-silk curtains, thriving in the interregnum between persecution and science. His maternal grandfather was the parish-beadle, and wore a long blue coat with brass buttons, during official hours and when he was reading his Bible, and carried an imposing japanned staff. George often proudly made the round of the graves with him, and went with him to his garden up the Bristol Road at five in the morning, and lit his pipe for him with laborious flint and steel, and brimstone-match of "satanic fumes." His paternal grandfather he never saw. Losses of business—he had had a position of some small value—unsettled him and drove him to the north.

The account will be found most conveniently in the earlier chapters of his *Sixty Years of an Agitator's Life,* though I have generally drawn on earlier documents. He was the second child and eldest son in a family of thirteen.

The boy saw little of his father in the early years. Men often worked in those days from five in the morning until nine at night, with no half-day on Saturdays, and his father was a valued worker and foreman in a large foundry. His children saw him on Sundays, when he would don his drab breeches and long boots with white tops. He was a grave, kindly, thoughtful man: quite unlettered, but with intelligence, a feeling of dignity, a strong silent will, and more than ordinary skill at his work. He was never addressed by his fellow-workers in the familiar terms they used to each other, and he quietly neglected the customary ritual of homage to the masters. He had "a pagan mind," complying without a word in religious usages, but apparently thinking that Providence was so very exacting in the duties of this world that, if one attended soberly and well to these, one could not be far astray.

The mother was more actively religious in feeling. She was equally strong in character, and had a good share of practical capacity. Before her marriage she had one of the home-workshops that then abounded in Birmingham, and she kept it for some years after George Jacob's birth. With so many children to rear, she still controlled the business of making horn-buttons in the adjacent shed, until the larger methods of industry destroyed it. She was one of the last in Birmingham to surrender.

The joint industries and sober habits of his parents brought comfort to the home in his childhood. The year of his birth was a black one in the annals of Birmingham. The cessation of the demand for warmaterial had caused distress in the iron-trade, and at the same time the quartern loaf went up to *1s. 8d.*, and potatoes to *1s. 2d.* per peck. Even the skilled artisan, whose wage was two or three times that of the factoryhand, had little luxury beyond his large family in those days. However, the children could help in the buttonmaking, as George Jacob very quickly learned to do, and they lived well. He retained to the end a boyish recollection of stealing down one night to contemplate a sucking-pig, flanked by toothsome auxiliaries, in preparation for a festive supper. It was not until his twelfth year that their circumstances were straitened. But he was a delicate boy. His death was periodically shifted a few years ahead by the elderly prophets of the place: though few of their grand-children can have lived to hear of it. It is clear that he was thoughtful beyond his years and full of nervous energy.

Of his early education there is little to be said. Most of the children of his class still educated themselves and each other on the streets until their eighth or ninth year, when they became workers. But the school-question was taking shape. Sydney Smith said that " there was no other Protestant country in the world where education was so grossly and infamously neglected as in England," and philosophers and statesmen were trying to work out the problem, how far it was possible to reduce the criminality and coarseness of the people by schooling without giving them ideas "beyond their station in life." The Quaker Lancaster had founded the British and Foreign School Society in 1814; and its menace to the Church, with its

undenominational teaching, was met by Dr. Bell's "National Society for promoting the education of the poor in the principles of the Established Church." Robert Owen and his followers had initiated experiments in secular education. Vast numbers of Sunday Schools gave instruction— though of that, Mr. Kay says, " it will be most charitable to say little "—and many widows and other dames, who could read a little, and sometimes even write, earned a slender living by joining in the work.

The historian of Birmingham boasts of the schools of his town. About 1820 it had one blue-coat school, one National and one Lancastrian school—representing what the wags called "the fight of Bel and the Dragon "—a few dameschools and many Sunday Schools, to a population of 100,000 souls. Young Holyoake attended a dame's school for a time, as he states in a fragment of an early diary. The mistresses of these institutions were often unable to write their names. They gathered their dozen pupils in a ring about them in their cottages, and, with the interruption of domestic duties or attending to the shop, taught them to read the printed pages in the dialect of the district. The strain was not great, and at the age of seven or eight the boy began to earn his living in the evenings after school, by soldering the handles on lanterns. That he "often burned his fingers " we can well believe; but, when we remember the miserable pay of unskilled workers at the time, it is curious to hear that he came to earn 3*J. 6d.* a week at the work. For a time he controlled some new steammachinery for making buttons that his father had bought. His neck-kerchief was caught in this one day, and he was only saved from losing his head prematurely by a neighbour rushing in at his cries. He must have been in his eighth or ninth year at the time, as I find a letter of Smith and Hawkes, the owners of the Eagle Foundry, telling in 1849 that he has been in their employment for thirteen years. In his ninth year he began to accompany his father to the foundry at six in the morning.

For a few years the quick, nervous

boy had no other education but the founding and forging of metal and the day-long clangour of the shop. He very soon showed that he had his father's love of and skill in fine metalwork. But we may trace first the more direct influences in the formation of his mind and character. In his eleventh year he began to attend the Carr's Lane (Wesleyan) Sunday School. It seems to have been a little more advanced than many, as it had a sand-class— a class in which half a dozen children were taught the rudiments of writing by scrawls in a layer of fine sand. To this select circle Holyoake did not attain, though he attended the school for five years. He did no more than the customary reading of the Bible and Watts's hymns. The lessons were not made attractive. With one eye on the sluggish fingers of the clock and another on the sun struggling through the dull ground-glass windows he used to envy the boys who had not the privilege of a Sunday School.

His religious interest was quicker, and probably helped him more than the slight secular training. His mother attended at Carr's Lane, where the Rev. Angell James—whom he quite expected to have wings under his black coat— taught sturdy doctrines. The mother sent a thrill round the supper table one Sunday night by bringing home the assurance that there were children in hell not a span long. The boy shuddered at such doctrines, but his mother presently took him to a Baptist chapel nearer home, where the Rev. Mr. Cheadle expressed comforting doubts whether there was any hell at all. The discrepancies stimulated him, and he became an assiduous chapel-goer. Visiting ministers spoke of him as an " angel-child." In his twelfth year, however, his piety was seriously chilled. It was a year of commercial panic and great distress, and the means of the family suffered heavily. The rector of St. Martin's sent in his charge of fourpence for church-rate; but coppers were scarce, and were all needed to save a younger sister from death. The next week the charge came again, with a half-crown added for costs. Fearing that the bed might be taken from under the child, as a neighbour had experienced, the mother hurried to the office to pay. She was kept waiting for five hours, and found her child dead when she returned. George himself contracted rheumatic fever at her grave, and was very ill for six months.

Many of these details are from Miss S. D. Collet's sketch of his life, of which we shall see more later.

The incident probably lay like a charge of powder in the magazine of his memory, rather than had any explosive effect at the time, but we must remember that he was precocious. In his twelfth year he made with his own hands an elaborate model in steel of a fire-grate, which shone proudly on his mother's shelf. However, he continued his young pilgrimage among the chapels. By his fifteenth year he had advanced so far as to set foot in a Unitarian chapel; though he remained near the door, and kept an eye on the ceiling, so as to be able to escape if the roof fell on their terrible doctrines. On Sundays he prayed all day long at one place or other; and then there were mothers' meetings, at which the boy was asked to "engage in prayer," and Friday-night meetings, and endless others. The deacons of his original chapel warned him that a rolling stone gathers no moss, which was probably an encouragement to wander. In Inge Street was a small Paedo-Baptist Chapel— though "what that meant not a single worshipper knew"— and he was appointed teacher in its Sunday School. He had read Boston's *Fourfold State* and similar monumental works from his mother's shelf. At another time, when still a small boy, he used to go out to Harborne with John Collins (later Chartist lecturer and prisoner) to teach in a Congregationalist Sunday School. With a cold mutton-chop, thoughtfully provided by his mother, in his pocket, he used to take the hand of his big friend during the eight-mile walk through the snow. After his lesson and Collins's sermon were over, they went to the deacon's cottage to eat their dinner and contemplate "an almost invisible fire in a spacious grate." As each lesson, like each service, was opened by prayer, and

included prayer, and closed with prayer, there was much to his credit. He said long afterwards that his mind ached to think of it. He trusted that the Atonement covered "the sin of prayer."

But the vague wandering of his mental tendrils soon came to an end. One of his last religious experiences in the old order of ideas was to listen to a new and fiery preacher, whose pale thin face in its frame of long black hair gave him a prophetic value. He preached the allsufficiency of faith. The youth tested it by going to chapel without his coat in bad weather, and caught cold. Then he startled the prophet by coming to his home and demanding an explanation, which proved ambiguous. He turned to profane instructors. While educational theorists wrangled over methods, and the clergy fought for their theological interests in the schools, and the wealthy tried to determine what amount of schooling was compatible with the submissiveness of the worker, a band of reformers, headed by Dr. Birkbeck, founded the first Mechanics' Institution, at London in 1823. Lord (then Mr.) Brougham sent Dr. Coates to found one in Birmingham in 1825, and Holyoake found his way to this in his seventeenth year. It included a library, readingroom, and museum of mechanical models and scientific specimens. Lectures were delivered weekly, and classes were held nightly in mathematics, elementary science, drawing, Latin and French, and a few other subjects. Junior pupils paid *is. 6d.* a quarter, and adults three shillings. He elsewhere calls it Paedobaptist. But there are several small inaccuracies in his autobiographical volumes, and I have been at pains to trace the correct record. He also wrote verses in a religious magazine about this time.

In this admirable school Holyoake made rapid progress, under teachers who were as competent and anxious to form character as to inform the mind. One of the most energetic workers was William Pare, a follower of Robert Owen and afterwards Governor of Queenwood. His influence on Holyoake was indirect but decisive. More direct and valuable was the tuition of two Uni-

tarians, Daniel Wright and Hawkes Smith; though Smith was also a defender of Owen's social theories. Wright was a capable teacher, a vigorous political worker, and a man of culture and character. Young Holyoake used to walk home with him across the badlylit town at night, and won his regard. The Unitarians were not admitted to be a religious body in Birmingham, and they certainly had a secular tinge in comparison with their neighbours. Their Sunday School offered lessons in logic and mathematics, and they were well represented on the staff of the Institution. But they never pressed their critical views, and Holyoake passed almost unconsciously through a Unitarian stage before he became an Owenite. They were content to train the minds of the young men under their charge in habits of precise and fearless thinking, and they had a sufficient trust in the nature of things to feel that this would lead them into paths of truth.

Another movement of the time that helped to quicken the minds of the workers was the "Society for Promoting the Diffusion of Useful Knowledge." It was set afoot by Lord Russell, Mr. Brougham, William Allen, and a few others, who do not seem to have noticed how much the name might be conceived to reflect on the "Society for the Promotion of *Christian* Knowledge," which they copied. While even Cobbett looked with little favour on the education of the workers, they were convinced that a more intelligent people would tend to be less vicious. Their *Penny Magazine* soon reached a circulation of 200,000 copies a week, and they published also a *Penny Cyclopaedia,* an *Atlas, Journal of Education, Gallery of Portraits,* and other useful works at a low price. Their publications were convenient for the pupils of the Mechanics' Institutions, as the books used in the National and British schools were childish and ludicrous. In the course of time, however, the Society fell into disrepute with the workers. It would not fulfil its promise of educating them in social as well as physical science. Frederic the Great had said that he would not have a throne based on the ignorance of his subjects. The French Revolution had obliterated whatever traces of that feeling remained in the minds of rulers. The Emperor of Austria was bluntly declaring that he wanted "good subjects," not learned ones. The Papacy extinguished for another thirty years every spark of interest in the dangerous science of political economy. In England a few, like Brougham and Russell, were compromising. Mental and natural science they were prepared to encourage, but they dare not promote social studies. Yet they were teaching young men to demand them.

Holyoake made rapid progress in grammar, logic, mathematics, astronomy, and mechanics. His geometrical exercise-book, which is preserved, is a model of neatness, finish, and accuracy. Instruments were dear, and he made himself an elaborate and ingenious pair of compasses of sheet-iron. They were shown to Mr. Isaac Pitman in 1836, when he distributed the prizes, and he gave the youth a set of instruments, with the remark that "it was a pity a mastermind should be so crippled." He may have been amused when the slender youth of nineteen replied that he hoped to show his gratitude " by renewed exertions in the cause of science." How he kept his promise, and proudly reported on the November meteors to the Birmingham Philosophical Institution in the following year, we shall see later. But we have said enough of the formation of his mind up to his twentieth year. He was happy in his tutors and, for the age, in his opportunities. He was not wholly a self-made man. The clearness, precision, conscientiousness, and almost unfailing refinement of his later work have their germs in his character, but they were skilfully tended in their early growth.

In the meantime his education in the broader sense was proceeding even more rapidly than his schooling. Before he reaches his thirtieth year we shall find men of distinction in the metropolis taking counsel with him. No excellence of training would have brought the young white-smith to that position in the space of twelve years from his learning to write. There was something in the atmosphere of his life that forced his spirit more actively. Religious inquiry must have aided, though he never appreciated this; but it was chiefly the characters of industrial and political life at the time that quickened his observation.

The first feature of the life about him to fall with irritating effect on his mind was the condition of the workman. He had been working in the Eagle Foundry, with his father, since his ninth year, and had become a very promising mechanic. His little grate and his compasses showed skill and originality. He also invented a power-drill, the first that was known in the large iron-works. Friends had his name entered in George Stephenson's note-book, and one is tempted to think that an engineer of distinction was lost in him, whatever was gained. The work was thoroughly pleasant to him, but the conditions of work soon disgusted him. His father was respected in the foundry, but the treatment other men received gave him an impression of tyranny and injustice. A shopmate of good character was transported for ten years because he attempted to take away a file valued at a few coppers. Strong men hit their knuckles with their hammers from nervousness when the master was about. The more sober had to conceal any money they saved, and to dress badly, lest their wages should be reduced.

The Eagle Foundry, under Unitarian masters, was not an especially bad works; and the earlier law forbidding combinations of workers had been repealed in 1824, and a more moderate Act passed in 1825. Francis Place had been devising in his famous room at Charing Cross for ten years how to secure the right of combination, and he had triumphed just before Holyoake became a boywhitesmith. Unfortunately the years that followed were very lean ones in the calendar of trade and industry, and the new Trades' Societies brought little improvement. The strikes they initiated generally failed, and the distress became greater than ever. Iron was replacing wood in a thousand ways, and the new demand for iron rails (for trains) was of interest to Birmingham; yet, with the exception of 1823 and 1824, the fifteen years after the Peace were years of short work and great distress.

The precocious boy would quickly learn that he had entered a rebellious order. In the year that he became a worker there were large and bloody riots, especially in Lancashire. A thousand power-looms were broken up in broad daylight at Bury, and the waves spread to the eastern counties, to Scotland, and to Ireland. In the summer there was a terrible drought, and harrowing stories were read in the papers of people standing all night by the springs and fighting over the trickling streams. The jails were overcrowded, and were stinking hotbeds of fever. Men and youths were hanged in batches for crimes of a quite secondary order of social injury. Men sold their bodies to the surgeons, to get part of the price (about sixteen guineas) down; while body-snatching and the "finding" of dead bodies became a skilled industry. The ricks flamed nightly over the country. By 1830 the unchanging misery and gray prospect had engendered a feeling of revolution in the stronger workers, and almost obliterated the trace of humanity from the weaker. Trade Unionism had failed, men said. The weavers of Lancashire and Cheshire were earning from four to six shillings a week. Their children of seven and eight worked by their side for twelve hours a day. They had started in the early morning with a breakfast of rough bread and tea (generally an infusion of mint-leaves, often merely hot water coloured with burnt crusts), and at night, after a supper of potatoes, they flung their tired bodies undressed on the straw. Their parents knew only one relief when money *was* available—drink and, Ludlow and Jones say, "general unchastity." They left the public-houses late on Saturday night, and returned on Sunday morning.

"When the hour for church approached, the churchwardens, with long staves tipped with silver, sallied

Progress of the Working Classes, p. 17. Lloyd Jones was a Manchester working-man at the time. He tells how he and his neighbours had their pikes ready for the event of the Reform Bill not being passed in 1832. The helplessness and degradation of the bulk of the workers are amusingly shown in a story he tells. A Reform-Bill lecturer went out from Manchester to lecture in one of the large villages. As he drew near he saw streams of men pouring toward the village. At last he observed to one of them that there was likely to be a good meeting. "Nay, mon, it's nobbut a dog-feight," was the reply.

forth, and seized all the drunken and unkempt men they could lay their hands on; and these being carefully lodged, and a pew provided for them, were left to enjoy the sermon, whilst their captors usually adjourned to some tavern near at hand."

The peasantry were equally impoverished and debased. The reports supplied to the Government by magistrates related that the labourer's wage had fallen to *2.d.* a day in many places, whereas they could not keep felons on less than six shillings a week. The better-placed peasants earned about nine shillings a week (for the work of the whole family), and bread was *iod.* a quartern loaf. Artisans had much better pay, but work was scarce.

In these circumstances of the nation agitation was the moral duty of every thoughtful man, and young Holyoake learned his first lessons in that form of activity. There was a considerable body of men who had profited by the new education, and these, in increasing numbers, now joined in the demand for political reform. The suffrage was the magic wand that would turn the blighted land into an earthly paradise. They must root out corruption, and capture the field of politics. There were plenty of able leaders. Large towns like Birmingham and Manchester were not represented in Parliament, and their merchants chafed as much as their workmen. There had been a meeting of 60,000 people at Birmingham eleven years before to protest against its dis-

ability and propose a violent remedy. In 1830 the agitation for the Reform Bill surged through the land, and a sharp lad of thirteen received a first and impressive lesson in politics.

CHAPTER II GROWTH IN POLITICAL CONSCIOUSNESS

On October nth, 1830, all Birmingham was assisting in spirit at a remarkable dinner that was taking place in Mr. Beardsley's furniture-repository, not far from Inge Street The Birmingham Political Union was applauding the second French Revolution, the success of which they had just learned. The Union had been formed in 1830, and, electoral reform being the panacea of the hour in the workshops, its blue rosette quickly fluttered on thousands of breasts. Attwood, the Royalist-Radical banker, took the chair. Holyoake hints that Attwood's real interest in electoral reform was due to a notion that a reformed House might pass his novel financial scheme, but history shows that there was more depth and sincerity in his feeling. He was a sonorous orator and heroic political worker. It was computed that during a single election he kissed 8,000 women and a proportionate army of children. He now presided over the 3,700 diners, and when they were well warmed with band and chorus and ale—a pint of beer each to dinner and a quart afterwards—he courageously toasted the revolution which had "burst asunder the shackles that fifteen years of fraud, tyranny, and guilt had forged for the nations of Europe." The oratorical explosion rang through the county. Merchants, shopkeepers, and workmen poured into the ranks of the Union, until at length it numbered 200,000 members.

For the next eighteen months its bands, banners, and blue ribbons enlivened every corner of Birmingham, and Holyoake retained throughout life a vivid recollection of the wonderful meetings that were held. No citystate of ancient Greece ever throbbed with a more intense political life. Bramber, with a population of 97 sodden souls, returned two members to Parliament: Birmingham, with an alert population

of 100,000, was refused representation. Peasants flocked in from the villages about, to listen to the endless oratory of the beer-houses and fire the county with bucolic enthusiasm; and other Unions sprang up over the country. They adopted an ominous military form, and drilled and marched and countermarched with flags flying. But the military air was neatly explained. They were going, Attwood said, to supply the new king with an army twice as large and brave as that of Wellington, with which he could crush the borough-mongers who hampered his benevolent designs.

With the spring of 1831 began a year of agitation at Birmingham that is almost without parallel. In March eager crowds gather day and night at the stoppingplaces of the London coaches. Lord Russell's Bill is in the Commons. He is defeated, and appeals to the country, and the spires of Birmingham ring out their peals—men snatch the keys from the hands of reluctant clergymen—and the rainbow-garment of flags flutters gaily over the town. In September there is another outburst. The Bill has passed the Commons. What will the Lords do? There must be no vagueness about the people's mandate. The Union issues an invitation, and in a few days more than 100,000 men and women surge through the streets of the town, and up to the waste-ground on Newhall Hill, where there is a vast natural amphitheatre for their gatherings. "I have been told," Attwood roars over the arena, "that with all my immense power I shall not be able to control the oligarchs, but I answer, we will get 200,000 strings: we will place each of these strings in the hands of a strong and brave man: and we will twist those strings into a thousand ropes, and twist those ropes into one immense cable, and by means of that cable will put a hook into the nose of the leviathan, and guide and govern him at pleasure."

Already the Bill is in the Lords, and, as the five days wear on, men gather in crowds about the newspaperoffices and coach stations. "My days were passed within a few yards of the Union offices," Holyoake says. On October 8th the rumour flies that the coaches have brought no London papers, and the streets are full of grim debaters. At last the news comes that the Lords have rejected the Bill: the Bishops have turned the scale against it. There is no rioting at Birmingham; as there is at Canterbury, where the mob spits on the archbishop, or at Bristol, where they talk of converting the cathedral into a cavalry barracks. But the sextons of the town toll a funeral knell, and black flags fly at every spire and pinnacle.

In April the Lords pass the Bill, and propose to mutilate it in committee. That week thousands of copies of a pamphlet giving instruction in the use of fire-arms are sold in Birmingham, and iron-workers employ their leisure in shaping rods that look like pikes. The safety-valve must be opened again. All day long on Sunday, May 6th, blue-ribboned regiments of workers march along the roads to Birmingham from everywhere within forty miles. There are no railways yet in the Midlands. Dusty and tired, but with indomitable fire, they sing their war-songs, and find rough quarters for the night. At nine in the morning, like a great gray flood they sweep into the town—150,000 of them, with 200 bands and 700 banners—and swirl through the narrow streets, and spread over the familiar waste-ground, until every foot is hidden, and the line of houses round it is black with tiny heads. "Will you not rather die than be the slaves of the borough-mongers?" Attwood roars, and the echoing roar spreads over Birmingham. 'If we are to have Polignac," says another orator, "it shall be with Polignac's fate." His fate is fresh in everybody's memory in 1832. With mighty volume, and 200 bands, the great crowd raises the favourite hymn:—

"Lo, we answer! See, we come!
Quick at Freedoms holy calL"

Mr. Salt appeals to them to vow their purpose "in the face of Heaven and the God of justice and mercy." The word passes round. All hats are doffed, and 150,000 voices tumultuously repeat the fervent phrases: "With unbroken faith,

through every peril and privation, we here devote ourselves and our children to our country's cause."

There is little work done in Birmingham that week. Men line the routes of the mail-coaches on the Tuesday, and passengers shout down to them that the Government has been defeated. All work is abandoned, and pale, eager crowds throng the streets. An express-rider gallops in in the middle of the night. The King has accepted the resignation of the Cabinet, and sent for Wellington. Down in the mud, under heel, go the medals of the Union: they have "God Save the King" on them. Tory and Royal names of streets are torn down. The "King's Head" over the publichouses is swathed in crape: the "Queen's Head" ominously disappears. The bells are muffled this time. Five hundred of the most wealthy inhabitants, who have hitherto held aloof, now walk in procession to the Union rooms in Great Charles Street. "Newhall Hill at three" is the shrewd order, and "Come like brothers, arm in arm, wearing a noble aspect as men going to an assured victory." Like brothers they come, arm in arm, ten to fifteen abreast, to the familiar *agora.* Then they melt again into little groups, and any child in Birmingham can hear them telling of past days in England when there was civil war and men beheaded obstinate kings. They crowd round the barracks, where the Scots Greys, the hope of Wellington, are booted and saddled day and night, and supplied with ball-cartridge. Many of the soldiers belong to the Union, and they have dropped anonymous letters on the streets, saying that they will lift no arm against peaceful demonstrators. So they will be free to march on London. They will join other Unions, and camp on Hampstead Heath, and show the king what they mean.

On the Sunday morning (May 13th) thousands of them go to the barracks, where they have always been admitted in their holiday clothes. The gates are closed now, and through the bars they see the troopers rough-sharpening their swords—a thing not done since Waterloo. The march on London for that night

is countermanded, or replaced by a gathering of 200,000 on Newhall Hill. But their leaders are in London, with Francis Place. And on the Friday morning at six the town is awakened by the deafening, exultant clang of all its bells. Wellington is defeated: Grey is recalled: the King has yielded. Once more the streets are alive, and they march out to meet heroic Attwood, and then on to the Hill, where the banker-orator solemnly gives thanks to God for his country's escape "from a most tremendous revolution."

So our fathers won the suffrage; so Holyoake learned his first lesson in politics, and it sank deep. He was now turned fifteen, and an exceptionally thoughtful and impressionable lad. Such lessons, however, must have been largely subconscious in effect in 1832. As his mind developed, the vivid memories would find their logical place. And we have seen that the next five years were assiduously employed in training. He happily resisted the fascination of the language-classes at the Institution, and pursued studies of disciplinary value. Economic study would have been even more useful, but it was in almost as bad odour in England as in the Papal States. He says that during twenty years of his own recollection one needed as much courage to mention "social science" as to quote Darwin or Lyell. People seemed to have a remarkably definite conviction that a young man could not study the social order of England at that time without sinking into revolutionary sentiments. The Owenites would presently introduce him to that dark science; meantime he was learning precision of method and expression under good teachers.

It was from the industrial side that the next great educative impulse came to him. The workers returned to the bench in 1832 with unbounded trust in the Reformed Parliament, but as the months passed their note of confidence died away. It is not the place here to appraise the work or the failure of the new House. I need only observe that it was soon greeted with discontent. The *Westminster Review* called it "a donothing

Parliament, wavering between impotence and mischief." The workmen discovered that the "Worshipful Company of Ten-pound Householders " had no idea of extending the suffrage to themfelves.) Trade Unionism was restored to honour as the social panacea. A combination-fever spread through the industrial world, and young men were impressed by a ritual of initiation and thrilling pretence of secrecy that fitly represented the new magical power. One was taken blindfold into an inner room, giving mystic passwords, and then found oneself facing a skeleton or a large crude painting of death, while elderly brothers in surplices administered dire oaths, and others stood by with tin-foil battle-axes or real naked swords. Holyoake went through the performance.

Birmingham had, in fact, once more become the centre of the popular movement The new Unionism had fallen under the lead of Robert Owen, who seemed at last to be within reach of his noble ambition. He had persuaded the powerful Builders' Union to erect a grand institution at Birmingham, and at the end of 1833 they walked in gorgeous procession and laid its first stone. The frail, ineloquent cotton-spinner had become the idol of the workers. He had appealed in vain to masters and rulers to realise his national ideal, and now, after the failure of electoral reform, which he had slighted, he spread it amongst the people as a vast scheme of selfhelp. The *Pioneer,* a penny unstamped paper that the Owenites published at Birmingham, was read in every workshop. "At a very early period," it announced, "we shall find the idle possessor compelled to ask you to release him from his worthless holding." What the grand plan was, and how Holyoake enlisted in its advocacy, we shall see later; but the Owenite-Unionist scheme of 1833 was wrecked in a few months. Owen bubbled on from plan to plan. In January, 1834, founded a "Grand Consolidated Trades Union," and in a few weeks it had half a million members, but their oaths and ceremonies undid them. Two of their delegates, who fell into the hands of the police at Exeter, were found to be in possession of cutlasses, masks, white robes, and figures of death. A village-worker, who had ordered a six-foot picture of death for initiating purposes, was, with others, transported for seven years; and the Unions hastily dropped their theatrical properties, and fell into weakness.

It was in this atmosphere of sullen rebellion and this world of dramatic effort to evade or displace an oppressive burden that the youth's mind opened. He was at first repelled from extreme doctrines by their taint of Owenite heresy, and he held the more patient attitude of the church-goer. Before he was out of his teens this repugnance was worn away. It was not so much intellectual criticism that affected him as the apparent indifference of the Churches of his time to the poverty, suffering, and coarseness of the workers. The bitter experience of the death of his sister had—he afterwards stated during his trial—led him to consider what place the clergy occupied in relation to the national cry for social betterment. They seemed to be wholly silent "Our pastors and masters," he says somewhere, " held then the exclusive patent for improving the people, and, though they made poor use of it, they took good care that nobody infringed it." The Bishops had turned the scale against the Reform Bill, and they were equally opposed to all schemes of national education. Nor were the Nonconformist clergy more prominent or practical in their sympathy. They remained within the narrow field of ecclesiastical work, and gave little heed to the struggling movements for education, the freedom of the press, better conditions of labour, the reform of the jails and the penal code, the saving of the children, and the removal of municipal and political corruption. From Mr. Angell James, Holyoake heard that "young men must be content in the station and with the lot which Providence had assigned them." It was, therefore, natural that, as his interest in human affairs deepened, his attachment to the Churches insensibly diminished. They chose to move in a sphere apart.

But he retained his general religious belief until his twenty-fourth year. There was grave shaking of heads over his association with the Unitarians; but his tutors never sought to alter his creed, and he thought that "three Gods were not too many to attend to the affairs of this vast universe." It was reserved for a second great wave of feeling to wash away the last traces of his belief.

Thus his mind grew toward its maturity in a world of large intellectual incitements. Everybody felt that the key to the golden age was on the eve of being discovered, and there were yearly announcements of the discovery. Strict Owenites found it in the secular formation of character: followers of Mr. Ashley put their hope in the passing of the Factory Acts: Cobbett had faith in electoral reform: Russell and Brougham in education: Trade Unionists in combination. Others advocated reform of diet: one reformer going about with pockets bulging with grey peas, which were *his* panacea. One poor enthusiast went about bravely in a white robe, telling people they were already in heaven, and death and suffering were an illusion. Co-operative Societies were known in many places, and Labour Exchanges, and Halls of Science. Richard Carlile had a too drastic remedy in his scheme of "Somatopsychonoologia." A *Co-operative Magazine* (London) pleaded that the trepidations of courtship were the radical evil, and proposed to start the new world by marrying a hundred handsome tailors by ballot to a hundred handsome young ladies. Another Owenite invented a "Satanic mitrailleuse," which was to make an end of war and heal the world.

The first of all these philanthropic schemes to engage Holyoake's attention, and lead him to a definite vein of thought, was phrenology. Gall and Spurzheim had visited England, and by this time there were thirty societies in the country, with several journals. Archbishop Whateley embraced it, so that the current charge of materialism could be met. Spurzheim had initiated George Combe to the mysteries, and in 1838 that apostle visited Birmingham.

He had married a wife on phrenological principles, and the happy issue confirmed his belief; though critics reminded each other that the lady had 800 a year. Holyoake had read his work, *The Constitution of Man,* and eagerly accepted the position of assistant during his course of fourteen lectures. He bared his head courageously to the expert for proof of his suitability to hold up the casts to the audience during demonstrations. The material recompense of his work was slight. Combe gave him a cheap edition of his *Elements of Phrenology* and a nose-less bust that would not go into his box on leaving. When others hinted that he ought to have a fraction of Combe's large receipts, and wrote Combe to that effect, the phrenologist shook his admiration by replying that there was no contract, and that the young man "had imperfectly held up the casts." The imputation was felt to be severe, and Holyoake for eight years afterwards carried about with him a polite letter to Mr. Combe, whom he at last met and forced to retract (but not pay) in Scotland in 1846. The letter, dated August 1838, lies before me—probably the most widely travelled of all epistles. The young man complains that he was engaged for only one hour each evening and occupied for three. "It appears," he says, " you deem it unbecoming in me to form an Expectation, and presumptuous to make a Claim; but were I to do the latter Custom would sanction it and Gentlemanly feeling would give it immediate attention." As to the imperfect holding of the casts, "without any strong manifestation of No. 10 I believe myself perfectly capable of holding up a lump of Plaster to the gaze of any assembly that ever met to hear your lecture." When he ran Combe to earth in 1846 that gentleman haughtily replied that he was "the only assistant who ever hinted that he expected a pecuniary remuneration or who would not have felt affronted at my offering to pay them.' They seem to have met on equal ground about 1850, and Holyoake writes of Combe with respect.

When Combe's friend and bust-maker, Bally, afterwards treated him with worse meanness, Holyoake's enthusiasm was damped, yet the experience was important. Combe was a liberal thinker; not at all atheistic, but without belief in the creeds, and a strong advocate of the material basis of mind and character. His didactic and apparently scientific manner impressed the young man, and prepared him for the great Owenite dogma that "man's character is made for him and not by him." The train of thought suggested—though much attacked in the *New Moral World*—was followed keenly by Holyoake and his fellow-pupils, who had abandoned their classes at the Mechanics' Institute to follow the lectures. They got skulls of animals and puzzled over marks of cerebrum and cerebellum. A Churchman, Dr. Brindley, attacked phrenology, and the reply from Holyoake's Unitarian tutor was so decisive that the young man moved slowly nearer to Owenism, which Mr. Hawkes Smith equally defended.

From his twentieth year (1837) we trace his growth with some ease, as the innumerable letters and papers he has left behind go back to that date. He is on the Committee of the Mechanics' Institute, and evidently known in Birmingham. In November he watches the shower of meteors on behalf of the Philosophical Institution. After working all day in the foundry, he remains on its roof all night, for three consecutive nights, mapping the shooting-stars. The cold he caught and the need to purchase medicine for himself and colleague were quite on the lines of scientific research, as one read in biographies, and a letter of thanks from a Philosophical Institution was recompense enough; though the philosophers awarded him a guinea also for the same work in 1838 and 1839. It is clear, too, that he was already well known amongst the Owenites; but his connection with this school is so important a link between the old reform-ideas and his later views that I reserve it for continuous treatment.

His health began to fail under the strain of study, work, and investigation. Down to the summer of 1838 he worked as iron-workers did in those days. Since 1834 he had in addition devoted the whole evening to study. After a hurried tea every night he retired to the attic and bent over his books from seven until midnight, often until two or three in the morning. After a time he went so far as to spend a whole night studying by candle-light once a week. He copied out two or three mathematical works with all their diagrams and a lavish embroidery of fancy penmanship, and evolved an elaborate system of memory-training that proved remarkably effective. On Sundays he added teaching-work, and gave lessons in logic and grammar at the Unitarian school. In later years, when he was asked the secret of his longevity, he explained, quite seriously, that he had always "avoided excess in food, in pleasure, in *work,* and in expectation." The truth was that he nearly killed himself in his youth. His health began to suffer after the phrenological evenings, and an unpleasant experience with the phrenologist's friend proved the last straw. This M. Bally, an "evasive Swiss," induced Holyoake to bring him customers, and promised to make a plaster-cast of his own head in reward.

"At last the auspicious morning arrived when I was to be immortalised in plaster. My hair was combed in appropriate order. I had put on our best family face, for my ancestors had pride of race. At last the factory-bell rang nine. Between that and ten breakfast had to be eaten, Bally to be visited, and the cast to be taken. But breakfast that morning took little time. I soon left the Old Wharf wall (above which the Foundry stood), vaulted along Paradise Street (I still speak of Birmingham), and by a quarter past nine I was in Upper Temple Street at M. Bally's door. A ring of the bell brought the maid down, who informed me that M. Bally had gone to Manchester the day before."

It was not long before his nerves broke down, and, as the doctor recommended a walking-tour, he decided to go to Manchester on foot in search of the Swiss. He started, with five pounds in his pocket, on September 3rd, 1838. He lodged in cottages, dispensed with breakfast, expended twopence on a midday meal, and had a basin of milk for supper. His experiences were pleasant, as country-people welcomed the talk of "a pale-faced young traveller of unforbidding aspect, and his head full of town-ideas." Derbyshire showed him hills and glens for the first time. At last he reached Manchester, and at once sought the Social Institute in Salford. He explains that his name would be known to the Owenites through their journal, the *New Moral World,* though I do not find his name in it until 1840. That night he tossed in fever at a Socialist friend's house, but it was only a matter of fatigue, and he found M. Bally the next morning. The encounter was characteristic. With the fine restraint and quaint moral dignity that distinguished him throughout life on such occasions he delivered a brief and quiet ethical address on the door-step to the confused absconder, and politely wished him good-morning. In his diary he relates that he saw Robert Owen at Manchester.

The rest of his tour must be read in his own lively *Sixty Years of an Agitator's Life,* I, 67.

narrative. He went in a canal-boat to Liverpool, spent "enchanted days" amongst the docks, and at last boarded a small steamer for the Isle of Man. As he awaited the sailing, he was hailed from the quay, and found the Liverpool Social Missionary (Owenite) looking for him. It is clear that he was somehow well known amongst them. At Douglas he made a second venture in journalism. He wrote a letter to *Mona's Herald* (not the *Manx Herald,* as he states) on Mechanics' Institutions, and received a roast chicken and a bottle of port for payment. As the letter (dated September 24th, 1838) is very brief and meagre, the pay was princely, as such things go; but he seems to have impressed them as a distinguished visitor in Mona. How he wandered on foot through Wales, taking a boat from Douglas to Bangor, and fell in with a group of Coventry tailors doing the same *grand tour,* and cheerfully clubbed with them, and at last reached Birmingham, after five weeks' absence, with a few shillings left out of his five

pounds—all this he has told in his own sparkling way, and I may not repeat it. It is one of the most piquant narratives of the *Wander-Jahre* of young philosophers.

He returned to the foundry for the winter, but his health was not completely restored, and, though the swing of the hammer ever remained a pleasure to him, his mind had outgrown the narrow world of the workshop. For some time, indeed, he dreamed of emigration, either to India or to Australia. In the following spring he married the lady who was to share his hardships so bravely and his honours so modestly in the ensuing years. He had had an experience of courtship a few years before that brings him nearer to us, perhaps, in his youth than anything else he has recorded. A pretty *Sixty Years,* Vol. I, chs. xiv and xv. I have made some corrections on the authority of his early diary.

girl came into the foundry one day in his eighteenth year, and he fell in love with her at sight for her "gipsy beauty." He courted her for two years, but failed to obtain a single solitary walk with her. Then he determined to seek philosophic solace in his books, and wrote to tell her so. He was called to the door a few days afterwards, and found the blushing "Zingara" standing there. She dropped his opened letter nervously on the door-step, and turned away. He walked in silence by her side to her home, but their natures were veiled in too tremulous a sensitiveness for them to see and act in the natural way. He did not see her again until he was summoned to her death-bed.

His second love-story began and proceeded on lines on which a young bookworm could move more easily. It engaged his scholastic interest. At the Unitarian book-store kept by Mr. Belcher he found a young lady in service whom he grew to regard as a likely "partner in propagandism." She read *Chambers' Journal,* and had ideas and self-possession. I find a letter in which Mr. Belcher speaks of her with warm praise, after five years' service in his establishment. A young lady who wrote letters like this could come nearer to

such a young man than the poor "Zingara ":

"As to the famine, on account of which a fast is ordered, I am disposed to think that by the time it reaches her Majesty there will be other means resorted to for its removal than praying, and more honest and manly means might be resorted to on the present occasion. I question whether the famine much affects the landowners. Why not allow the land to be cultivated for the support of poor wretches who are suffering, instead of idly praying? It does not say much for the humanity of the Being the people are directed to call upon if the sight of their misery does not elicit His attention without a formal prayer."

This is the kind of language for which Holyoake would go to jail in a couple of years. They were married in the registry-office, a bold and ominous innovation in their families. One of the Owenite leaders, William Pare, had been appointed registrar; for which Birmingham was roundly denounced in the House of Lords, and brought to repentance, by the Bishop of Exeter. The marriage was a most happy one, and the partnership in feeling, suffering, and action was complete. "I can fancy," an Owenite friend wrote him from Coventry, "that I see you seated beside your intellectual companion working out a problem in mathematics, or giving or receiving other general instruction. Oh! what a delightful contemplation. The imagination may dwell upon it for hours, and the knowledge that such cases are very rare should make the prize more valuable." The spectacle was imaginary, but Holyoake ever esteemed the "prize" he had chosen, in Owenite fashion, with his "moral and intellectual faculties." Mrs. Holyoake never entirely shared his agnosticism, but she urged him to be honest and fearless. "Do what you think right, and never mind me."

The marriage took place on March 10th, 1839. Holyoake had warned the young lady that he contemplated a career of some adventure and risk, and she very quickly had cause to appreciate it. Early in July we find him applying to the Birmingham Botanical Garden for the position of lodge-keeper. His employers, Mr. Belcher, the Unitarians, the Mechanics' Institute, and the Philosophical Institution, warmly supported his candidature, but it does not seem to have succeeded. However, he left the iron-works, and for two years his position was very precarious. In August or September he was employed as guide at an exhibition of machinery that was held at Birmingham. His father (so his sister Vol. 1. D states) was one of the founders of the Exhibition, and his little steel grate was amongst the exhibits. He there made the acquaintance of Lieut. Lecount (R.N.), who startled Birmingham clergymen with "naval oaths of rotund quality and explosive as shells." Lecount was the author of *A Hunt after the Devil,* and afterwards contributed at times to Holyoake's paper. Before the exhibition was over his tutor, Mr. Wright, died suddenly, and Holyoake was appointed to succeed him at the Mechanics' Institute. The pupils of the senior classes themselves petitioned for the appointment. "In our opinion," they write, "there is no individual so well qualified as Mr. G. J. Holyoake to succeed our revered and much-lamented tutor.... Mr. Wright was evidently attached to him, and always recommended his conduct to our imitation.... We think that he is the only person competent to fill the place."

The work was thus begun under happy auspices, but Holyoake's views, now openly expressed to the Owenites at their meetings, seem to have disturbed zealots. In December (1839) friend Hollick, now an Owenite missionary at Sheffield, addresses him in his sprightly way as "High and Mighty Secretary of the Mech. Inst., Professor of Mathematics, Chirography, etc., etc., etc." A month later he writes: "I am exceedingly sorry to hear of your leaving the Ex. Com. Examination Committee of the Institute, both on account of the treatment *you* have received and the loss *they* must have experienced. You must, like all public characters, make up your mind to immolation on the altar of that Demon of Discord—party-spirit."

Holyoake had expressed disgust with the whole Institute, and even asked Hollick to take him as an amanuensis; for his lively friend had written an imposing account of his activity in the north, and his being currently described as "Anti-christ." There is no situation to be had in Sheffield, Hollick replies, except in the police-force, where everybody is busy "breaking houses open, discovering pikes and infernal machines, capturing Chartists, etc." But he urges Holyoake to apply for the office of Social Missionary in the Owenite movement.

There was evidently serious friction at the Institute, and Holyoake left it in January 1840. For three months he gave lessons in a private school in the town. A letter from the owner, Mr. Tolly, on April 4th thanks him very warmly for his assistance, and the writer feels sure he will never find a "better" assistant. Meantime, in March, he had taken an engagement as book-keeper to a Venetian-blind maker, Pemberton. The salary was only eight shillings a week, but the work was light. The younger brother of his employer was the gifted actor and lecturer, Charles Reece Pemberton, who was much attached to Holyoake. His health failed, and Sergeant Talfourd, Mr. W. J. Fox, and other friends assisted him, but he died in March. Holyoake was one of the few friends he loved to have with him at the last, and the first publication of Holyoake was a short memoir of Pemberton. He also attempted to raise funds for a memorial to the actor; but Mr. Fox and others were unfavourable, thinking it unworthy that the many who had done so little for Pemberton in life should put marble over his grave. There were other bits of employment He wrote advertisements, at seven and sixpence each, for a firm whom he persuaded "that to tell the truth about their wares would be the greatest novelty out." The occupation did not last long. He gave literary assistance to uncultivated mechanics who were engaged to write technical treatises. He also advertised private lessons in mathematics at his own home, but the experiment was darkened by "a drab

knave," his first pupil, who came to him for a number of lessons, in attire that made bargaining as to terms seem superfluous, and declined to pay in the end because there was no formal contract.

A Sketch of the Life and a few of the Beauties of Pemberton. Leeds, 1842.

But 1840 was a lean year for the young married couple. In their little cottage on the edge of the town (12, Sandpits) they just contrived to keep out of debt, and had a useful schooling in economy. "Eleanor" had the happy thought to grow a bed of mustard and cress to give taste to the monotonous bread and butter. Neighbours saw through the thin show of bravery, and one would come along with her mug of porter and tactfully force the young mother—their daughter Madeline was born in May—to take a neighbourly pull at it. The life of an apostle could not very well be harder. Holyoake leaned to Hollick's suggestion, and made his fateful entry into the ranks of the Owenites.

CHAPTER III THE GOSPEL ACCORDING TO ROBERT OWEN

Birmingham had, we saw, become one of the chief centres of Owenism in 1833, and some of the best teachers at the Mechanics' Institution were staunch Owenites. The boy must have been well aware of their activity, at least from his sixteenth year. But they were "infidels," and, much as he varied his bold exploration among the chapels, he avoided the Owenite meeting-house in Well Lane. As the fence of his Baptist beliefs grew thinner, he began to peep timidly at his much-maligned neighbours, and to discern features less repellent than he had been led to expect. At last an amusing accident took him amongst them. He heard his mates telling that Robert Hall was to speak on a certain date, and went with eagerness to hear the great Nonconformist preacher. To his horror he found that he had imperfectly caught the name, and he was listening to the suave heresies of Robert Owen.

They seemed less damnable than he had supposed, and he began to resent the injustice of his comrades' strictures on them and to associate more with

Owenite fellow-students like Hollick. To do them justice in workshop-debates he attended their meetings, where he learned their real doctrines. As, about the same time he sold a pretty edition of the Bible that he had—rumour quickly changed the story into "burned his Bible"— fingers were pointed at him. His early diary puts his first hearing of Robert Owen in June 1836, and notes that in the following January he "spoke for the Owenites." His intimate friend Hollick had just become a young apostle of the movement, and in February he writes to Holyoake from London, where he had gone with Robert Owen. The young reformers of the world were not puritanic in speech, one gathers:

"You ask if London is really 'the mart of genius.' It may be of genius, but I'll be damned if I think it is of geniuses. 'Does it swarm with sterling talent?' It may, but, like sparks in a flint, it is latent, and requires to be struck devilish hard to fetch it out.... When I first came here, they told me it was a pity I had come before a *London* audience. I might have done if I had continued in the country. London audiences were so *very* intellectual, etc.... This was the first Sunday I was there, before I lectured. At the conclusion of my lecture I received two rounds of applause, a thing they had heard traditions about, as having been heard of in remote times, but not belonging to their own age."

He hinted that Holyoake would shine even more brightly in the metropolitan firmament, and urged him to apply for the position of Social Missionary. It was early as yet to seek that distinction, and Holyoake continued to attend the services. He taught in the Socialist Sunday School, and sometimes read the lessons at the hall. I find a letter of Robert Owen's preserved by him, dated April 1838, praising the "excellent arrangements" made for his Birmingham lectures; though it is not clear that it was addressed to Holyoake. We saw that he was known at that time to Owenites in the north. A nervous and sensitive youth, with mind early expanded to large ideas of reform by the distress he saw about him and the constant agitation of his political atmosphere, he could not fail to be arrested by the new ideas of co-operation in industry and the effect of surroundings on character, which were the two clear notes of Owen's teaching.

Robert Owen, whom even Sir Leslie Stephen calls "one of the most important figures in the social history of his time," was then in the last phase of his development. His ample plan of salvation was to distribute the nations into model industrial communities—a kind of combination of garden-city, farm-colony, and Bohemian club—where the products of labour should be clubbed, and the mind and character diligently cultivated. Reybaud describes his system as a mixture of the practices of Abraham with the ideas of Baboeuf. His first task was to prove by an experiment at New Lanark that his educational ideal—his partners in the business prevented him from making it industrially co-operative—could achieve splendid results. The New Lanark community became the social wonder of Europe between 1800 and 1830; though other communities, like Orbiston (which he did not control), failed. But, while kings and statesmen admired, they declined to break up their kingdoms into Owen's pretty co-operative cubes, and, the clergy being alienated by Owen's outspoken heresy, the idealist appealed to the people. Francis Place and other practical reformers listened to him with infinite weariness, but the mass of the workers heard him with enthusiasm.

The right of combination, that Place had secured for them, seemed to have proved futile, and at the precise time when Holyoake began to think the thoughts of men there had been some reversion of the feverish workers to political action. The Birmingham Political Union was revived in 1837, and Holyoake joined it; he wrongly speaks of it as a gun hung up on the wall to rust in 1832, and never taken down. He also entered a secret political society, of the character that has a fascination for young men of all ages.

'' The object of the society I found to be to cut off Lord Palmerston's head. Things were bad amongst workmen in those days, and I had no doubt somebody's head ought to be cut off, and I hoped they had hit upon the right one. The secretary was a Chartist leader named Warden, who ended by cutting his own head off instead, which showed confusion of ideas by which Lord Palmerston profited."

This was in 1838, the year of the publication of the People's Charter, and the society probably merged in the new Chartist Union, as Holyoake was an early Chartist. His relations to that body will call for ampler treatment a little later, and in fact he never joined wholeheartedly in their work; but our narrative will not be quite intelligible unless we insert a few words on it.

Chartism was born of the discontent of the workers and the Radicals with the measures passed by the Reformed Parliament. Radicals like Roebuck, Molesworth, Colonel Thompson, Crawford, Hume, Daniel O'Connell, etc., joined with working-class leaders. A committee was appointed, and they issued the famous Charter with its six points—manhood suffrage, annual parliaments, the ballot, abolition of property-qualifications, payment of members, and equality of electoral districts. How the red-hot oratory of the popular leaders gave a revolutionary glow to this sober programme, alienated the Radicals, and gave the Whigs some ground for their savage repression of the movement, we shall understand when Holyoake comes into contact with men like Feargus O'Connor and Ernest Jones. Suffice it to say here that trade was very bad and distress *Sixty Years*, II, 77.

acute between 1837 and 1842, and Chartism set the country aflame as easily as the sun fires a parched moor. The great Reform-meetings were dwarfed by the huge gatherings of from one to four hundred thousand men that were held over the country, from London to Glasgow, in 1838 and 1839. Sleepy Bath, that would not to-day furnish forty of its daughters to welcome the most fascinating of heretics, then saw 4,000 of its women assemble to greet

Henry Vincent, the red revolutionary. In the north great streams of men poured out on the moors at night, their countless torches grimly lighting up rough banners that bore skulls and red caps of liberty, or such mottoes as "More pigs and less parsons"; in the large towns Radical orators like Attwood stood side by side with the O'Connors of the people. At Birmingham in August they met to the number of 200,000. Attwood swore that 100,000 men would march to release him if the Whigs dared to arrest him; and the herculean, handsome, fiery O'Connor— who had deserted O'Connell and Ireland, Gammage says, on the maxim that it was "better to reign in hell than serve in heaven"—urged them in a voice of thunder to "go flesh every sword to the hilt." Holyoake says that, at all events, many of his mates had pikes and files stuck in wooden handles.

The Government issued stern orders, and in a few months hundreds of the leaders were in jail. At Birmingham Holyoake watched eagerly, but took no part in, the riots that ensued. His friend George White, a reckless young Irishman, who was, Gammage says, "quite at home in battering the head of a policeman," and who impudently forced the magistrate to supply him with sherry and sandwiches during his defence, was imprisoned; so were Collins, and Lovett, and Harney, and others he knew. The authorities of Birmingham had borrowed a force of the new police from London. The workers, who saw in the establishment of the police a new device of Whig despotism, scorned the "blue bottles" and "raw lobsters," routed them when the mayor brought them out, and were in turn chased and cut down by the cavalry. They had turned off the gas, and the maddened troopers chased them about Holyoake's quarter by the light of burning houses. His wife and he were nearly cut down, as they went out to inquire about a friend. Opposite him in the little street off the Bull Ring, the centre of the riot, he had for a neighbour during the riot-week Harney himself—a dark, moody little man with the pen of a Marat.

Attwood and others presented a protest to the House containing 1,280,000 signatures, threatened a general strike for a month, and counselled a run on the banks and abstinence from excisable articles; but the Government triumphed. Chartism was, for some years, "exhausted by the disasters of 1839," and we may leave it until its revival in 1848, when Holyoake becomes active in it. In the intervening years he is merely on good terms with its branches, wherever we find him. His hope is centred in Owenite education, rather than in political agitation, and to this we must return.

Robert Owen had been introduced to the Birmingham Political Union in 1832, and he had lectured on his system to an audience of 8,000 people in Beardsley's Repository. It reminds us at once of Leslie Stephen's description of Owen as "one of those intolerable bores who are the salt of the earth," and of Holyoake's statement that when Owen called a meeting you could never be sure when it would terminate, to find that the meeting lasted from 11 a.m. until 4 p.m. But Owen depreciated political action, and politicians distrusted Utopias. The Socialists—as the Owenites were commonly called, though they differed fundamentally from modern Socialists—remained a small but vigorous body. They opened a Labour Exchange in Bull Street, where the workers directly exchanged the products of their industry without the mediation of money (or by the use of tickets indicating the pure labour-value of the goods). Owen himself slighted these crude Co-operative experiments (which soon failed), and insisted on the adoption of his comprehensive scheme of a new world. His organ, the *New Moral World,* announced that "the reign of truth had now commenced on earth, and would prevail for evermore." Of this new world he was styled the "Preliminary Father," or, at a later date, the "Social and Right Reverend Father." In 1838, when Holyoake met him, he was in his sixty-seventh year. Genial and amiable to all, of tireless energy and tireless patience, with great dignity of bearing, admirable voice, and graceful gesture, he still exercised a remarkable sway over thoughtful men, and had more than a hundred thousand avowed followers. Holyoake would see him again in 1839, when the Congress was held at Birmingham, and the two previous associations he had founded were merged in "The Universal Community Society of Rational Religionists." The Central Board of the Society was located at Birmingham, and the *New Moral World* issued there.

I have said that Pare and Hawkes Smith and others of influence over Holyoake were Owenites. We find a *Birmingham Co-operative Herald* as early as 1828. It cannot be questioned that Holyoake largely regarded the post of Social Missionary as a means of livelihood and of escape from his disagreeable position. At the same time the pay was far smaller than he could have earned as a mechanic, and his heart was wholly in the work. The Manchester Congress in 1838 had appointed six Social Missionaries (Lloyd Jones, Rigby, Green, Buchanan—father of the novelist, Campbell, and Hollick), and stationed them at London, Birmingham, Leeds, Manchester, Liverpool, and Glasgow. The whole kingdom was majestically divided into six dioceses for them, and an episcopal salary of £80-£100 a year was guaranteed. When four more missionaries were appointed in They did not advocate State-action at this time, but voluntary association in communities; nor could any one at that stage of municipal development dream of "municipal trading." 1839, the optimism of the Owenites was only equalled by the terror of their opponents. A petition was solemnly presented in Parliament, from the clergy, traders, and magistrates of Birmingham, praying for attention to the movement. The Bishop of Exeter took up the " holy war " in the House of Lords, and vainly endeavoured to make the peers' flesh creep by a tragic account of their partition of the kingdom into Socialist dioceses, and a stern denunciation of "the horrid blasphemies and immoralities " of the *New Moral World.*

It will appear presently how these

strictures had an unforeseen effect on the band of adventurous spirits into which young Holyoake now sought admission. Early in 1840, when the trouble at the Mechanics' Institute became serious, Hollick urged him to apply to the Central Board. From some cause or other he long hesitated, but at the Congress that was held at Leeds in May Hollick submitted his name.' All present spoke highly of him, his friend wrote, though many regretted he "had not a more powerful bellows." Holyoake says somewhere that "others concluded that, in a party widely credited with subversive and dangerous purposes, an unaggressive voice like mine might confuse prejudice, if it did not disarm it." It was probable that the next vacancy would fall to him, and not improbable that Mr. Mackintosh would soon retire from Birmingham, and leave that honourable position to him. In June the Birmingham group purchased a chapel (in Lawrence Street) for holding their meetings, and there is a letter expressing their great indebtedness to Holyoake for collecting funds and attending to the legal business. He also sent up to the central officers a suggestion that he should write books for use in their schools, and was vaguely encouraged. We shall find them amongst his later publications.

The blasphemies were not serious. The " immoralities" were probably found in Owen's " Lectures on the marriages of = by the priesthood," which: Mr. Podmore describes as "a high-pitched and indiscriminate condemnation of the whole institution of marriage." He has, perhaps, not taken sufficient account of Holyoake's assurance (History of Co-operation, I, 139, and elsewhere) that, Owen being careless as to misinterpretation, the lectures were not published as he delivered them, but " made up of abrupt notes made by a hearer." Elsewhere (Measoner, May 23, 1849) Holyoake declares of the lectures that "Mr. Owen has repudiated them." As has happened to many marriage-reformers, Owen's stress on the spiritual link threw the legal or ecclesiastical contract into comparative shade.

In September he gave a series of lectures to the Worcester Owenites, and they pressed him to come to them as station-lecturer. "They have in Worcester," he wrote to the London executive, "an apology for a Mechanics' Institution. They want a *real* one; which I think I could soon supply to them." The Birmingham Board reported that " his morals were unimpeachable, while of his mental acquirements much, very much, might be said, without doing adequate justice to him." The Central Board approved his acceptance of the post, but regretted that they were not in a position to grant him a salary. However, the Worcester people had promised to raise a small salary for him, and at the beginning of October he set out for his mission, leaving his wife and child at Birmingham. He had at last his share of the world to conquer.

His letters at this important period of his career suggest a shrewd, business-like, self-possessed, and industrious young man, his adolescent zeal well salted with discretion. The letters written to him, or about him, especially from the Socialist branches, plainly show that he had charm of character and an impressive address. He was in his twenty-third year, much (though imperfectly) cultivated—the Birmingham Board speaks of his command of "all philosophies, ancient and modern," and more judicial correspondents respect him—refined in bearing and speech, and, though weak in voice, well trained in delivery, witty, and sententious. I knew him only in his last eight years, when his ceaseless humour, his refined and dignified bearing, his neatness and felicity of phrase, and his obvious solidity of character, won all who met him, and inspired younger men. It was something to learn, as the research for this biography went back into dark days, that he had never been otherwise: that at a time when his mind was immature, and his life cast in the hardest circumstances, the best traits of his character were never obscured. His grave, well-cut features, framed in dark long hair, did much to disarm those who came to hear him retail the "horrid blasphemies" of the Rational Religion.

But the auditors were few, and his first theatre of public action not likely unduly to elevate him. Their Hall of Science (in Garden Street) was a small workshop hastily turned into a temple of humanity, and their fragment of "the new moral world " was a very tiny patch of Worcester. They met twice on Sundays for service in it A few naturalist or humanist hymns (poems by Shelley, Elliott, etc.), and a reading from some edifying work, preceded the lecture. These hymns were often pretentious and pedantic, but Mr. Podmore's strictures on them in his life of Owen are hardly justified. He says that justice does not seem to have been included amongst the virtues they sang, and that the omission "will help to explain the indifference of the Socialists to all the great democratic movements of the time." Owen's whole scheme was based on a demand for industrial justice; and although the "Father" himself depreciated the Radical political reforms—he called them "small ware" in comparison with his own more vast and more radical scheme—most of his followers were not at all indifferent to them. They fraternised with the Chartists everywhere, and often worked in the Anti-Corn Law movement.

Owen himself did not fail to point out the partial reforms that were involved in his broad principles—the industrial principle of co-operation and the moral principle of the effect of good or bad surroundings and of culture on character. No reformer of the nineteenth century had less limitation in the application of his principles, though his methods were impracticable, and his system had to die to disclose its fertility. Nearly a century ago he advocated infant-schools of a kinder-garten type (the first London infant-school was founded by his disciple, Wilderspin, in 1820) and the legal suppression of childlabour: an eight-hour day for the adult worker: co-operation in production and distribution: the general diffusion of the elements of science and art: the corrective treatment of the criminal and the reform of jails: the substitution of arbitration for warfare: greater freedom and a wider life for woman: the emendation of the divorce-laws, the poor law, and the licensing law: the suppression of the national lottery: the collective ownership of the land: and the admission of Jews, etc., to Parliament. All these ideas were urged in his journal and by his missionaries, and from him Holyoake inherited them. No doubt he was wrong in fancying that reforms are brought about in a wholesale fashion; but experience has shown that, when men do take them up with the single intensity of purpose that is requisite for attaining them, the old limitations return, and the sectional reformers are apt to be contemptuous or hostile to each other. The breadth of Owenism had advantages.

Robert Owen, I, 475. The reader must recollect that it was an age of poor hymns. Even the Unitarian hymn-book had such verses as:—

"On Cherub and on Cherubim
Full royally he rode;
And on the wings of mighty wind
Came flying all abroad."

Most of Owen's missionaries were not men of a type to impress England as their leader did. Their work was a failure, and they were disbanded in four years. Holyoake himself had a large ideal of his mission, and brought energy and character to it. The "Hall of Science"— in some places their structures were known as "Social Institutions"—was understood to mean a centre for the cultivation of *social* science, a thing then dreaded by the wealthy and frowned upon by the religious. Holyoake went further, and taught mathematics and physics; though his flock became cautious when he introduced "laughing gas," and to his astonishment sent the subject, a heavy carpenter, in a series of somersaults along the room and down the stairs into the street The pay was apostolic. Out of his sixteen shillings a week he had to maintain himself at Worcester and his wife and child at Birmingham, where the mustard and cress must still have flourished. After a time he increased his income by teaching mathematics at a girls' school in the town, under the decent disguise of " Mr. Jacobs." He then,

in December, brought Eleanor and the child to Worcester, and could spare himself the occasional 26miles walk to go and see them. He never had the faculty of pressing for money, as some of his colleagues had. One of them had a trick of admitting an audience free, and then locking the door and refusing to open it until they had subscribed the price of a sheep or a cow for the Queenwood community. Lectures at other centres brought little profit. He gives an amusing account in his *Last Trial for Atheism* of a lecturing adventure at Cheltenham, where he had to squeeze the food out of his host, and in the end pay the travelling expenses for himself and his wife.

The apostolate was dreary and dispiriting, and he soon appealed for a regular diocese. He was proposed at Birmingham as a delegate to Congress, but Charles Southwell was appointed. A friend sends him a dark account of the manoeuvres of Southwell's friends, but the letter is chiefly interesting because it shows that Socialism is already dying at Birmingham. There were only 34 members at the meeting (though 43 votes were recorded!), and the society is deep in debt. The new moral world was curiously like the old bad one, when one got fairly inside it. However, both he and Southwell Tvere appointed missionaries, and at the end of May he left for Sheffield. The Worcester officers testified that "his general demeanour as a private individual had been most open, free, and unaffected, which with an urbanity of manner and kindness of disposition has gained him the respect and admiration of all with whom he has had to do." I fancy the lively, if not flippant, paragraphs he had sent weekly to the journal of the movement had a good deal more weight with the Sheffield people.

In May he set out with enthusiasm for his larger sphere, little dreaming that in another year he would be in a Midland jail. The Central Board had a big way of doing things on paper that accorded with their theory.

It drew up a formidable charter of the new diocese Vol. 1. E created for

Holyoake. The territory he was to evangelise comprised "the town of Sheffield and generally that part of the county of York not included in the Leeds district: the towns of Derby and Nottingham, and generally the county of Nottingham and that part of the county of Derby north of a line drawn immediately south of the town of Derby, etc." In brief, it included 33 large towns and villages innumerable.

In point of fact the work at Sheffield proved more inspiring. The hall was a substantial building in Rockingham Street, there was a day-school in which he had full scope for his ideas, and he attracted friends of distinction. His pasdagogical work showed genius for teaching. He taught writing in such a way that children would easily scrawl their own and their mothers' names in a week, and in a few weeks could write well. His " Pestalozzian school," with fifty pupils, won him regard. Sheffield seems to have known him before many months. In the winter the pantomime of the town was "Jack the Giant-killer," and the hero was an open impersonation of the young missionary. The actor, Mr. Young, was friendly to him. George Julian Harney, the Chartist, came to Sheffield, and lived for some time with him. Ebenezer Elliott, the democratic poet, was attracted by a pamphlet that Holyoake wrote on "The advantages and disadvantages of Trades' Unions." A letter from the poet to him runs:

"Dear Brother,

"Not having seen the paragraph you allude to, I cannot answer your letter. But if ever I offend you, pray come to my breakfast table, and let us settle it over a cup of coffee. I am not aware of having written or said a word that ought to offend you or any of you—and I am myself a Socialist, if I understand myself—remaining The system may conveniently be read in *Bygones,* I, 33. He first teaches the child to make a "straight stroke" and "a round O." The other letters of the alphabet are then shown to be combinations of these. He proceeded largely on the sensible principles lately popularised by Mrs. Boole,

"Your brother,

"ebenezer Elliott."

Holyoake appropriated one of Elliott's poems for the Rational Religion, but substituted the word "Cooperation," in defiance of metre, in the second line of:

"Behold 1 behold! the second ark—
The Land! The Land!"

Elliott laughingly suggested another cup of coffee, but he was really not an admirer of Owenism. He urged the workers "not to be deluded by your Owens, Oastlers, etc."; and on one occasion, when Holyoake and others lunched with him, he gave them his lines:

"What is a Communist? One who hath yearnings
For equal division of unequal earnings;
Idler or bungler, or both, he is willing
To fork out his penny, and pocket your shilling."

It was, of course, mere parody of Holyoake's teaching—"the best definition in our language of what Communism is *not*" he says—but Elliott was a forgivable man, and his friendship a distinction. Other men of familiar name entered his circle. There is a letter to him from Mr. Samuel Smiles (then editing the *Leeds Times,* to which Holyoake contributed) which shows appreciation. He describes one of Holyoake's articles as "cleverly and brilliantly written." Holyoake suggests that Smiles borrowed the phrase "Selfhelp" from himself.

Distinction was on its way, but money tarried. In offering him thjrty shillings a week, the president of the society had pleaded that they were "deuced poor." Their collections on Sundays came to about twelve shillings, and they had fallen from three orations to one, as the receipts for the other two did not pay for gas. For this Holyoake had to teach for five hours a day, lecture on Sundays, and visit his diocese. When the work proved too much, he paid a curate (Paterson) out of his own salary. Meagre additions were made to it by a little journalism (the *New Moral World, Sheffield Iris,* and *Leeds Times),* a little literary revision, and a little private teaching. Money was so scarce that

when the Huddersfield society invited him to deliver their anniversary lectures, and could offer only ten shillings for expenses, he walked there and back—thirty miles each way—to save the money. The unpleasantness increased when he knew that the raising of his salary was a perpetual theme of discussion in his own society. "Weary of my engagement," he notes in his diary in the summer.

His relations with the central authorities of the Rational Religion did not long remain, if they ever were, cordial. Owen himself was not the kind of leader to detect and encourage talent. He was full of his vision, and he regarded the missionaries only as indifferently helpful transmitters of it The younger man saw that the vision was too broad, and the movement in need of specific aims. He sent up the manuscript of a mathematical work (probably his *Mathematics no Mystery),* and urged attention to education, which–AfH was then much discussed. Owen, a born educationist, looked at the manuscript and discouraged publication. The general secretary begged Holyoake to work rather at the presentment of their general principles than at small educational measures. "The day has now arrived," Galpin wrote to him, in July, "when, with unity of action, our society may carry the world before it." Holyoake knew well that the society was in a state of decay, and his suggestions of definite reforms were good. But Owen's eyes were blurred with his besetting vision, and the decaying frame of his movement was now torn by a storm that hastened its end, and swept Holyoake into more adventurous fields.

The attack made on the Socialists in the House of Lords had drawn hostile eyes on them. It was discovered that they took money at the doors of their Halls of Science, and that this practice was illegal under 39 George III, c. 79. Small-minded zealots at once urged the authorities to move against them. They replied that they were assembled for "religious worship," and that they were a " congregation of Protestants called Rational Religionists." The enemy at

once claimed that missionaries who made this plea for their institutions should be called upon to make a public profession, on oath, of the Protestant faith, and many of them were summoned to do so. The editor of the *New Moral World,* Mr. Fleming, urged them to take the oath, and this seems to have been the general feeling of the officials. Lloyd Jones took the oath at once: Robert Buchanan hesitated a few weeks, but at length "swore himself into the position of the Rev. R. Buchanan." They were supported by the officials, and the Central Board became very anxious to restrain all its lecturers from referring to religion.

This procedure on the part of a movement that stood for truth and sincerity above all things was repugnant to Holyoake, nor was his disgust lessened when he heard the editor of the *New Moral World* say at Sheffield: "If you offend people's prejudices, the capitalists will never lend us money." Money was, in fact, urgently needed for the communal experiment they had started in Hampshire, but Holyoake and a few of the more ardent and unaccommodating spirits rebelled. They at once opened a crusade for the outspoken criticism of theology. John Watts (of Manchester) wrote to the Central Board that they seemed to be developing "the souls of stockjobbers." Jeffery (of Edinburgh) wrote to Holyoake: "All the bright anticipations which we had associated with the social body are doomed to disappointment if it become nothing more than a Joint Stock connection of men whose only *principle* in the movement is *the principal* they may advance for the sake of profit." Holyoake, with characteristic openness, wrote and circulated a pamphlet charging the Central Board with sacrificing principle to expediency—the war-cry of the dissenters. Within a week or two he received a circular letter from the general secretary, which gave three months' notice of dismissal to all the missionaries, unless they were individually reappointed at the Congress in May. A later letter assured him of the Board's sense of "the value of free discussion and the course adopted by Mr. Southwell, Mr. Hollick, and yourself," but the Congress disbanded the missionaries from lack of funds, and afterwards reappointed "the Rev. Lloyd Jones" and one or two others. When Holyoake, a few weeks later, fell into the hands of the police, Mr. Galpin wrote: "I have always admired the bold and honest conduct of yourself and party "; but he wrote to a Cheltenham Socialist that the proceedings "did not surprise the Board," and they would not stir in the matter.

This was the beginning of organised anti-Christian activity in England, and it is interesting to see how it was directly due to a petty and unjust manoeuvre on the part of some of the faithful. For our purpose—the interpretation of Holyoake's character and career—it is a cardinal point. He was still a Theist (as Owen always was) at the end of 1841, and his interests were almost entirely social. He had been content so far to let the Churches go their different way, as well as they might. His mind now swung round to a more critical consideration of the Churches and their doctrines, and the events that rapidly followed moved him from indifference to hostility.

His colleague at Bristol, Charles Southwell, began to publish an atheistical journal, the *Oracle of Reason,* and he had the support of William Chilton, a Bristol printer, and Malthus Ryall, a London engraver. Southwell had been a soldier and an actor, and his rhetoric was resonant and melodramatic. Though he was the youngest of thirty-three children (not thirty-six, as Holyoake says) by the same father, he was a man of fire and energy. Bristol knew him as a vigorous and naughty lecturer in some obscure "Hall of Science," but when he began to issue a weekly penny paper, having a sale (at first) of 6,000 copies, he could not be overlooked. He wrote of the clergy: "They pour their poison of lies into the ear of cradled infancy—nay, they debauch reason in the very womb, and only in the grave can their multitudinous dupes find repose for their terrified and exhausted sensibilities." The clergy and

their "multitudinous dupes" demurred to having this bellowed by a strenuous actor from the shades of Bristol arches, or circulated in the workshops, and they raised the cry of blasphemy. Ryall egged him on. "Throw away the foil, sabre, or single-stick," he wrote to Southwell, "and come to bloody noses and black eyes." But after the issue of No. 4 of the *Oracle* Southwell passed from the editorial chair to the dock, and was sentenced to one year's imprisonment and a fine of 100.

Holyoake had joined "the defiant syndicate of four," because the only alternative seemed to be the company of hypocrites. He did not know the men, or he knew only Southwell, and that slightly. Indeed, if their language is at times trying, we may remember the irritation caused them by their colleagues, the tactics pursued by their religious opponents, and the coarse character of much of the religious life about them. They quote in the *Oracle* such passages as this from Dissenting literature of the time: "O Lord! dung us with Jesus Christ, that we may bring forth much fruit meet for thee.... Souse us, O Lord, in the powdering tub of thy grace, that we may become tripes fit for thy heavenly table." On the other hand, men of their own way of thinking were being treated daily in the courts much as the Jews had been in the Middle Ages. There were many cases in which men escaped charges of assault by proving that their victims were atheists, and therefore ought not to take the oath. One instance will illustrate the incredible and exasperating situation that existed so late as the forties. A respectable London bookseller appeared before a Clerkenwell magistrate to prosecute a man for stealing a book. "Stand down, sir, I will not hear you," said Mr. Combe on learning that he was not a theist. But as other witnesses were available the thief was committed, and the magistrate bound over the bookseller to prosecute. "I think"—he began, asking leave to withdraw the charge in the circumstances. "Oh, we don't care what *you* think: we don't want your thinkings here," said the clerk. "No, certainly

not," added the magistrate, "we don't want the thoughts of such a man here." But we shall see enough of this presently. Atheists were outlaws, and it is hardly surprising that some of them used the language of outlaws.

Holyoake had still a vague belief in God at the end of 1841, but the prosecution of Southwell at Bristol let loose a flood of feeling in which the last lines of his creed were obliterated. For some years afterwards he freely described himself as an "atheist." He did not mean— very few atheists do mean (Holyoake says Chilton was the only dogmatic one he ever met)—that he could disprove the existence of Deity. That is not the meaning of the word. His view was, he wrote at the time, the view of Pythagoras: "I know nothing of Gods." It is the attitude he afterwards made popular under the name of Secularism and Huxley called Agnosticism. He found human problems so absorbing and pressing that he desired to keep aloof from theological ones. This had been so entirely his attitude up to 1842 that he had not noticed the collapse of his belief. But he was now naturally drawn for a time into an aggressive mood.

On January 9th he announced a lecture on "The spirit of Bonner in the disciples of Jesus: or the cruelty and intolerance of Christianity." The police noticed the flagrant placard, and sent a few officers to the meeting. No action was taken, but it was hardly for lack of material. His "curate," Paterson, read the lesson, which was the very article in the *Oracle,* on "The Jew Book," for which Southwell had been imprisoned; and in the warmth of his feeling Holyoake fully defended it and its author. "Christianity had once more produced the *iron* evidences of her divinity," he said, and he must examine them. The lecture was published, and forms the third of his pamphlets. It reads strongly, of course. Respectable Socialism is described as "shivering for two years with the wet blanket of orthodoxy about its shoulders." The rigorous treatment of Southwell has proved "the cradle of my doubts and grave of my religion." The truth more probably is that it led him to tear away a veil of which he had been half conscious, and discover his real lack of faith. He had known Southwell at Birmingham, but his pathetic and sincere references to the "martyr" are undone by the papers before me. Friends were subscribing a pound a week for the prisoner. In the caterer's manuscript-list of " necessaries " supplied I find about four shillings' worth of cigars a month, much bear's grease, some silk handkerchiefs, and a generous supply of bottled stout.

"Prepare yourself for a separation," Chilton wrote to Holyoake. Mr. Fleming at once went to Sheffield to stamp out the spreading fire. Holyoake was got away/on some pretext, to Bradford, and Lloyd Jones took his place. He would not spare the young man who had fastened on him the name of the " Rev. Swear-at-once" (Buchanan was the "Rev. Swear-at-last"). Holyoake found great dissension on his return *(Movement* No. 51), and friendly members told him he would be wise to look out for a fresh place. He accepted Chilton's invitation to undertake the editing of the *Oracle.* Chilton deprecated "coarseness and vulgarity," and himself contributed a long and remarkable series of articles on "The Theory of Regular Gradation," which presented the doctrine of evolution with learning and acuteness, seventeen years before *The Origin of Species* was published.

Holyoake began to edit the journal with its eighth issue (February 12th). "The Great Lama never dies," were his introductory words; but the Great Lama altered his tone. In his first article, claiming continuity, there is only one phrase that the most sensitive person could object to. The article so clearly displays his characteristic qualities of style in fair development that a passage will be read with interest:

"Because the tortoise once beat the hare by its perseverance, laggards in reasoning have fallen in love with laziness; and, with sagacity in perfect keeping with the subject, can conceive of nothing so effective for the establishment of truth as sleepy error. The

bounding fleetness of the hare was its virtue; its reliability to relax its efforts its vice; but wiseacres have extolled and imitated its failing and totally neglected its good quality.... Error is ancient and full-grown; truth infantine, and by overcareful nursing a rather weakly child. Unloose its swaddling clothes—give it exercise, and fear not but that its fair proportions will soon be developed— that it will soon grasp the club of Hercules and dash out the brains of ignorance."

The mind is obviously immature, but the expression is curiously developed. The epigrammatic force, the apt and facile imagery, and the precision of phrase that distinguish Holyoake's later works made an early appearance. Another passage (February 26th) will show that he was reading:

"In the days of Aristotle, when men were so full of theory that practice was of little repute, hidden meanings were useful, peradventure. To the schoolmen, who love jargon because it seems learned, and write unintelligibly of necessity, having no distinct and natural view of things; to such worthies mystery is like darkness to lovers of evil deeds, a perpetual letter of recommendation. But no one can deny that the spirit of modern times is most anti-supernatural, so completely so as the very genius of practicability could desire."

One can gather a large crop of fair epigrams from these articles of his twenty-fourth year. "Forbearance, like eating, is capital in moderation; in excess it leads to disease." "The age wants, not footmen for falsehood, but warriors for truth." "It falls," he says of a new and intellectual religion, "like the moonbeams, not to warm but to freeze. Its rays are colder than the shade." When the *New Moral World* speaks of the "young atheists," he coolly retorts: "Many a commonwealth has owed more to the warmth of youth than to the cold prudence of greybeards." Some phrases are clearly due to the fact that so many friends whom he knows to be sincere men—Chartists, etc.—are in jail with felons. "Civilisation, instead of being a fertilising stream, freshening and invig-

orating the verdure of mind, lies like stagnant pools on the face of society, causing sad malarias to attack the advocates of freedom." The wonder is that he wrote so little that one cannot read with ease to-day. It was left to Ryall to "come to bloody noses "; and Holyoake did not, as a fact, control the copy editorially at all. He was always far away. However, Chilton, the other chief writer, was refined and scholarly, and the paper read well—and suffered proportionately in circulation.

Southwell himself was impressed with Holyoake's effective method of hitting hard without violence. Writing to him from Bristol Gaol, he requests Holyoake to alter freely any expressions he disapproves of in the articles the prisoner smuggles to him.

"There is," he says, "no man I ever met with whom I would sooner live or sooner die.... You will say old Southwell is running strangely, not aware perhaps that I have been long considering how we may hereafter enjoy, in generous freedom, each other's society. I am not without hope that the authorities will soon see the folly of meddling with the press, but you will do well to prepare for the worst. I would much rather, *very much rather,* some one else of stiffer constitution and of less value in other respects should pass the ordeal, but though hell gape, mind ye, my determination is to swim or drown with ye."

We know that there were no prison-rigours softening the temper of Southwell. The truth is that Holyoake won the respect, and often the enthusiasm, of nearly all who came to know him in those days. If to his sterling character, clear judgment, and ready command of phrase there had been added a sonorous voice and powerful frame, the story of Owenism might have run differently. For two or three months he edited the paper, nominally, from his house at Sheffield (179, Broomhall Street). In the spring he went down to Birmingham. He may have had some idea of setting up at Bristol, as the situation at Sheffield was unpleasant. From Birmingham he started on foot for Bristol—a ninety-miles journey—as he could not afford the coach-fare. It proved a much more adventurous journey than he expected, for he "fell among thieves by the way." CHAPTER IV TRIAL AND IMPRISONMENT

Holyoake left his wife and family at Birmingham on May 22nd, 1842, and set out on foot for Worcester. In those days even the open trucks of the third-class passenger were a luxury beyond his purse. On May 24th he moved on to Cheltenham, where he was to lecture. I have recounted how he visited Cheltenham in the preceding year, and drew a sermon from the Rev. Francis (afterwards Dean) Close. To that cleric's indignation, he was now announced by sundry placards to give a lecture on "Home Colonisation, as a means of superseding Poor-laws and Emigration," on May 24th. The title and the intention were innocent enough, but the echoes of the Bishop of Exeter's fulmination were still rumbling in sleepy places like Cheltenham, and the vicar made preparations for his reception. He sent three men to detect heresy in the lecture.

Socialism did not seriously menace the position of the Church in Cheltenham. I have stated how Holyoake had found the little group of Socialists there so poor in 1841 that he had to "dispute every inch of hospitality with his host. " A group of about a hundred Chartists and Socialists—mostly men and youths, but with a sparse sprinkling of adventurous ladies—now gathered in the Mechanics' Institution to hear the lecture. Mr. Close's spies were disappointed, for Holyoake adhered strictly to his subject, and made no reference to religion. But

Owenite lecturers always invited questions from the audience, and one of the envoys, a local preacher of a darkly zealous order, seized the opportunity. He asked why there had been no mention of chapels in Holyoake's description of the home-colonies he advocated. The lecturer had, he said, "told them a good deal about their duty to man: what about their duty to God?"

The question was stupid and irrelevant, if not malicious, and in ordinary circumstances might have been disregarded. But the Owenite world was bubbling with excitement over this very question of concealing one's opinions about religion, and Holyoake was full of indignation that one of his colleagues should be in jail for expressing his views. Owen's original instruction to the missionaries in such circumstances was: "Should you be challenged to discuss the dogmas of the Christians, state that you have not time for such discussions, which tend to increase the general insanity of the world upon these mysterious and endless imaginations of the human brain." But Owen had himself acted otherwise. At the beginning of his public career (at the London Tavern, in 1817) he had been challenged in much the same way as Holyoake now was, and he gave a defiant answer. The recent dishonour of their body through the temporising policy of some of its leaders made it impossible for Holyoake to hesitate. He knew, further, that there was a local charge of cowardice. A Cheltenham teacher, named Sperry, had published Socialistic sentiments, and had retracted under pressure of a threat of dismissal; though he was dismissed all the same. Few will question that it was, in the circumstances, more manly to meet the question. It was indiscreet; but it is well for the world that there have been indiscreet men in it at times.

Holyoake's fatal reply has been quoted in so many forms—even Mr. Podmore gives it in the inaccurate words of the hostile witnesses at the trial—that I will give it in full:

"As you, sir, have introduced religion into this meeting, which I have carefully avoided in my lecture, I will answer your question frankly and sincerely; and as you say we cannot have morality without religion, I will answer that too. Home colonisation is an economic scheme, and as we can ill bear the burden of a God = a system of worship here, he may lie rather heavy on their hands there. Our national debt and our national taxes hang like millstones round the neck of the poor man's prosperity, saying nothing of the enormous gatherings of capitalists in addition to all this; and in the face of our misery and want we are charged twenty millions more for the worship of God. This is utilitarianism *versus* divinity, and I appeal to your heads and your pockets if we are not too poor to have a God? If poor men cost the State so much, they would be put like officers on half-pay. I think that while our distress lasts it would be wise to do the same thing with the Deity. Thus far goes the political economy of my objection to build chapels in community. Again, I never like to propose to others what I shrink from myself. I am not religious—my creed is to have no creed. But what do I hear? That morality cannot exist without religion? Preposterous! Religion in my opinion has ever poisoned the fountain-springs of morality. Connect them together! Hark ye! Morality alone is lovely—has a sweet, balmy, and healthful reputation, and sheds honest influences over mankind. Who that has felt its power would degrade it by connecting it with religion? Read the mental degradation and oppression of your race, and there you read the history of religion: look at its bloody instruments of torture and its fell subjection of honesty, when men would "shun the revolting homage it demands: and there we read its character! Why, its fierce and inhuman myrmidons have immured, within these three months, Charles Southwell in Bristol jail; and while the friend of my bosom lies there I wish not to hear the name of God, I shudder at the thought of religion, I flee the Bible as a viper, and revolt at the touch of a Christian—for their tender mercies may fall next on my head. This, sir, is no reason why the people in communities may not introduce religion there, but it is the reason why I do not introduce it into my lectures, and I trust you will take it as my apology for not recommending god-worship in home-colonies."

The words created no disturbance. They were accompanied with general laughter and followed by general applause, and Holyoake cheerfully resumed his pilgrimage to Bristol jail. In a day or two, however, he received a copy of Mr. Close's paper, the *Cheltenham*

Chronicle, in which he read the following paragraph:

"atheism And Blasphemy.

"On Tuesday evening last a person named Holyoake from Manchester delivered a lecture on socialism (or, as it has been more appropriately named, devilism) at the Mechanics' Institution. ... He impiously remarked that if there was a God he would have the deity served the same as the Government treated subalterns by placing him upon half-pay. With many similar blasphemous and awful remarks, which we cannot sully our columns by repeating, the poor misguided wretch continued to address the audience. To their lasting shame be it spoken that a considerable portion of the company *applauded* the miscreant during the time he was giving utterance to these profane opinions.

"We have three persons in our employ who are ready to verify on oath to the correctness of the above statements. We therefore hope those in authority will not suffer the matter to rest here, but that some steps will immediately be taken to prevent any further publicity to such diabolical sentiments. —Ed. *C. C."* I take the account from the *Oracle* (June 4th), the earliest and most authentic version. There was much discussion later as to whether he said: "I do not believe there is such a thing as a God." There is no such phrase in this contemporary report.

vol. I. F

Whatever one might think of Holyoake's impulsive and unpremeditated remarks, there is no difference of opinion on the conduct of his opponents. Close at once admits that the witnesses are in his own employment, and "to prevent further publicity" transfers the "blasphemies" from the little audience of ioo to his own audience of several thousands, and then to general notice. But this is only the temperate beginning of the drama. The next issue of the *Cheltenham Chronicle* contained a further paragraph:

"Holyoake, The Blasphemous Socialist Lecturer.

"In reference to a paragraph which appeared in the last *Chronicle* regarding this monster, the magistrates read the article alluded to, and expressed their opinion that it was a clear case of blasphemy. In order to check the further progress of his pernicious doctrines, the superintendent of police was ordered to make every exertion to bring him to justice."

It must be remembered that a charge of blasphemy at that time did not mean a charge of hurting the feelings of one's neighbours and so possibly provoking disorder. That civil gloss on an ecclesiastical law came later. The offence was, in essence, purely theological, and Holyoake held, as all hold to-day, that prosecution for such offences was tyranny. The other Cheltenham paper *Free Press),* of lay ownership, censured the prosecution, and pointed out that Holyoake was naturally embittered by the imprisonment of his friend. "Oh! when will Christians cease to act as though they disbelieved the power of the doctrines they profess?" the editor wrote.

Holyoake did not hesitate. He took to the road at once, and on the evening of June 1st, a blazing day, he walked boldly into Cheltenham. At his friend's house he learned that the Chartists had announced a meeting in the Mechanics' Institute for the following night. They were not only friendly to him, but were themselves interested in the right of free speech, and they put the room at his disposal. The news quickly circulated that he would speak at nine o'clock on June 2nd, and a good audience assembled. He entered secretly, so that the police might not arrest him prematurely, and began his lecture.

"After I had spoken about an hour in vindication of free speech in answer to public questions, the superintendent of police entered, armed with all the available force. They formed a handsome addition to the audience, and as they ranged themselves against the walls on either side of the room their shining hats formed a picturesque background to the meeting. This determined me to speak an hour longer—not having foreseen such an opportunity of extending liberal views in official quarters."

So his light pen dealt with the scene thirty years afterwards, but it was grim enough at the time. The courts of England were evil places for a heretic to enter in those days, and the jails of England were deadly. Some of his Chartist friends were done to death, and others brought to the brink of insanity, in them. His health was frail, his nature exceptionally sensitive, his young wife and child wholly dependent on him. But I will tell the pitiful and repellent story in as brief and sober a narrative as is possible.

Sixty Years, I, 148. But I generally follow the contemporary journals and his *Last Trial for Atheism.*

His speech that night had been temperate and persuasive—it may still be read—and he ended, not with a note of defiance, but with a courteous and gentle appeal to his hearers. He then asked the superintendent to show him the warrant for his apprehension. No warrant had been issued; in fact a magistrate said afterwards that on such a charge "any person in the audience had a right to take him without a warrant!" However, Holyoake went quietly with the police to the station, the whole audience joining in the procession.

He was brought before the magistrates the next morning. Two of them were clergymen, and they did not think fit to quit the bench while a charge on which they could hardly be impartial was heard. The prosecuting solicitor, Mr. Bubb, will be acknowledged by any who read the proceedings to have been "a particularly gross, furious, squabbuilt, vulgar person." He did not attempt to refine the charge. "Any person," he assured them, "who denies the existence or providence of God is guilty of blasphemy," and, without troubling about the quality of Holyoake's remarks, he treated him on that sole ground as a contemptible ruffian —except that he untruthfully represented Holyoake as speaking before children. Nor were the magistrates less partial. The witnesses—one of whom was a prizefighter—had no written notes of Holyoake's words, but were allowed to swear "to the best of their belief." It happened that one of Holyoake's friends, in offering bail, said that "to the best of his belief" he was worth £$o. He was at once dismissed, and when Holyoake pointed out the equality with the witnesses' testimony, one of the clerical magistrates rebuked him for "quibbling."

He was committed for trial, and handed over to the police. When he returned to the station he was put through an examination, not in physical condition but in theology, by the police-surgeon, a Mr. Pinching. And when the doctor's long arguments failed, he observed that he was "sorry the days were gone by when we could send you and Owen of Lanark to the stake instead of to Gloucester Jail." He was shut in a filthy room, with a too obviously verminous person, but was presently told he must walk to Gloucester. If he could have remained twenty-four hours at Cheltenham, where he had friends, he might have arranged bail in less than the fortnight it actually took. They fastened a pair of irons—a pair at first so ill-fitting that they tore his skin —on his wrists, and he was brought out between two burly policemen, and made to walk through the town in this damning guise. They intended to make him walk the nine miles to Gloucester, but as they passed the station—railways were then beginning to spread their iron net over the land—friends were allowed to pay his fare and that of his guardians to Gloucester. But the irons were not removed, and the people of Gloucester saw the same spectacle of a pale, refined, delicate young man, guarded with every indication of the last criminality, and were told it was "the blasphemer" from Cheltenham. His pockets were searched, his notebook and papers taken from him, and he was put in a cell "with the fetor of death in every corner." A grating at the top sent enough dim light on the filthy bed to show the troops of lice, and, worn as he was, he dare not lie down that night. He sat on the edge of the bed all night, and'reflected on religion.

After his disappearance his Socialist and Chartist friends held an indignant meeting at Cheltenham, and some of them resolved to defy the clergy. His host, George Adams, sent for a parcel of atheistical literature, though he was not an atheist, and put copies of the *Oracle* in his window. The police sent an agent to buy one, and at once secured a warrant for his arrest. His wife, a handsome and spirited woman, defiantly continued the sale, until she too was arrested on going to see her husband in prison. A policeman accompanied her home to get her baby—a child at the breast—and she brought it into the jail. They wanted to put her in the common room with the drunken and debased women there, but she obtained permission from the superintendent to pass the night with her child in the police-kitchen. She had left four other young children in her home; and when indignant neighbours took these into their houses, her landlord came and locked the door and took the key away. She was released until trial on a light bail, but her husband remained in jail, and, as he suffered from inflamed eyes, nearly lost his sight in the dank and draughty cell.

Holyoake remained in jail for a fortnight. On his first appearance in the common room, the experts in criminality he found there refused to regard him as one of themselves, and treated him with respect. They gave him some of their mint-tea (the common luxury of the poor at the time) to help him to swallow his coarse bread, and he used what influence he could for their improvement. The assizes would begin soon, and, having no funds to employ counsel and little trust in their conduct of such a case, he had to prepare his defence. He meditated an elaborate argument, but the chaplain refused to let him have sent in most of the works he needed. At last his friends, who were active at London and elsewhere, appealed to the Home Secretary. Sir James Graham had already spoken in the House of the "grave irregularities" committed in regard to him, and he retained an open ear to petitions.

Bail was found, and he set out on foot for Birmingham to see his wife and child. He lectured for the Socialists in Lawrence Street Chapel. But the metropolis was now buzzing with his name. Journals of influence were commenting severely on Cheltenham and its ways. In the *Weekly Dispatch,* especially, W. M. Thompson and Captain Williams (" Publicola") wrote scathing paragraphs, and Mr. Roebuck elicited strong censure on the magistrates from the Home Secretary in the House. The general public were at least able to appreciate the determination of the Cheltenham authorities to wring an oath (in connection with his bail) out of a man they were prosecuting for atheism. To London Holyoake soon proceeded, walking most of the way. It seemed an "enchanted city" after the provincial towns, and it furnished him with useful friends and some funds. The first night was spent in a summer-house in Ryall's garden, working out the plan of defence. Collections were made for him in the Owenite room, the Rotunda in Blackfriars Road, and elsewhere. Captain Williams attended his lecture at the Rotunda, and published a lengthy abstract of his plea for free speech. Holyoake was in poor condition and nervous, but he is described in the *Dispatch* as having "uttered many striking truths of an original character, which elicited considerable applause." Mr. Ashurst, who became a warm friend, and Sergeant (then Mr.) Parry assisted him with his legal preparation. One day he went down to the House, and was hailed by Mr. Roebuck, the distinguished Radical politician, who was befriending him there. Veterans in the cause of free speech were filled with admiration. George Julian Harney wrote from Sheffield: He was not three weeks, as he says somewhere, but two, in jail, and there are other slight slips in his record. I find him lecturing in Birmingham on June 17th, and writing from there on June 26th. Other letters show that he is in London in the middle of July. He was back for trial on August 2nd. However, he has underrated rather than exaggerated the brutality of the proceedings.

"friend Of The Human Race,

"In forwarding the enclosed amount of subscriptions received by me up to this date,.allow me to observe that you must not judge of the number of your friends in Sheffield by the small amount of money subscribed. Hundreds of your Chartist (to say nothing of your Socialist) friends are too poor to give even a penny, and fervent are their wishes for your triumph over your persecutors. Another martyr has been sacrificed at the shrine of tyranny. Samuel Holberry, convicted at the York Spring Assizes of 1840 of sedition, and sentenced to four years' imprisonment, expired in his dungeon (York Castle) yesterday morning, at a quarter past four. As if in mockery of his dying agonies an order of release came from the Home Office a day or two before his death, with the conditions annexed that he should find bail himself in £200 and two sureties of 100 each to be of good behaviour! His poor wife (whom you have seen at my house) was refused permission to see him only two or three weeks since. She is distracted. Shall there be no retribution for this foul and bloody murder? When, oh when, will the human race rise in its might and trample in the dust the monarchic, aristocratic, priestly, and profithunting villains who oppress, plunder, and murder them?

"That the fates may preserve you from the torture under which poor gallant noble-hearted Holberry has sunk into his grave is the heart-felt hope of, "My dear Holyoake,

"Fraternally thine, "george Julian C. Harney..

"Sheffield, June 24th, 1842."

There was no melodrama in Harney's hatred of Whig and Tory, but there is more significance perhaps in the attitude toward Holyoake of Richard Carlile, who had spent ten years in jail for uttering unpopular opinions. They met by accident on Blackfriars Bridge, and Carlile invited him to attend his lecture that night at the Hall of Science (City Road). Carlile hated atheism, and taught "Sacred Socialism" (Socialism allied with a liberal Christianity). Holyoake, after the lecture, opposed his plea for a symbolic interpretation of biblical statements. He contended that "the moral test of the Scriptures was sufficient, and the only one that had popular education in it, and needed neither ridicule, nor bitterness, nor scorn to enforce it." Carlile was still ardent as a youth in the cause of free discussion, but he had quarrelled with his old comrades, and had grown sensitive and somewhat morose in his isolation. He was invited by Ryall to address a meeting on behalf of Holyoake, and consented, on condition that he be "not called upon to play the second fiddle to any man who has not the same experience and standing on the question." He was a very difficult colleague to them all with his mixture of red republicanism and Sermon on the Mount (" but I am not such a Christian," he naively wrote to Ryall, "as to be passively spitten upon and smote in the cheek "). He joined in the fray, and the sequel is instructive for our purpose. Before his death (a few months afterwards) he quarrelled violently with most of them, but Holyoake fired his enthusiasm. In his last letter, after some controversy with even Holyoake, he wrote: "I court his further acquaintance, and he may ever command my respectful attention." Of Southwell he said: "I feel a dignified gratification that I have never sought his company anywhere but in his imprisonment."

From the admiration of London Holyoake returned to spend a few days at Birmingham before his trial.

"It was a bright summer afternoon when I set out alone from the house of my eldest sister, in which my family resided, in Aston, Birmingham, to proceed to Gloucester Assizes. It was not in my power to leave any provision for those I left behind, owing to the unforeseen and unsought apprehension which had befallen me. My little daughter, Madeline, ran from her mother's knee to the door, when she found I had gone, and called after me down the street. Her sweet clear voice arrested me. I looked back and saw her dark eyes gleaming. I never met her glance again, nor heard her voice any more."

Back he went to the heavy atmosphere of Gloucester. His friends had insisted that he should not be tried again by the Cheltenham magistrates, as they intended and as the normal course involved, and the Home Secretary put a measure through that transferred all trials for opinion to the assizes, where there would be an independent judge. The Gloucester Assizes opened on August 2nd, and Holyoake and Mr. and Mrs. Adams were there from the start. There was no intention of proceeding against the wife, but she was put to needless suffering by not being informed of this, and kept about the court for ten days. Holyoake procured counsel for Adams, through his friends; but when the barrister concluded by an expression of his client's "contrition," Holyoake called to Adams: "Don't permit him to do that unless you are really contrite." His sense of honour—it was no mere defiance—must have seemed Quixotic even to some of his friends. Adams protested that he was not contrite, and he got one month's imprisonment.

As Holyoake had intimated that he would defend himself, Mr. Justice Erskine decided to take his case last; and when it came to Saturday, and there was some presentiment of a long speech, the trial was set down for the Monday morning.

On that morning the Shire Hall was crowded with an excited audience. Country-gentry, ladies, and clergymen mingled with sober groups of Chartist and Socialist workers, and sipped their wine and nibbled their cakes as the long hours passed. It was not intended by the prosecution that the case should last long. The jury—"seven farmers, one grocer, one poulterer, one miller, one maltster, and one nondescript shopkeeper," as Captain Williams wrote — were not improved in temper by the protracted neglect of their business, and Holyoake had no care whatever to conciliate them by small considerations. When his name was called, a pale, long-haired, suspicious-looking young man entered the dock, and peremptorily ordered the jailer to hand him up a large corded box. The court looked on in amazement and despair, as he occupied twenty minutes in silently arranging his mass of books and papers! Then a sonorous indictment set forth that George Jacob Holyoake, "labourer"—a deliberate and malicious untruth—did "maliciously, unlawfully, and wickedly compose, speak, utter, pronounce, and publish with a loud voice"—"which I never had," he says—certain terrible things "to the high displeasure of Almighty God, to the great scandal and reproach of the Christian religion," and so on. Worse and more really censurable blasphemies were more common in the streets of England at that time than they are now, but Holyoake's flash of impulsive humour was dressed in a legal San Benito.

Holyoake's distrust of barristers did not please those of the profession who were present. One of them gave an unflattering sketch of him as "a wretched-looking creature, scarcely emerging from boyhood, whose wiry and dishevelled hair, 'lip unconscious of the razor's edge,' and dingy looks, gave him the appearance of a low German student."

There is no need to dwell on the evidence, but Mr. Alexander's opening of the case for the prosecution almost deserves to be preserved in full. In all seriousness it is a perfect parallel of the immortal speech of Sergeant Buzfuz. One extract from it will suffice:

"The defendant, on the 24th of May last, issued placards for a lecture to be delivered in Cheltenham. In these placards he announced, not the diabolical, the dreadful topics which he descanted upon, not anything which would lead the reader to imagine or expect what really took place, but he gave out his subject as a lecture upon Home Colonisation, Emigration, and Poor Laws. Mark this, gentlemen of the jury! Had he given in his announcements any hint of what was to take place, his end might have been defeated, and no audience attracted to listen to the blasphemous expressions you have heard set out in the indictment. But he did obtain an audience, a numerous audience, and then declared that.... and —though it pains me to repeat the horrible blasphemy— that he would place the Deity upon half-pay. ... It may be urged to you that these

things were said in answer to a question, that the innuendoes must be made out. Innuendoes! I should think it an insult to the understandings of twelve jurymen—of twelve intelligent men—to call witnesses to prove innuendoes. But I shall place the case before you, and leave it in your hands."

It reads like a caricature of legal manners. In view of the facts we have given it was, a concentrated mass of untruth.

Mr. Alexander's case was contemptuously brief, and he sat down with an instant expectation of justice; but the clock struck hour after hour, and Holyoake's voice grew stronger, and his argument gave promise of infinity. When he had spoken for six hours—he began at a quarter to twelve—the judge sent the governor of the jail to ask him, courteously and patiently, how much longer he would be. He thought "three hours more would suffice," and, after a brief adjournment, he resumed his speech, and continued it until ten minutes to nine! Captain Mason, the governor of the jail, afterwards pleasantly observed that he deserved six months for the speech. The jury must have thought it not without ability for a "labourer," but as it rather proved every man's right to utter blasphemy whenever he felt disposed than answered the actual indictment, they found him guilty. They may have recollected that a Gloucester jury had been regarded with suspicion some time before for acquitting a Mormon preacher who was charged with blasphemy for saying that " Euclid was as true as the Bible." Mr. Justice Erskine had suggested a way of escape. He said that if Holyoake would convince the jury that he merely meant that the incomes of the clergy ought to be reduced (which was clearly the positive idea of his words), he would recommend a verdict of not guilty. But Holyoake detested the very shadow of compromise. He pleaded for free speech, and the judge had no alternative. He said that Holyoake had spoken from impulse, had not connived at the putting of the question to him, and could hardly have avoided answering it; but he had spoken with "improper levi-

ty," and he must be "imprisoned in the Common Jail for six calendar months."

Erskine's conduct was strongly censured in some of the London papers, and Mr. Parry described it as marked by "ridiculous onesidedness." Holyoake, on the other hand, spoke of him even at the time with respect, and described his bearing as "most dignified and urbane. " He afterwards dedicated his *Short and Easy Method with the Saints* to Erskine, and said he had had, "on the whole, a fair trial and a patient hearing." He might have used stronger language with perfect justice. Erskine was a religious man, and sincerely believed atheism to be a source of crime. He could not possibly be free from bias. But, though his attitude and judgment were unduly severe, his courtesy and patience were remarkable during the long speech, which he could justly have curtailed.

There is no need to summarise or analyse the speech. There were excellent points made, and able passages, but it was weakened by its length and its lack of symmetry. He dealt at length with the proceedings at Cheltenham and in the House, the newspaper comments on the case, the philosophy of theism, the tenets of Socialism, the law of blasphemy, his own career, and anything he could connect with the charge. His long quotations—from Socrates, Rousseau, Godwin, T. More, Lord Russell, Chalmers, Burke, Blackstone, Mosheim, Bulwer, Channing, Guizot, etc.—would have of themselves taken hours to read. Erskine must have felt that he would hear again of so original and spirited a young man. Richard Carlile, who was in court, spoke of his defence with rapture. There were passages that subdued the court, and made ladies weep. But the undoubted ability shown in the speech was too much distended. A pithy, graceful, two-hour speech, such as he could well write, would have been better. But he had been pompously told by the magistrates that he would not be heard at all: he had a tradition of long self-defences before him—one Chartist a few years before (Benbow of Chester) had spoken for ten hours and a half: and he had a rare audience and still rarer liberty. He felt that, as we all feel now, there was an iniquitous law in the land, and he willingly suffered as a protest against it. He benefited a far wider range of critics than the opponents of theology; and we who wander freely down the broad avenues to-day may think with gratitude of the resonant axe and stout heart of the pioneer.

The story of his adventures in prison is familiar, and I need do little more than add a few details from forgotten sources. He experienced at once that imprisonment was to mean something more than detention. He had had no food for thirteen hours, though ladies in court had offered him some of their tartlets; and the inexorable regulations forbade the giving of food out of hours. A cup of water and a small apple from a kindly warder's pocket made his supper, and he tossed feverishly all night on his hard bed. Then began the grim routine of daily life. Until his health gave way, and the doctor was compelled to interfere, his diet consisted of gruel, coarse bread, and potatoes. The rice that was substituted for potatoes twice a week had "a blue cast, a saline taste, and a slimy look." After two months he was allowed a bit of salt beef twice a week, but " I could not often taste it, seldom chew it, and never digest it—I should say it was rather leather *mode* than *a la mode."* Later his friends, who were busy with their slender subscription-lists (chiefly for his family) and indignationmeetings, often sent him human food. The cells were dirty and damp, and exercise had to be taken in a tiny yard that made him giddy. He often thought of Holberry's death from these causes in his northern jail, and of another Chartist prisoner who had succumbed since in a Midland jail. It was fortunate for him that the Home Secretary was known to have acted to his advantage.

But, apart from the great danger to his delicate health, the moral privations were worse than the physical. Visitors were rarely admitted, and they could only stand with him for a few minutes, and generally speak through repellent bars which he could allow no lady to

face. In the earlier months he was cheered by the letters that came. Carlile, who was also his first visitor, wrote enthusiastically:

"My Dear Holyoake,

"I had not made a proper estimate of your worth to society until I heard your defence yesterday. It was certainly the most splendid of the kind ever delivered in this country. More power, as physical power, in delivery might be found; but more moral power, more sweetness, more beauty, more persuasion, could not be found. I could scarcely restrain myself from jumping into the dock to embrace you on several occasions. I envy not the man his earthy, clod-like, vicious religion that, after that defence, should condemn you. It is not my Christianity, nor that of the Bible, nor that of the Natural and the Spiritual worlds, that could so condemn you; but the same Pharisaical righteousness that crucified the Saviour, gave the poison-cup to Socrates, and that has destroyed, banished, or persecuted the wise and good of all nations.

"I shall not be idle: will fill the *Oracle of Reason* weekly, if that help be needed. The moral world shall lose nothing in progress through your imprisonment. I will either join you, or shame the authorities of your imprisonment. At a moment of leisure I shall write to the judge and to Peel. I know nothing of the character of Sir James Graham, to write with effect to him.

"I advocate all your principles, but my dearly purchased experience has put them beyond the reach of indictment. It is not that I fear imprisonment, but that I have grown wiser and stronger. I have as much resolution now to suffer for the battle of free discussion as in 1817 when I began. I have a second letter to-day pressing me to come to Bristol. I propose being there on the 29th, but I have a great taste for three nights in the theatre of Gloucester. On Sunday I visit Stroud to preach on Radborough Common.

"Let your imprisonment be like a rod in pickle for your enemies. This was my sustaining resolution through nine years. I feel as if I had been well pick-

led, and will lay it on those who now need tickling with it. Take care of your health. Six months' imprisonment would have been felt by me as a joke. I have taken as much voluntarily rather than yield or ask for liberation. Adieu and strengthen. Respects to Adams. Have just sent Mrs. Adams a large bundle of books.

"Richard Carlile."

The good feeling with Carlile was somewhat disturbed when he heard that the veteran was describing him as "a Christian." This was at the meeting on Radborough Common, which gathered together 3,000 people in a rural district: a sufficient answer to those who pretended that they initiated prosecutions solely to prevent the spread of obnoxious opinions. Carlile's words were published, and the *Oracle* took umbrage. Holyoake did not feel that the epithet was flattering after his recent experience of Christians, and he disliked Carlile's use of religious terms. He wrote him a pleasant letter with a view to mitigate the effect of the controversy in the *Oracle.* It began:

"My Dear Sir,

'' My residence on the banks of the Severn has one convenience. I enjoy such a happy propinquity to dock bells, basin bells, cathedral bells, and jail bells, that should I *re-bel* it might easily chime in with the others. But my residence has this disadvantage. It makes me resemble Homer in that unenviable particular in which 'nothing but rumour reached him.'"

Firmly and courteously he intimated that he could not share Carlile's "Sacred Socialism." In a long reply

Carlile regretted that he had become "infected with

Southwell's cavalier method of adopting the most repugnant of titles," and maintained that Socialism Vol. 1. G was dying of inanition and Chartism ending in folly. They parted with mutual respect, as I stated earlier. Carlile died soon afterwards, but his wife and daughter communicated with Holyoake long afterwards in terms of affection.

Many other expressions of regard came to cheer the prisoner. Mr. Parry wrote a long letter, from which I quote a little:

"My Dear Sir,

"I take shame to myself for not having before expressed to you by letter that sympathy which I trust you will believe I have always had with your disinterested struggle against an unjust and arbitrary law. It was only, however, a day or two since, in calling at your friend's, Mr. Ryall, that I learned there was a possibility of communicating with you at Gloucester Jail, and I now avail myself of that possibility at the earliest moment open to me.... Judge Erskine has been roughly handled in the *Weekly Dispatch* for his ridiculous onesidedness. But from judges we must never expect either enlarged or generous opinions. Their minds are too cramped by education and too fettered by precedent to understand, much less to enunciate, the genuine principles of mental freedom. Indeed the whole of English society is impregnated in respect of theological belief with the most slavish prejudices. You know, alas, too well how atheism fares: but deism, Unitarianism, or almost any other ism than that which swallows the whole mess of superstition at one blind gulp is hunted out of society just as we hunt noxious vermin out of our houses.... I admire the bravery of men like yourself determined to protest against this growing social disease which, unless timelily resisted, threatens to absorb all independence of thought and action...."

A friend sent him this extract of a sermon preached by Mr. W. J. Fox at South Place Chapel:

"While on the seashore, with the waves of the ocean boasting as it were in their freedom, I received a letter from a poor fellow in Gloucester Jail, asking me what I thought of the Christianity that had put him there for the expression of his honest conviction. He is a young man who is not able to perceive and acknowledge the existence of a superintending Providence. He was giving an exposition of a system which, though visionary, is beautiful, and leads the mind to an elevated state of enjoyment. When a question was put to him on the

subject of his religious opinions, he did not shrink from a declaration of those opinions, unconnected as they were with the subject, on which he had been discoursing.... The person to whom I refer is Holyoake, the friend and able disciple of Charles Reece Pemberton."

Cheerful letters came from his humbler friends. One letter reached the jail with the postal address:

"George Jacob Holyoake, Esq., who is engaged in a six months' study of the love, joy, peace, and long-suffering of Christianity and of the beauties and mysteries of our holy religion, in one of her Majesty's seminaries for the spread of learning and piety, that is to say, the Jail, Gloucester.".

His Irish friend, George White, sent him merry greetings from the neighbouring jail at Warwick. "How are you getting on in your country seat? I think we had better act like the aristocracy in future, that is, give up our old surnames and adopt the title of our respective country seats." Southwell wrote: "You seem to have gained golden opinions of all sorts of people. Good judges say that you made the very best appeal for liberty that has yet been heard within those halls called Courts of Justice. There's honour for you."

But all this alleviation of his sufferings was denied him during the latter part of his time, when he needed it most. He was not allowed to see any friends, or to write to them, even to his wife. All his letters were confiscated. When he complained of these privations, some of the visiting magistrates took occasion to denounce him before the other prisoners as "the worst felon in the jail and the most atrocious"—to quote a letter written at the time. He thought he foresaw serious conflict with the authorities, which might have dangerous and degrading consequences. He held a brave view of life, and felt that duty to his wife and child forbade him to take his life, except under intolerable hardship. But he marked a circle with a stone round one leg of his iron bed, so that, in case of need, he would be able to tilt up the bed, lay his head on the circle, and then pull it down so as to drive the leg

through his brain.

One of the visiting magistrates was the brother of Sir Astley Cooper, and a humane man. He would tell Holyoake in a gruff way that he was "a fool for being an atheist," and then add that "he could not be one—he did not look or speak like one." His son was chaplain of the jail, and Holyoake suggests that his conversion was "a family speculation." The chaplain insisted that Holyoake should attend chapel, but a prisoner for atheism could plead that that was rather an incongruous demand. They did not care to carry him into chapel, as he protested they must, and he escaped most of the usual services amongst a herd of felons. One day the chaplain invited him to the chapel out of hours, and gave him an oration to himself. He asked what Holyoake had to say, but his quaint patient insisted that "the place was too cold for reasoning," and that he would only discuss with him on equal terms. They adjourned to a warm cell, and had some argument. When the chaplain offered him a cheap Bible, Holyoake objected that "it was not respectful to God to present His Word in that curmudgeon form "; he "would accept a betterlooking copy, with marginal references down the centre, such as might assist him in trying to reconcile what appeared to him its many contradictions."

Another clergyman who sought to convert him was an aged and usually quiet Wesleyan minister amongst the visiting magistrates. One day he quoted the psalmist's opinion of the atheist to Holyoake in presence of his fellow-magistrates and the prisoners: "David says you are a fool." Holyoake, instead of entering into a long explanation that he did *not* say there was no God, and that very few men—least of all, fools—ever did, merely replied that he "no more admired rudeness in the mouth of David than he did in the mouth of a magistrate." Another clerical magistrate, with more penetration, lent him Paley's *Natural Theology* and Leslie's *Short and Easy Method with the Deists.* Holyoake wrote pamphlets in reply to both—which we will see presently—"to show that they had received careful attention." When commissioners were sent to examine the jail and were interrogating Holyoake, he said amongst other things that "county magistrates did not seem very bright, and had no clear idea of their duties."

When they wished to enforce the prison dress Holyoake declared that they would have to come and dress him every morning, and he escaped the indignity. He was also successful in obtaining permission to sit up until nine o'clock. But the Home Secretary, who sent down the order, had not directed that he was to have a light until nine o'clock, and the local authorities ruled that he should not. The device with which he partly met their tyranny was singularly ingenious. He stuck pins in two rows down the sides of the cover of a book, and ran threads across. When a piece of paper was thrust up under the threads, it was practically ruled, with tangible lines, for writing purposes. He hid the contrivance, and wrote letters and articles for the *Oracle* in the dark. The evenings were long and cold, for the winter soon came on, but he must have written his pamphlets in the daytime. In the common-room of the jail he opened a school for the prisoners, who were almost all illiterate, and tried to impress them. One wonders if any of these Gloucester gentlemen of 1842 came to see the humour, at least, of a prisoner, who had been put away and was being treated with barbarity as socially dangerous, using his time to discharge those social duties that the country so criminally neglected.

The darkest and most dangerous hour of all was in October. The governor one day called him into the yard, and handed him a letter from his wife. Their little girl, Madeline, a child of "much beauty and promise," had died. If he had known at the time the whole circumstances of her illness, his name might have been added to the list of sensitive men, Chartists and Atheists, who succumbed, or nearly lost their reason, in the jails of England in the nineteenth century. She had contracted a fever while her little frame was enfeebled

through poverty. Friends were subscribing to send a little weekly to Mrs. Holyoake, but they were mainly poor workers, and it was "the hungry forties." The money came irregularly, and wife and child knew hunger.

It was represented to Holyoake that he might obtain his freedom by sending up a petition and promising to abandon the advocacy of Socialism. He refused to do so. As the time for his release drew near, it was again suggested to him that, if he would promise to refrain from propagandism, they would find a scholastic position for him and his wife. Again he gave an utter refusal. "My wife," he said later, "would have resented it if I had done it on her account. So when I was free I took the warpath again." He was released on February 6th, 1843, and after a round of grateful visits in Gloucester and Cheltenham rejoined his poor wife at Birmingham.

Thirty-six years afterwards, while a Co-operative Congress was being held at Gloucester, a number of the delegates came before the jail in the course of their sight-seeing. "Take off your hats, lads! That's where Holyoake was imprisoned," one of them cried, and their heads were bared in memory of his suffering.

CHAPTER V THE END OF OWENISM

Holyoake's resolve to return to "the warpath of opinion" needs no explanation. The policy of repression has rarely silenced any but the less earnest and therefore less dangerous. You must burn your heretic, or else leave him entirely alone. Tolerable martyrdoms are always good advertisements. The only effect in Holyoake's case was to make him feel more acutely that there was tyranny in the land. When George Combe made a careful study of his young assistant's cranium, he seems to have overlooked the bump of "combativeness." He knew Holyoake as a quiet, refined youth, modestly exhibiting his ingenious compasses and his ornate copy of Euclid, and he discovered in him "a strong organ of form," "causality considerable," "individuality," and other obvious qualities. Although Holyoake confesses to a boyish ambi-

tion for pugilistic fame—one of his sisters had a pugilist beau—few could at that time have discerned a restless agitator and fighter on public questions in the bookish youth. But he came to find himself in a world where one could not hold a single great ideal without fighting, and he learned to fight; and the prison-cure for his impetuosity had the not unusual effect of trebling it. In fact, it was somehow a world in which all the men he most respected disappeared at intervals into a jail.

During the next few years he remained an Owenite, but he naturally associated with those Owenites who felt that the times demanded an aggressive campaign against theology. The only question that occurs to one is whether his good taste or good temper suffered from the terrible experiences he had endured. It is pleasant to find that he returned to the fray with all his old humour and restraint. His address to the readers of the *Oracle* (Feb. 18th, 1843) after his release opens:

"My Friends,—It is now six months since, cut and hacked, I fell, not merely in the language of the parable, but literally, among thieves. Of my new acquaintances, the saints, I am afraid I must say, as W. Hutton said of an untoward sweetheart, 'there was little love between us at first, and heaven has pleased to decrease it on a further acquaintance.' Christians profess to draw men to Jesus with cords of love, but were it not for their judicious foresight in telling us that they are 'cords of love,' I guess that few would find it out."

The article was a temperate plea for freedom of speech. As he soon took to the lecturing field, he wrote few articles in the *Oracle*, which lingered lustily for another year; and it is only when prosecutions multiply among his friends that his writing loses its philosophic temper. One might withhold admiration if it were otherwise.

One of the first scenes of his renewed lecturing activity was Cheltenham! A large audience gathered, and he defiantly repeated to them the words that had brought trouble on him, on the plausible ground that he "had been called upon to pay a certain price for free speech, and that, as he had paid the price, he had purchased the right." There was little danger now in exercising it. The Cheltenham magistrates had been so severely censured in the House, and so widely ridiculed in the country, that the fight was over in that part of the land.

The words are originally in *The Merry Wives of Windsor.*

One of the Cheltenham papers (the *Free Press)* had openly defended him from the first, and his speech at Gloucester had made a good impression. The foreman of the jury told Carlile that they themselves were impressed by it, but they were clearly directed to say guilty. He gave other lectures at Worcester, Coventry, Leicester, and Northampton, and made his headquarters amongst the Socialists at Worcester.

A faded handbill that lies before me invites people to '' come and hear the Liberated Blasphemer" in the Social Institution at Leicester. The titles are, "Christianity as displayed in the recent prosecution for blasphemy," and similar inevitable themes. These lectures were now his chief source of income, but with admission fixed at " one penny " we cannot assume that his experiences proved profitable. Even at this period, however, his lectures were often purely constructive, and we shall find him return more fully to social interests presently.

One offer of employment that came to him at this time is interesting in many respects. Readers of his *History of Cooperation* will remember how, in 1847, Ryall and he made a visit to a communal settlement at Ham Common. The settlers were imbued with the ideas of the mystic Pierrepont Graves as well as Robert Owen, and lived austerely. They walked out to Alcott House by night and "found it by observing a tall patriarch's feet projecting through the window. It was a device of the Concordium to ensure ventilation and early rising. By a bastinado of the soles of the prophet with pebbles we obtained admission in the early morning."

They had raw cabbage for breakfast, and, when his wife asked for salt, she was begged to keep it hidden under her plate so as not to deprave the taste of the weaker brethren. It was from this Spartan home that an offer of teaching employment came to him in 1843. It ran: I find this interesting statement in an unpublished letter of Carlile's.

"Probably you have heard of a very small community now associating together at Alcott House, Ham Common, Surrey, under the name of Concordium: a sort of industrial college, at this present time, having a printer and printing press, tailors, shoemakers, bakers, gardeners, and other labourers: both sexes associating kindly together as one family, and though not manifesting any great doings as yet, are to be highly commended for their sincere and resolute opposition (in practical habits) to the principles, practices, and manners of the Old Immoral World—reprobating war, slavery, and intemperance, and gluttony, and bigotry, not only in profession by wordy declamation, but by discontinuing and discouraging all habits that tend and lead to the above horrors. The Concordists at Alcott House wish to form a school there, and are desirous to meet with a competent educator, previous to agreeing to receive any more children into the establishment, there being four now there. The diet is exclusively limited to breadstuffs and farinaceous food and fruits, fresh and dried, of every sort that can be obtained, and all kinds of vegetables, and water is the only drink supplied. Neither milk, butter, cheese, eggs, nor any species of flesh meat, nor animal food: neither tea, coffee, nor any of those artificial stimulants do the Concordists partake of, or supply to others. There are married couples, and parents and children now in the Concordium. The working members receive no wages, but are supplied with lodging, food, clothing, washing, baths, firing, candles, and whatever is needful, for their giving their services to the Concordium. About eight hours daily is the usual average for them to work: eight for sleep: and eight for bathing, recreation, meals, and improvement."

Holyoake had by this time mastered the coyness of the cigar, had vainly tried to rise to the level of vegetarianism, and was fond of tea and other "horrors" of the Old Immoral World. He did not go to Ham Common. Indeed, his taste of metropolitan life had been so pleasant that he could no longer settle in the provinces. "Londoners," he afterwards wrote, "are the lapidaries of the nation: they polish the diamond found in the provinces." On May 7th he severed his connection with the Worcester Society, and went up to London. On the day of his arrival he noted in his diary: "Penniless. If I starve in a garret I follow illustrious precedents."

Immediately after his arrival "Branch 53" of the movement invited him to become its secretary, at a salary of ten shillings per week. They met at the Rotunda in Blackfriars Road, and Holyoake lectured there occasionally, but more frequently in the provinces. He also gave classes "for the study of literary composition, logic, and oral investigation " at Bailey's Coffee House, Soho, under the auspices of the "London Theological Association"—a group of free-thinkers. For these he charged a fee of sixpence a week, or five shillings a quarter. But fresh imprisonments constantly occurring, he was compelled to found an "Anti-Persecution Union," and devote most of his time in 1843 to combative work.

Paterson, his Sheffield curate, had briskly succeeded him in the dangerous chair of the *Oracle,* and was following the "bloody noses" method with vigour. Like Southwell, he had had military adventures, and was acquainted with strong language. As he edited the paper from London, he had the fiery Ryall at his elbow. They took a shop in Holywell Street, and, their articles not attracting sufficient notice, they began to enliven the windows with large cartoons illustrating incidents described in the Old Testament. The London public now came in crowds. It was stated in the press that 20,000 people a day visited the place. The *Standard,* apparently with a view to dissuade people from going, gave prominent notices of " the abomination," "the den of infamy," etc.

There seemed to be more ground here for prosecution than in the casual remark of a studious youth, and the police intervened; though it was unfortunate that their chief witness to the harrowing nature of the placards, a sergeant, was convicted not long afterwards of taking bribes. All this, of course, was before Holyoake came, and had not his support. However, a more effective crusade was at that moment opened by the police at Edinburgh, and Paterson and Southwell and other adventurous spirits buckled on their swords and hastened there.

The Anti-Persecution Union had at first little success. The Owenites were not only divided in opinion, but were giving every shilling to save their community in Hampshire, of which we shall see more presently. It was, moreover, a very calamitous period for the workers of the country, and few of the middle-class people would enter a Hall of Science. The impotence of the heretics was bringing really barbarous treatment on them, and the wonder is that so few men of intelligence and character intervened. At London, about this time, a young atheistic speaker was arrested, and, on the police stating that he had also "talked about brothels," the shuddering magistrate punished him severely. What he had really said was that the Dean and Chapter of Westminster ought to be ashamed to draw rent from such places, as they then did; but the boy's father and friends were refused admission to court, and there was the customary caricature of justice and more fuel for the literary fires of the atheists.

A case then arose that provided a more respectable base for the operations of the Union. Stories were reaching England of the persecution of Protestants by the Catholic authorities at Madeira. A native Protestant woman was condemned to be hanged there in 1844 for denying the divinity of the consecrated wafer. She was Portuguese, and England could do nothing but express its amazement. But in 1843 an English Protestant, Dr. Kalley, had been put in jail by the authorities, and a pretty situation resulted. Holyoake at once

wrote to the prisoner, and offered him assistance from the Union's funds. "Your alleged offence," he wrote, "is against the mother of God. Mother or father, it makes no difference to the Anti-Persecution Union." It made a vast difference to other people. Kalley himself had the good sense to decline their aid politely, and entered on a long correspondence with a view to convert Holyoake. But the full irony of the situation was seen in Scotland. In September a meeting was called at Edinburgh, with the Lord Provost in the chair, to express indignation at the persecution of Dr. Kalley at Madeira. Paterson and Southwell went there to join in the indignation, and the Lord Provost and his friends, meeting to protest against the repression of heresy in Funchal, promptly handed them over to the police as blasphemers. Paterson was sentenced to fifteen months' imprisonment, and matters became somewhat entangled. The atheists published letters from Paterson in Perth jail, which sent "love to Dr. Kalley and all friends"; while the good folk at Edinburgh, who had put him in jail, were urging the Government to take up Dr. Kalley's case, and were at the same time carrying on a fierce war with the local group of free-thinkers because they demanded freedom of speech. Aged men like Finlay and sensitive young women like Miss Roalfe (who had gone from London, and reopened the book-store of an imprisoned Scotchman) were lodged in their jails for selling criticisms of the Bible, which the officers were expressly sent to purchase. The humour of the matter was complete, and the rhetoric of the atheists exultant, when, in the end, the Government did take up Dr. Kalley's case and demand his release and 1,200 compensation!

This state of things readily accounts for the warmth of the language that Holyoake occasionally used at that time. Some idea of the effect on the more sensitive of the heretics may be gathered from a letter of Carlile's widow to Holyoake, in which she exclaims: "Although my exertions in the cause of human redemption have been produc-

tive only to myself of poverty and all its concomitant evils, yet were no other to be found in the world, I would still struggle single-handed with the enemy and overcome it, or die in the attempt, and my last words should be—Free Discussion." Miss Sharples—she was not legally married to Carlile, as he had an insufferable wife living—had herself been a lecturer in early years, and, though her strength was too worn with long endurance for her to do anything, her spirit fired others. Little groups of free-thinkers gathered in various parts of London; and into one of these, a few years later, a gifted and fiery youth was to be drawn who would carry the direct war on theology all over England once more, under the name of Charles Bradlaugh.

Many of the titles of Holyoake's lectures show that he was not wholly absorbed in critical work, and he continued his educational efforts. It is plain, indeed, that his concern for free discussion was a broad social interest, though the circumstances gave it a narrower look. In August (1844) he published the pamphlet he had written in jail, *Paley Refuted in his own Words,* which eventually ran to a sixth edition (in 1866), at a price of sixpence. It is rather pretentious, but fairly acute and informed. He shows acquaintance with all the literature of the time bearing on the subject, which his colleagues rarely do. His chief objection is that Paley "suddenly abandoned, at the very moment when its assistance seemed to promise curious revelations, the analogy which had been the guide to his feet." In other words Paley proved an architect to exist, and then scouted all analogy in tracing the features of this architect With some cleverness he reasons that intelligence is always displayed in proportion to organisation; and so, if analogy is to be our guide, the Supreme Architect should have vast organisation, whereas Paley denied that he had any. He also stresses those darker features of the universe that Paley conveniently ignored. It is interesting to see that, even at this earliest date, his last note is not criticism, but an appeal for positive moral and social culture instead of dogmatic speculation. His Unitarian biographer, Miss Collet, says that, though somewhat crude, it "manifests decided intellectual power in conception and arrangement." It was published by Hetherington, and is incorrectly marked in the catalogue at the British Museum as first published in 1847.

In December (1843) he engaged in a new enterprise that occupied much of his time. The *Oracle* had suspended its utterances some weeks before for lack of funds, but it was practically the same journal that appeared on December 16th, under the editorship of Holyoake and Ryall, and with the name of the *Movement.* Its motto was Bentham's phrase: "Maximise morals, minimise religion." Holyoake endeavoured all through to keep their positive and educational aim in rank with the negative one. When the authorities threatened heavy action, he could sincerely reply: "We have not written from bravado, but from simplicity, and we have known no policy but that of not knowing expediency." The paper professed atheism, but made it clear that theirs was the attitude afterwards known as " Agnosticism," and sometimes called by Holyoake "Limitationism." The police took no action against it: nothing that Holyoake ever wrote was actionable for its form or content. He set up from the start the strict standard of "decency" which he so well maintained throughout life. But his writing in the *Movement* is riot of good quality, as a rule. It has few flashes of his distinctive power of phrase. His colleague Ryall continued, with some moderation, the "fisticuffs style," as Southwell called it, but the journal never attained either popularity or notoriety, and it only lived fifteen months.

Early in 1844 he published his *Practical Grammar.* It took appalling liberties with the staid science of the grammarian. The *Athenaum* thought it " readable," and the *Spectator* felt it to be "written in the conjoint style of *Punch* and an ultra-Radical setting the world to rights." Its temper was sturdily practical. In dealing with the parts of speech

be omits "thou " altogether, and explains: "The curious I refer to the first grammar they meet with, where, it being a subject of little or no practical importance, they will find it displayed in all its roots and branches." Hazlitt is his favourite model, and his "examples," which are often funny stories or jokes, depart terribly from the professional path. His rules for composition are of Spartan rigour. The little work was certainly useful in training young men to speak and write clearly and precisely, and became popular. A little later he followed it up with a shilling *Handbook of Graduated Grammatical Exercises.* The idea of the work is probably one of those he had proposed to elaborate for the Owenite authorities. It shows very well the character of the classes on "grammar" that he used to give to young men. It was published by Watson, at *is. (id.* I find a third edition announced in February 1845. VOL. I. H

During 1844 Holyoake had less trouble with his opponents than with his friends. He had written a strong eulogy of Paterson's character and courage in the first number of the *Movement,* and Southwell and the other Scotch workers took umbrage. A few stormy letters from Southwell swept into Holywell Street, but Holyoake wisely declined to be drawn into a quarrel. It was the beginning of the long series of intestine wars of which he was to be a spectator, or more. From the days of the Pauline and Petrine schools no propagandist movement has been free from these unpleasantnesses. He continued to send money to all the victims of the " Scotch war," and he succeeded in inducing Mr. Joseph Hume, the prominent Radical, to appeal to the Home Secretary on their behalf. Hume protested at first that Paterson had been put away as "a nuisance," but he afterwards (March 27th) wrote more satisfactorily:

"I have read and return the sentence on Mr. Paterson, and I shall see Sir James Graham on the subject of the petition and act accordingly. It has long been my opinion that every man should be allowed to publish and to sell what

he pleases—without that there is *no liberty of the Press,* and without the power of communicating opinion we cannot say that we live in a country that enjoys freedom of opinion."

Mr. Arthur Trevelyan (brother of Sir Walter) also wrote strongly in support of their work, and became attached to Holyoake. "I will thank you," he wrote in May, "to propose me as a member of your Atheistical Society." He was a thorough Owenite, and wrote an article in the *Movement* on "The insanity of mankind," and an address to the Home Secretary, in which he described all the ministers as "moral lunatics."

The work was useful, and won many friends, but it had no remuneration, and the home remained at an apostolic level. When "Branch 53" fell into decay, and his secretarial salary ceased, he must have lived on little more than a pound a week. He tried to secure the Rotunda for a "Philosophical Institution," with Mrs. Emma Martin as lecturer, but it was refused, and he made a tour in the provinces, using the Manchester Hall of Science as his headquarters. "During my stay in Manchester," he says, "I occupied a room in which a former inmate hung himself. It was hinted by a pious friend that I, having no religious restraints, would probably follow the same example. But I quieted all apprehension on this score by the assurance that, in my profession, I did not like to be *tied* to any particular *line* of practice. " He went with the intention of propagating social philosophy, but was asked everywhere to lecture on religion. "Inquisitive parties made their appearance at the Hall of Science to satisfy themselves that I do not wear horns, nor carry eyes in my elbows." At Rochdale, Stockport, and especially Oldham, he had crowded audiences. At the last place "three policemen graced the assembly by order of the magistrates, and there is hope that before this time the whole bench have been benefited by my labours." The lecture at Rochdale has historic significance, as we shall see later.

In the summer he made an effort to bring to London Mme. D'Arusmont, the able and spirited Scotchwoman who is still well known to woman-workers by her maiden name of Frances Wright. It was she who had started, with great power and brilliance, the womanmovement in America, to which Lucretia Mott and others lent their aid. She was on a visit to Scotland in 1844, and Holyoake begged her to join them in London He was from the first—like all Owenites—an advocate of woman's cause, and had just made an effort to establish Mrs. Martin in London. But Mme. D'Arusmont declined the invitation with every indication of respect and sympathy.

"I thank you from my heart," she wrote, "for your welcome to my native island and your invitation to visit the friends of liberty in London. I need not say that all my sympathies are with you, or that my services are sworn for life to the cause of Truth and Justice. But seeing the narrow limits prescribed to individual strength and existence, and the immensity of the field open to individual exertion, the soldiers of the great army of the universal 'Movement' have to divide the work, and to select each his post of attack and defence. Having selected mine in early youth, I feel pledged by honour and commanded by prudence not to exchange it for any other until the strongholds of Error and Misrule shall be there carried, and a first example of Wisdom and Justice in the administration of human affairs shall be there opened by a people master, in principle, of the soil, and sovereign to will and to execute the emancipation and salvation of the human race."

A more important episode occurred in the autumn of 1844. From the earliest issues of the *Movement* Holyoake had indulged in polite criticism of the Owenites. "Socialism will be criticised in the *Movement.* The present policy of Socialists I think not sound—the interpretation of Socialism not correct—the measures neither so vigorous nor practical as they might be; but they *may* be right. I arrogate no infallibility: I only venture to explain differences. I question not the Central Board's integrity—assume no dishonesty; I only impugn

their judgment, and desire, if indeed I am able, to improve, not condemn." Soon he came to apply to it a verse well known to readers of the time:

"Day after day, day after day, It sticks—nor breath, nor motion;
As idle as a painted ship
Upon a painted ocean."
-" i

The quarrel was at first conducted in prfjpiir-Owenite spirit. In June Mr. Galpin wrote him a pleasant letter, wishing "to exchange a few ideas with you rejaiiye to human progression, for although we are apparertily.in two different spheres of operation, yet I think I could have spoken to you that which would have strengthened' rather than weakened you." The conservative officials always treated Holyoake quite differently from the other radicals. In August, when Owen was about to depart for America (with heavy heart), Holyoake and Ryall sent an address assuring him that they were of his party, and that there is "no difference in the affection we bear you." They urged their readers to go to the public breakfast in Owen's honour. But Holyoake soon afterwards touched a sorer point in the Owenite body than the question of religion, and there was much resentment.

As Owen's grand plan was the salvation of the world by home-colonies (or model communities), it was imperative to exhibit at least one of these successfully in England. Land was bought for this purpose in Hampshire in 1840, comprising two farms of 500 acres. "We see it announced," one of the dailies wrote, "that the Socialists are about to establish an Epicurean stye on a large scale in Hampshire. We trust that popular indignation will protect that fair corner of this Christian isle from so hideous a pollution." The chief building was begun in 1842, and Owen's followers watched its progress with immense enthusiasm. No expense was spared. Even the kitchen and basement-rooms had a deep mahogany wainscot, and hundreds of pounds were spent on walks and promenades. Artists sent pictures for the dining hall, and students of science gave specimens for the school.

No mere " 1844 A.d." was cut into the stone, but the large deep letters "CM. 1844 " announced to the natives/the real Commencement of the Millennium. Unhappily" the inaugurators of the millennium—highmitKJBiomen and women they were, often making great sacrifices—had too much individuality for communal life ahtl too little agricultural skill for colonisation. Pressing appeals for funds, rapid changes of governorship, and the return of disappointed colonists, gradually apprised the Owenite world that the great plan was miscarrying. From 1840 until 1845 it was the main theme of their Congresses and thei crushing burden of their officials.

To this enterprise Holyoake turned his critical attention, without malice, in 1844. Correspondents had urged him to do so, and it was known that the *New Moral World* was suppressing letters. On October 14th he left London to visit the community at Queenwood, and he afterwards published his reflections in a series of articles in the *Movement.* They are reprinted to a great extent in *Sixty Years* (ch. xxxvii), and I must omit the pleasant observations about his journey. The railway officials sent him to Farnborough, where he learned he was forty or fifty miles from his destination. The delay was not without interest. Louis Philippe, Guizot, and others, were just expected there from Windsor. He mingled with the crowd of police, "deeming that the best place for not being seen by them," and was so close to the French king—heartily detested by all radicals—that he "could have shot him half a dozen times." The portrait of the king sketched in the *Movement* is not flattering. "His cheeks hung like collapsed pudding bags. His frontispiece struck me as resembling Jupiter's with the brains out. His head baffled all my phrenology—it is something between facetiae and mathematics—half comical and half conical." Prince Albert "looked as though he were very well fed, and never thought where it came from "; while of the Queen he says: "Her pretty Saxon face, beaming both with maternal affection and thought, quite prepossessed me in her favour." At three o'clock he resumed his journey, and ended with a nine-miles walk from Winchester to Stockbridge.

He had to pass the night at a village on the way, and he improved the time by sharpening his social philosophy on observation of rustic life. The average wage of agricultural labourers in the south and west at that time was seven or eight shillings a week, with a few extras. In little one-storey cottages of two rooms large families huddled together with little notion of decency and none of cleanliness. Their food was mainly a coarse bread (*1s.* the loaf) and potatoes. Tea was five to eight shillings a pound, and was eked out or replaced entirely by mint or burnt crusts. Beef and mutton they never tasted, though some kept a pig and had pork on Sundays. Snails were not disdained in those days. The one point of brightness in their lives was the ale-house, with its rich odours and clean sanded floor; and the horizon of each one's prospect was bounded by the workhouse wall. Holyoake had just come from the north, where he had been taken through factories at Oldham, and seen men, women, and children working in a baking and foul atmosphere for twelve or fourteen hours a day. Decidedly it was not a world to take quietly and respectably.

These half-developed rustics looked with bovine wonder on the colony of "Zozialites" that had been planted amongst them. In that stately three-storied structure, with stained glass windows to its dining hall, a princely kitchen, a ball-room, and all the rest, they were told to see the model of what every English worker's home would be like under an equitable system of industry; though their clergy disturbed them with suggestions of sulphur in its magic. Thirty thousand pounds had been spent on it. Mr. Pare had advanced 5,000, Mr. Galpin.£8,000, Mr. Bate his whole fortune of £14,000; and thousands of workers had invested all their savings in it. By this time, 1844, the shadow lay full upon it. Bravely the communists struggled and economised. Tea and sugar had already disappeared, but they still sang their cheerful music after the thin communal meal. Holyoake saw at a glance one reason of the terrible failure. The land was flinty and poor—better suited for "a colony of gunsmiths." In fact, one was impelled to the conclusion that " it was chosen with an eye to insolvency, under the impression that the chalk-pits in the neighbourhood would be convenient for 'white-washing.'" It was miles away from markets, and so only possible as an agricultural colony; and for its success as such "nature had done little, and the directors less." Owen and his colleagues had built it in "a panic of pride"; it was "squanderisation, not colonisation." The most hidden material of it was of the costliest character. The ball-room and class-rooms (it was to a great extent a school) had "richly finished ceilings." "A long vinewall was erected that probably cost a guinea a yard." In a word, he openly charged the directors with foolish extravagance, bad book-keeping, unwise choice of locality—in fact, unwisdom in everything. His note was not bitter, and, although the situation seemed hopeless, he concluded with a powerful appeal to Socialists.

He was still working with the Owenites. In the issue of the *Movement* in which he concludes his articles (November 13th, 1844) he is announced to lecture at the Social Institution, 5 Charlotte Street, Blackfriars Road, and Southwell is to lecture at the Hall of Science, City Road. Some of the Owenites strongly supported his open criticism, but others, and especially the officials, held him largely responsible for the catastrophe that soon came. The London papers announced the failure of Queenwood in 1845. The trustees "hired such stray ruffians as were to be had," and put the governor and his family on the lanes. They let the building, and it became a successful school (in which Tyndall gave lessons).

So foundered the stately ship that bore the last hopes of Owenism. Holyoake wrote afterwards that the establishment would have attracted sufficient capital if the clergy had not so grossly misrepresented it; and that then, under proper management, it would have paid, and made at least a useful college of reform. We may repeat that the seed of Owenism was to die before it could germinate. From its apparent disintegration have come some of the greatest modern movements. For the moment I need only point out that the Rochdale Store, the direct starting-point of the Co-operative Movement, was opened in the very year (1844) in which Holyoake made his pilgrimage to the bankrupt community, and Owen left England sadly for America.

The rest of the story of Owenism is soon told. "Branch A 1," the London centre of the Rational Society, read the articles with a not unnatural resentment, to which the *New Moral World* gladly gave expression. The articles were reprinted in pamphlet form, and the movement (and *Movement*) simmered with controversy. Mr. Lloyd Jones was his chief opponent, and when Holyoake made public that lecturer's attempts to destroy his position at Sheffield, feeling ran high. Mr. Arthur Trevelyan, Mr. Josiah Gimson (founder of the Leicester engineering firm), and some of the most important members, supported Holyoake, and the Manchester and Leicester branches expressed indignation at the treatment accorded him. In the midst of the quarrel, in July, a special Congress decided to wind up the affairs of Harmony Hall, with the effect I have noticed. The branches of the Rational Society rapidly dwindled. Their solid structures remained, and long sheltered the shrinking groups, but not even in the revolutionary atmosphere of 1848 could they restore life to the fallen cause. Holyoake always felt that the trustees were defrauding the shareholders, and in 1861 he supported William Pare in an action against them. They actually pleaded—quoting Owen's lectures on marriage— that the Rational Society was founded for immoral purposes, and so they could not be sued! But they were forced to sell out and divide the proceeds amongst the shareholders.

The pamphlet was published by Hetherington in January 1845, at twopence. Another twopenny pamphlet issued in 1845 by Holyoake was "A lecture on the value of biography in the formation of character," published by Watson. This was a lecture on C. R. Pemberton, embodying the early material he had gathered on his actor-friend. A larger work was issued by him shortly after, entitled *Rationalism: a Treatise for the Times*. This was a sixpenny exposition of his views.

The *Movement* did not long survive the Queenwood articles. For a few months longer its lively pages enable us to trace his work. He is co-operating with the Chartists, and on good terms with Bronterre O'Brien, the most cultivated of them. He still speaks at Social Institutions, and gives classes (especially at the North London Schools, off the New Road). His subjects are generally connected with religion, but touch every aspect of social reform. Fresh editions of his works are needed, but his writing in the *Movement* itself is negligible. In the issue of January 1st, 1845, he has the grandiose prospectus of a new undertaking. Believers have had their Pantheon; why should not unbelievers add an "Atheon" to the monuments of the metropolis? It will be a centre of "fraternal intelligence" for all countries (the first suggestion of an international bureau of progressive agitation), a labour-bureau for radicals, a seminary for atheist lecturers, and an editorial home for the *Movement* and the Anti-Persecution Union. It will have a museum of gods and idols and "blasphemy relics," and an atheistical library and reading-room. A balance-sheet of the accounts of the Atheon "will be presented annually in the *Movement."* Alas, for the grand plans! The Atheon appears no more, save for six timid lines in very small type; and in three months we have the last issue (No. 68) of the *Movement* and the '' Farewell address of Mr. Holyoake." Mr. Podmore observes that a direct offshoot of Owenism still flourishes in the north. This is the Rational Association Friendly Society, which has headquarters in Manchester and about 900 branches in the provinces.

At the beginning of 1845 their lecturing centres in the metropolis were:—
National Hall, Holborn.
Hall of Science, City Road.
Finsbury Institution, Goswell Road.
Social Institution, 5 Charlotte Street, Blackfriars Road.
Investigation Hall, 29 Circus Street, Marylebone.
Social Institution, John Street (" Branch A 1").
Social Institution, Whitechapel. The last-named failed in 1844 or 1845. There was also a centre at Roan Street, Greenwich. For a few months after the failure of the *Movement* he edited a tiny *Monthly Circular of the Anti-Persecution Union.*

It died of the usual malady, defective circulation. It had issued a fair balance-sheet in January, and Holyoake had then spent a month with the Leicester Socialists, whose president, Mr. Josiah Gimson, was attached to him. But the work and anxiety proved too much for him, and he fell seriously ill on his return to London. For several weeks his life was in danger. Miss Collet adds interesting details to his modest statement. He was, it seems, too poor to obtain proper medical treatment, and would not appeal to his friends. Fortunately, some of them—she mentions W. J. Birch, a wealthy supporter and a writer on Shakespeare—discovered and assisted him. He was nursed back to life to find that the paper was in debt, and he at once suspended publication. He met all its liabilities, even paying Ryall's salary out of his slender funds, and again faced the world without money or secure employment.

A little lecturing and a little journalism kept the home in precarious integrity at London for a few months. Another little work was added to his growing list of publications. *A Short and Easy Method with the Saints* is the second of his prison-productions. It is, on the whole, a plain and temperate censure of persecution, and is politely dedicated to Erskine. Knowing that "the worst quality of injustice is that it is contagious, and always infects its victim with its own madness," he is on his guard against the infection. Erskine had rebuked him for " improper levity," and he defends treatment by ridicule in some cases. "Like the rays of heat, which fly off polished surfaces, but penetrate dark grounds, so ridicule reflects from the burnished surface of truth, but scorches the black front of error." This sententiousness, with his humour and wide knowledge and dignity of personal bearing, won appreciation for his lectures, but it was an evil age for agitators of his school. The failure of Owenism threw masses of the workers back into a state of apathy. The prosperity of the country from 1842 to 1844 dulled the edge of the rhetoric of discontent, and the return of distress in 1845 had not yet restored its sharpness. Moreover, a rival agitation—the fight for Free Trade—was taking away attention from the older ones. A new panacea was having its turn, and it attracted most of the fresh discontent amongst the people. On the other hand, the left wing of the Owenite movement was split up and discredited by sordid quarrels. Paterson and Southwell accused each other of the grossest conduct, and Holyoake was assailed with letters about his " martyrs " that made him shudder. Ryall died in extreme penury, and their quarrels were vented over his grave. There is no reason for thinking that the grosser charges were founded, but there was a plain lack of moral backbone in the group, and Holyoake became more determined than ever to discourage criticism of theology apart from positive moral and social culture.

In the late summer he was invited to take the post of lecturer to the Glasgow Owenites. With his wife and two infants—Eveline and Manfred—he went to Liverpool, and took ship from there to Greenock. The society, which met on Sundays in a little chapel off Candleriggs, was small, and the fee proportionate. Unhappily, they had promised him more than they could easily provide, and he again had the unpleasant experience of finding himself a burden. Many of them found him too tame, and demanded lectures in the Southwell vein. He wearily offered his resignation. It seems, however, that the better part of them appreciated his work, and for six months continued to employ him. His ways impressed people. He found the place as dirty as Candleriggs generally, when he got there, and out of his own poor salary he paid a woman to clean the stairs and the causeway. The woman put it to neighbours that he had "clean principles," however dark his theories were.

While he was at Glasgow he made his most fortunate venture in literature. He learned that the Manchester Unity of Oddfellows wanted five lectures written, on Charity, Truth, Knowledge, Science, and Progression, and offered prizes of ten pounds for each lecture. It had been customary in the lodges to put candidates for the various degrees through a pseudo-mystic and ridiculous catechism, and they intended to substitute the reading of sensible and elevating lectures. Being an Oddfellow, Holyoake was interested in the reform, and the money would be welcome. He sent in the whole five lectures, written in attractive style. "Capital letters I printed, so that the beginning of sentences should be well marked. I left a broad margin, in which I wrote in red ink the subject of each paragraph. All the pages of each lecture were put into a separate coloured cover, bearing a cube in isometrical perspective, merely because it was ornamental, and mitigated the dullness of a blank cover." The arbitrators chose his lectures amongst those of the 79 competitors, and were not a little dismayed when they learned that they had chosen the work of the notorious atheist. Miss Collet says they were too honourable to withdraw. At all events Holyoake had the satisfaction of receiving his first literary fee of 5o, though he had left Scotland before the award was made.

Another incident of his life in Glasgow shows his constant effort to broaden the aim of his Owenite friends. I have already said that by this time another great panacea for all their ills was firing the imaginations of the distressed workers. Side by side with Owenism, Unionism, and Chartism, a movement was spreading vigorously through the land that promised to eclipse all their successes. From the passing of the Reform Bill in 1832 Manchester had raised the banner of Free Trade. As the power of the manufacturing class gained on that of the land-owners, they won numerous adherents, and with the fresh depression in trade the workers were disposed to listen to them. The AntiCorn Law League was founded in 1839, and it was conducted with such business capacity, and supported by such wealthy contributors and rousing orators, that it soon drew ahead of all competitors for public attention. The *Times* assailed it, in the interest of landlords, as "a gregarious collection of cant and cotton-men," and most of the Chartists and Owenites opposed it as a capitalistic and middle-class movement. But with workers and speakers like Grote, J. Hume, Molesworth, Roebuck, Eb. Elliott, W. H. Ashurst, Francis Place, Gen. Thompson, Paulton, Thomasson, Bright, Cobden, W. J. Fox, Villiers, Acland, Milner Gibson, Wilson, and Moore, it moved triumphantly through the land. At one meeting (in 1845) it collected 60,000 for its funds; in one year (1843) it distributed nine million tracts and leaflets. Peel attempted to meet it at first with a sliding-scale of duties on corn—"a thoroughly English device," says Holyoake, "worthy of a people who never precipitate themselves even into the truth; had Moses been an English premier, instead of making the commandments absolute he would have proclaimed a sliding-scale of violation." In 1846, seven years from its foundation, the League triumphed over its formidable opponents, and induced Peel to abolish the Corn Laws.

A gentleman who had offered the Oddfellows £50 for the copyright of one of the lectures withdrew when he learned the name of the author. Six years later, when the Friendly Societies' Bill was before the House of Lords, the Bishop of Oxford urged that the Manchester Oddfellows should be debarred from enjoying its provisions (though they had already been swindled out of £4,000) because of their "atheistical" lectures. He had not read them, and he withdrew his opposition when pressed to do so.

Of its brilliant career I must give no more than this summary, as it enters little into our story. Holyoake was a member of the League. Chartist leaders, failing to get support for the Charter from the powerful League, advised their followers to ignore or to attack it. Holyoake followed his own judicious view, and supported it; but he was not sufficiently known before 1846 to play any part in its work. At Glasgow in December he offered to speak at an important League meeting, but orators abounded, and he was not called upon. He would find that in Scotland an Owenite must be an Owenite and nothing more; and when the Owenites failed him, his condition was grave. A correspondence with Miss S. D. Collet at the time begins with the lady writing to him, as an influential man, to favour the publication of some of her humanist hymn-tunes; it closes—for the time (Miss Collet was a warm admirer of his)—with ten shillings' worth of stamps and an ingenious note:

"Dear S1r,

"Community of property is a favourite doctrine of Socialists. If you will believe in it practically to-day by calling the enclosed your own you will greatly oblige "Your sincere friends,

"S. D. Collet "and Bess1e Burgess."

He put aside pride, and genially answered that his wavering faith in the Communistic principle had been greatly strengthened, and had "received the *stamp* of permanency." Miss Collet also exerted herself to secure for him the management of a school that had been opened in connection with the National Hall, Holborn. This institution had been founded by Lovett (a Christian Chartist), Watson, Hetherington, and others, as a lecturecentre on social and political matters. Mr. W. Ellis endowed a school for it, and Francis Place, Watson, Mr. Collet, and others, recommended Holyoake for the mastership. Lovett, however, the prisoner for political heresy, was so prejudiced against the prisoner for religious heresy that he abused his position (as secretary) to thwart the application, and Holyoake lost a very desirable position. As a strong vote of censure upon Lovett was afterwards moved by Sergeant Parry and Mr. Collet, we may expect henceforth to find him in opposition to Holyteake. But before the matter was settled he had returned (in March or April) to London.

CHAPTER VI INTO A WIDER SPHERE

Holyoake returned to the metropolis in a mood of despondency and perplexity. It was a city of ruins. Little groups of Chartists and Socialists still met sadly at one or two of the old centres, but the causes they pleaded had almost passed out of the public mind. The *New Moral World* had sunk into the spacious grave of prophets of the millennium; the last "Social Congress" was over; and the Social Missionaries had disappeared, not in an odour of sanctity. "On Sunday morning," a correspondent had written to Glasgow, "we had the last dying speech and confession of Lloyd Jones. He does not intend to do or say any more with the Socialists. He told us that Socialism was a receptacle for all moral and intellectual delinquents—emptyheaded young men bordering on idiotcy, babblers and quibblers, longhaired, bearded, and vegetarians, etc." Chartism retained more strength, but it was torn by even more passionate quarrels and incriminations. Bronterre O'Brien, the quiet and judicious scholar of the movement, had been driven out by the bluster of Feargus O'Connor, who was now supported by the stentorian voice and iridescent oratory of Ernest Jones; while Cooper led another group at Leicester, Lovett and Collins a fourth (" Knowledge Chartism"), Vincent a fifth ("Teetotal Chartism"), O'Neill a sixth ("Christian Chartism"), and so on.

Into this chaos of struggling remnants Holyoake's Vol. i. *i*

London friends now invited him to come as peacemaker and reconstructer.

On the Chartist side Holyoake would soon discover his powerlessness. His feeble voice and polite rebelliousness were like a feather in the gusts of physicalforce oratory that then prevailed. We shall find that as soon as he becomes prominent in the movement he only hastens its dissolution. He turned more

hopefully to the survivors of the Rational Religion. Its finer and sounder ideals should be rescued from the contempt into which an alliance with ineffectual enterprises had drawn them, and the highminded men and women, who had sunk into a bitter silence at the failure of their schemes and the conduct of some of their leaders, should be restored to a confidence in humanity and progress.

As he cast about for some means of forming a centre for recrystallisation, he received a visit from the Grand Master of the Oddfellows, and was almost stunned to find himself in possession of ten crisp five-pound notes. He had never seen so much money before. At once, in the true knight-errant spirit of the time, he decided to start a weekly paper, with Watson as publisher, and on June 3rd appeared the first issue of the *Reasoner and Herald of Progress.* He had contributed for some time to the *Herald of Progress,* which was the organ of the surviving Owenites from October 1845 to May 1846, and its flickering life was prolonged by including it for a few months in the new journal. The new title was suggested by Linton. "It is not the arrogance of logical acuteness which is our assumed characteristic," Holyoake wrote, "but the determination of reasoning our way to the conclusions we proclaim and testing speculative as well as practical subjects by the tangible standard of utility." Its aim would be broader than that of its predecessors. "Infidelity has been too long a mere negation," he wrote in the seventh number; and in time he said: "We are not Infidels, if that term implies the rejection of Christian truth—since all we reject is Christian error." Thus from the first moment when he had entire control of a journal he defined critical work as secondary or incidental to constructive. The clergy would "chain the spirit of progress to musty records," and so he must fight them in the interest of progress. They are busy with a cry of " No Popery "— it was the great year of Anglican conversions to Rome —and he would substitute the cry of "No Poverty." His journal would be Communistic in social matters— from the

start he explains this to mean "the substitution of Co-operation for Competition"—Utilitarian in morality, and Republican in politics. In "tone and etiquette" he will be careful not to offend the most fastidious, but—it is a shot at the " respectable" Owenites —he will be sure that he *does* tread on people's corns before he apologises.

So, with a capital of fifty pounds and an appeal for support, he set out to conquer the old immoral world. The *Reasoner* continued for fifteen years, and it affords a valuable chronicle of the times, from the radical point of view, and an ample diary of Holyoake's activity. There is proof on all sides that its general dignity of treatment and sincerity of purpose won respect. A writer in the newly-founded *Daily News* gave an account of popular journalism on November 2nd, 1847. The Chartist, George Hooper, writing to Holyoake, said that the writer (Robertson, he thought) had "too profound a contempt for the people to understand its literature." However, he selected the *Reasoner* as a journal of high aims, "written with considerable ability and conducted with no small amount of tact." Its conductors were, he said, "by no means commonplace men: there is evidently a great deal of ability and power of special pleading in them." This was the expression of a hostile observer, and we can understand that more radical students of social questions were drawn to the paper. After a few months, when Holyoake made what he thought was a large appeal to his readers for 1,000 shillings, he was astonished to receive double the sum. He had won a numerous and honourable company of admirers. Men like T. Cooper (author of the *Purgatory of Suicides)* wrote familiarly to him—" from mere admiration of you and resolve to cling to you as a brother"— and men like Ashurst, Francis Place and Collet were drawn to him. Harriet Martineau "constantly and eagerly read his writings," she said. The *New Quarterly Review* spoke of him as a " highly important actor in the democratic drama."

The significance of the early years of

the *Reasoner* is more than personal. In the able articles he contributed to it we trace not only the broadening of his own mind, but an important tendency of the time. The earlier struggles of the century were mainly class-struggles. The Reform-Bill agitation had united middle-class and working-class reformers for a moment, and then sent them wider asunder, in a Chartist revulsion, when the franchise remained limited; and the Corn Law agitation had only reunited them to a limited extent The chronic divergence had lent a bitterness of invective to the popular campaigns that tended to maintain the classwar. Holyoake, with his greater trust in argument than rhetoric, his willingness to see principle in an opponent, and his sensitiveness to vulgarity and melodrama, was one of the few who thought a union, or at least a nodding acquaintance, of reformers possible. He fastened on the first principle that they *all* sought the betterment of the race, and would do well to compare and discuss their panaceas amicably. To make this possible in the three movements he was chiefly engaged in he sought to divest theological criticism of violence and give prominence to its moral principle—in his own words, "to place infidelity on a philosophical and moral basis, and draw a strong line of demarcation between liberty of conscience and the licentiousness of vice." He was converting it into what he would presently call "Secularism." Similarly, he sought to teach Chartists that persuasion was superior to pikes (especially when there was a disciplined army on the other side), and the sober education of the people better than inflaming them with scarlet rhetoric. The Owenites he would persuade that the economic future lay with Co-operation in the community rather than Co-operation in communities; that the new moral world could not be created in patches; and that modification of the old immoral world by education and right political action was not impossible. This ideal is perfectly plain in the first volumes of the *Reasoner;* and this is the actual line that reform took in the second half of the century.

Moderate men in the three movements—Chartists, especially, were already divided into moderates and extremists (or moral-force and physical-force Chartists)— joined with him, but the more fiery at once raised that cry of "trimming" which a conciliatory policy always provokes. Feargus O'Connor's organ, the *Northern Star,* replied to his polite criticisms that " mealy-mouthedness" was worse than "rudeness." Southwell, who had set up on a small stage at the Paragon Coffee-House in Blackfriars Road, alternately blessed and denounced him. Christians put his conciliatory air down to "the low cunning of the infidel." He genially inserted all their attacks upon himself in his paper, and made philosophic replies. He had the rare virtue of a real faith in the power of truth. Let the people be properly educated, and it must prevail. And with evening classes, educational books, and lectures, he did all he could to increase their enlightenment.

This is the general tenor of his work for a few years, and we may now look at it more in detail, and see how he bore himself in it. The first volume of his *Reasoner* reflects the desperate condition of the movements he is interested in. The third number of it has to record the forcible ejection of the manager of Queenwood, Mr. Buxton, by the trustees. The scant and sober details that Holyoake publishes are a small part of the correspondence that Buxton showered on him at the time: telling how he was violently put out of the building and the estate, how he pitched a tent in the neighbouring fields, and stole in at unguarded windows, and was chased by Mr. Finch's " ruffians " when he tried to take potatoes from the rotting heaps, and so on. Rival executives were set up, and anathematised each other quite orthodoxly; and the chief of these, the London Board to which Holyoake belonged, could only boast 187 followers in the whole country. Some of the Halls of Science had been sold, and few of them had more than twenty members. The "A 1" branch counted only 32 members, though it was now the only centre in the metropolis (besides South-

well's lively coffee-house), and it lowered its Owenite sign and put up "Literary and Scientific Institution." The merriment of the general public was increased when one of the leaders, Galpin, turned "white Quaker," and sent an urgent letter to his late colleagues to warn them that the second coming of Christ was at hand, and they would do well to hurry into his " Universal Church." The despondency of the body was so great that when Owen visited the country in November (1846) the Sheffield branch passed a vote of censure on him because he would not try to restore them. Holyoake gave classes in grammar and logic at the Mechanics' Institute in Gould Square, and lectured frequently at the John Street Institution. In the course of a year he had the satisfaction of seeing five other centres spring up in various parts of the metropolis.

He was not dismayed therefore when he lost his fifty pounds, and made no editorial profit, on the first volume of the *Reasoner.* He had made an impression, and won friends, and so he raised funds to continue it. An amusing document shows that he more than kept the esteem of his less heterodox friends at London:

"Memorial of the undersigned S. D. Collet, Sarah Lewin, and Elizabeth Burgess to G. J. Holyoake, discoverer of dismal doubts in doctrine and propagator of profound precepts in practice.

"Whereas it hath ever been deemed a meet and wholesome thing that the taught should testify their approbation or disapprobation towards the teacher, presenting him in the former case with a piece of plate, and in the latter with a cup of hemlock:—

'' And whereas the undersigned have, at various times, received instruction of a useful nature from the said G. J. Holyoake, for which they deem it right and fitting to express their gratitude:—

"And having learned with regret that the said G. J. Holyoake is accustomed to pen his erudite and doubtless world-convincing compositions from a writing-desk whose antiquated and ruin-like condition must excite in the spectator's mind mournful reflections on the degenerate state of things, besides affording no protection against the predatory incursions of minikin marauders:—

"The undersigned therefore hereby request the said G. J. Holyoake's acceptance of the accompanying writing-desk, with the wish that he may never pen from it a single sentence that he is not prepared to vindicate to all mankind."

The persistent admiration of cultured ladies like Miss Collet, so far removed from him in religious thought, says much for his character. A few months later she sent him word that she had spoken about him to Emerson, then visiting London, who told her "in a genial tone " that he had heard of him. A few years later (1850) she wrote a series of articles on him (afterwards published as a work, *G. J. Holyoake and Modern AtJieisni*) in the Unitarian *Free Inquirer.* She pleaded that, though many theists had respect and affection for "pure-hearted atheists," they "see atheism only as a negation of theism, and dream not of all the inspirations and associations with which—logically or not—it is connected in the minds of its most earnest votaries "; and "amongst the English exponents of atheism none occupy so high a place as Holyoake," who "bears a high character for integrity and usefulness, both public and private, in matters unconnected with atheism." Holyoake was—from 1844 to 1846 at least—a member of the South Place Chapel which the Collets attended.

During 1847 he published a supplementary volume to his grammatical work, entitled *A Handbook of Grammar,* of a similar character to the *Practical Grammar.1* To these he added his *Mathematics no Mystery, or the Beauties and Uses of Euclid.* This was built out of the note-books he had laboriously made at Birmingham.

But the year 1847 was chiefly filled with the struggle to maintain the *Reasoner,* which made steady progress. He also contributed to the *People's Press,* a liberal monthly that was published from the Isle of Man (to evade the stamp-law), and made excursions in provincial lecturing. A couple of weeks at and

about Northampton in January show the adventurous nature of this work. The landlord of the hotel at which a room had been *engaged* refused to let it for so forbidding a purpose as theirs, and Holyoake had to wander in search of another. The Quaker-proprietor of the Temperance Hall listened to him quietly and answered: "I will tell thee, friend, that I am favourably impressed by thee, and I think thee a sincere man—but I cannot let thee my Hall." They found a room at last, but when the landlord—it was in another hotel—heard of their difficulties he increased his rent fourfold. A renowned champion of the faith in the district, a teacher named Satchwell, came with a troop of supporters, and Holyoake, who was told that the man would not improbably use his fists when he became warm, brought him on the platform, but prudently kept the table between them. As Holyoake listened amiably to his lurid denunciation of atheists, the man pronounced him "worse than a devil," because devils " fear and tremble," while the atheist retained an ultra-diabolical "suavity." He begged the audience to look on Holyoake's smile as a piece of " low cunning," but they do not seem to have been convinced; and when their champion deserted his wife and eloped with one of their teachers in the following year, Northampton began to grow radical. His lectures covered many social questions besides religion, and were sometimes delivered to Oddfellows or to Mechanics' Institutes. The Great Western Railway Company gave him a free first-class pass in April to lecture at their Swindon Institute, and the local papers were complimentary.

The *Handbook* was first issued in five twopenny parts. These educational works ran into several editions, and were much used at evening classes. It has essays on the history and utility of mathematics, and the first book of Euclid, with notes. *Lloyds Weekly* said, in reviewing the second edition (October 31st, 1847): "Mr. Holyoake is an indefatigable labourer in the cause of intellectual progress, and he brings to his work a wellstored mind, a clear head,

and much ingenuity of purpose," The *Reasoner* quotes the *Northampton Mercury* of January 29th, 1848, for the elopement. The crude tactics of their opponents were everywhere helping the spread of atheism. A leaflet was at the time circulating in Scotland that gave an account of Mrs. Emma Martin's deathbed-recantation. It was ornamented with a coffin, and signed by several ministers. Mrs. Martin was then (and for years afterwards) lecturing at London in terms as heterodox as ever.

In 1847 Mme. d'Arusmont (Frances Wright) was again in England, and was persuaded to give a series of lectures on English history at South Place Chapel. After the fourth lecture the series was discontinued. The attendance was very poor, and Mme. d'Arusmont, who was extremely unwell, could not make the necessary effort with so little encouragement. Holyoake sent Watson to secure the manuscript of the lectures for his paper, and no little disturbance resulted. The first lecture was published, and a good deal of special advertising undertaken, when Madame suddenly claimed the return of the copy, and declared that it had been obtained from her under false pretences. She was a Deist; her object, in her own words, was "to bring men out of disputation into study, and out of theology and anti-theology (one and the same things) into religion." She accused Watson of representing the *Reasoner* as the organ of South Place Chapel, and denying that it stood for any special opinions. Holyoake was extremely annoyed at the loss and the odium incurred. While Southwell and his friends dropped hints about the *Reasoner's* lapse into Deism and " literary snobbishness," and feared that Holyoake's "amiable disposition to charm everybody" might put him in the light of a "trimmer," the more orthodox enjoyed the snub to his paper. The charge of deception is groundless. In a letter to Holyoake before the delivery of the lectures (May 6th, 1847) Mme. d'Arusmont says:

"Receive my warmest thanks for your note, and for the *Reasoner* which accompanied it. Had society more reasoners of his temper, it would lead a much quieter life, and have an infinite chance for acquiring some of that good sense and right feeling which it lacks."

There had been no special issue of the paper prepared for her perusal; and it seemed a legitimate distinction to secure copy from a liberal writer who could order the sending of copies to friends like Joseph Hume, T. Carlyle, and Guizot.

The truth was that Mme. d'Arusmont had been persuaded that the company she had entered was not respectable. Ironside, the Sheffield Owenite who had brought Holyoake to that town in 1841, had since modified his views, and seems to have been one of the culprits. Holyoake wrote him a politely indignant letter, of which two drafts lie before me, with the language gradually moderated to a strict ethical standard. "Those," he says, "who advised her to take away her lectures did rightly—if thereby more public good could be accomplished—but did they act justly to me when they proposed no compensation for losses which I incurred by their instigation? Greatly have I mistaken your character if you are more in love than I am with philanthropy which plumes itself upon a public virtue too exalted to estimate the sacrifice it makes of others." However, he obtained no further satisfaction.

By the autumn of 1847 he was able to survey a more satisfactory world of reform. Southwell had gone; Holyoake wrote an admirable letter to be read at his farewell-meeting, and Southwell came in time to condemn himself the "fisticuffs" method. On the other hand twelve London halls were engaged by his friends every Sunday, his classes at Gould Square were still running, and the support of the *Reasoner* was improving. He appealed for a thousand shillings, and got two thousand, as I have said. With part of this sum his brother Austin was established as printer of the paper. He had worked under Chilton, and he now took over the printing-business of his brother-in-law, Hornblower, at Clerkenwell. This was the beginning of the long and cordial as-

sociation of the two brothers.

The opening of Gower Street College about this time, another of the increasing efforts to free culture from clerical control, led Holyoake to take a singular and honourable resolution. The many marks of esteem he now received daily did not blind him to the defects of his cultivation, and he decided to attend some courses at the University. Mr. W. H. Ashurst—solicitor to the Post Office, made familiar to many readers by Holyoake as "a remarkable counsellor of propagandists"—Mr. W. J. Fox (of South Place Chapel), Mr. A. Trevelyan, and other friends, advanced money for the fees. Mr. Ashurst had helped Holyoake in preparing his Gloucester speech, and remained a generous and warm friend until his death. In religious matters he held quite different views from Holyoake—whom he called "a light shining in darkness"—but he shared the moral principle of Owenism, and helped all agitators of character and sincerity. In 1847 he lent Holyoake 50 for the payment of his fees at Gower Street, and was gratified and surprised, "as though his experience had not lain much in that way," to have it all repaid within a few years.

Austin had considerable ability, as had other members of the family. William Holyoake, the third brother, became an artist of distinction. One of his pictures hangs in the House of Lords, and he was for many years Curator of the Royal Academy School. The eldest brother, Horatio, kept a book-shop in Melbourne, and Walter became a photographer at London. The eldest daughter, Caroline, was extremely able and spirited. She took great interest in public questions and strongly supported her brother. Another sister, the youngest, and the only surviving member of the family, Selina McCue, still lives, in America, and I am indebted to her for some information. A correspondent who knew several of the brothers relates that they all had great charm of manner, and Miss Collet describes Caroline as beautiful.

As Holyoake's continuous diaries begin at this point we are able to catch a more

satisfactory glimpse of his movements, though the notes in the two score diaries before me are rarely more than bald references to events. On the first page, for instance, we read:

"Oct. 1. 1847. Presented Mr. Ashurst's introduction to Mr. Case.,, 2. Dr. Black, Gilbert Vale, Cooper, Fleming, and I met at Watson's. Took Vale to

Ashurst. Conferred with Shaen.,, 3. Lectured at Utilitarian Hall.,, 4. Accompanied Mr. Vale of New York to Mr.

Case. Looked into Dr. Allen's "Greek Exercises."

,, 5. W. Williams and Miss P. called. Becoming

blind.

,, 6. At Gould Sq. Sent for Mr. Bird.

,, 7. Progress in Logic interrupted."

There is something pathetic about the mingling of "Greek Exercises" with the matters of world-wide interest that are suggested by the names of his visitors. Most men who have by their thirtieth year attained a position of public esteem and utility are content to forget that they never plodded through the mazes of *Tvhtw.* It must have required enormous tenacity of purpose and a rigid sense of duty to settle down to such studies when the world was—as we shall soon see—ringing with revolution, and one had a score of platforms and several authoritative organs open, and a burning sense of a message to deliver. Yet through the next year or two of dramatic agitation Holyoake ground away at Greek and Latin and the higher study of logic. His health further hampered his studies. By October nth he is "blind with cold and inflammation," and in a few weeks is down with influenza. The inflammation of the eyes troubled him all that winter, and he was not the only invalid. "Malthus ill: two surgeons" is entered in the middle of his attack of influenza; and "Robespierre Holyoake born" comes shortly afterwards.

Of weak constitution and constantly ailing, faced with the dilemma of an increasing family and a small and stationary income, finding that energy which the study of the classical tongues demands from a busy man of his age, he was nevertheless commanding the attention of thoughtful men and women. He was urging women like Miss Martineau, Miss Collet, Miss Parkes (Mme. Belloc), Mrs. Hawkes (Ashurst's daughter, afterwards Mme. Venturi), and others, to start a woman-movement, and in an article in the *Free Press* he drew up a programme for them; he even suggested the title of a paper (*Woman's Journal)* that was adopted ten years afterwards. He was engaged in a discussion of the temperance question with Mr. Passmore Edwards, who championed total abstinence against Holyoake's defence of temperance in the more literal sense. He was corresponding on educational schemes with Mr. W. Ellis, and on land-schemes with Mr. Thomas Allsop (who subscribed to his journal at the rate of a shilling a number). But at the beginning In a long letter to him Mr. W. Ellis, a high authority on schools at the time, writes (May ist, 1848): "It will be highly gratifying to me to learn that a gentleman of your ability and acuteness can turn my unpretending works to good account." Mr. Allsop, a warm friend of Coleridge, observes, after reading one of his works (April 23rd, 1848): "I have been much gratified with the talent and temper of the work, and pleased but not surprised by the elevated views you take on all questions." Mr. Passmore Edwards writes to me: "I knew but little about G. J. Holyoake about the time you mention—1847—and only occasionally came in contact with him in after years, but always had cause to respect and admire him. He was, when I first knew him, and for years after, misrepresented, abused, and shunned, but by manly and useful conduct he gradually won general esteem." The debate between Holyoake and Mr. Edwards was on the subject of Cruikshank's "bottle" picture. Holyoake held it to be exaggeration, and all exaggeration to be mischievous. of 1848 all this activity was suddenly lit with the glow of volcanic fires, and Greek exercises must have suffered grievously.

At the John Street Institution he had joined Lovett and others in forming a society of "Fraternal Democrats" or "Friends of All Nations." From obscure corners of the metropolis came picturesque figures— Poles, Germans, Italians, etc.—who poured out glowing rhetoric in broken English on the state of things abroad. He began to realise that England was part of the map of Europe, and that the dream of revolution as a shortcut to the golden age was not quite ended. Cooper had to write and ask him to spare his readers any further account of his " Democratic Firebrands." One day (in September 1847) he was astonished to receive a letter from "the seven chiefs of the community at Ghent," telling him that some article of his "a fait sensation ici." Mr. Allsop, an authority in such matters, wrote him: "The time to which I adverted as near when I last saw you is now somewhat nearer, not only as a matter of self-evident fact, but as a matter of clear indication. We are on the eve of a mighty social convulsion." Cooper wrote him that Sir Harry and Lady Verney and T. Carlyle had invited him to tea and discussion. The letter has interest in regard to Carlyle:

"My Dear Holyoake,

"The baronet was very earnest in his questioning last night; and Thomas Carlyle boldly denounced abuses and laissez-faire, according to his wont. He declared his conviction roundly that the enactment of the Charter is at hand—though he does not believe it will result in immediate benefit to the people. Profitable employment for the people is what we want, he says, and says justly. We entered largely into that allimportant subject, and Sir Harry Verney eagerly and pointedly inquired what working men propose in that direction for themselves. I gave him some brief and imperfect account of Minter Morgan's plans, of Fourierism and communism, and, at his desire, have promised to send him a list of books unfolding what those plans and systems are."

He begs Holyoake to compile the list of books for him.

It would have been strange if the author of the *French Revolution* had failed to notice the indications of approaching disturbance. The workers of England were once more in a mood of great bitterness. Three successive times had their orators persuaded them that the carrying of a certain great reform would banish the misery from their homes: three times had they flung themselves against the conservative powers: three times had they, with fiery energy and blood-shed and much imprisonment, wrested the said reform from their rulers: and in the year 1848 they seemed to be no better off than ever. The Reform Bill, the Trade-Union law, and Free Trade were secured, but in town and country the squalor and ignorance and suffering were as great as ever. One half the population were still illiterate, and the average income of their scanty teachers (cripples, old women, vagabonds, etc.) was *£,22* a year. Their homes and surroundings were filthy beyond description. Paris and London had, half a century ago, sanitary systems far inferior to that provided in Babylon 4,000 years before. The stench and filth of the London courts were indescribable. "Lodging-houses" were found to consist of parlours, eighteen feet by ten, with beds of straw, rags, and shavings along each side, and every window stuffed: in such a room, swarming with vermin and serving (Kay says) for every domestic and personal purpose, one found as many as twenty-seven male and female adults, thirty-one children, and several dogs. In 1847 the cholera fastened on them with a deadly grip. In the country they still lived on turnips and coarse bread and crust-tea. The factory-workers were equally disappointed in their hopes. One whose memory goes back to those days tells me how, as a girl of nine, she would be roused at five, given a breakfast of bread and treacle and minttea, walk miles to her mill, work for twelve hours at the looms—the children were hidden when inspectors chanced to come along—drag her limbs home to a supper of bread and dripping (rarely potatoes and bacon), and sleep with the fifteen other members of the family in their dark and dank cellar-home until it was time to begin again. It is a typical story.

In spite of the repellent quarrels of its leaders, Chartism continued to thrive in such a soil. It is a mistake to describe it as shattered by the prosecutions of 1838. It reached its height in 1843, when it sent up to the House a petition signed by 3,300,000 people. It was then receiving subscriptions to the amount of 200 a week. But after 1843 internal dissension weakened it more and more. In 1847, though that was a year of commercial panic and terrible distress, its own convulsions threatened to destroy it. Then England was lit up once more by the glare of revolution in Europe, and Chartism drew up its forces for the last time.

As we have not only to consider Holyoake's attitude at this time in the Chartist body, but shall find our story for some years disturbed by the echoes of the revolutions of 1848, a very brief sketch of the outbreak may be useful. Since the Council of Vienna in 1815, when the work of the great revolution was undone by the restored monarchies, Europe had been living over a smouldering mine. From Naples to Stockholm, from Poland to Ireland, the revolutionary feeling still glowed in subterraneous clubs, and occasionally flamed out in Vol. 1. K the press or the open street. The French Revolution of 1830 brought momentary relief in France, and the Reform Bill of 1832 in England; but it was only momentary. Louis Philippe adopted the current kingly traditions; and the "water-gruel Whigs" were no less assailed by democrats in England. Austria and the Papacy lay heavy on the spirit of Italy, and the Carbonari and "Young Italy" spread the fiery cross through the land. The Liberals of Austria and Hungary and Prussia, and the Poles and Finns, turned and writhed under the oppression of the Holy Alliance. Norwegians chafed under the rule of Sweden; Swedes resented their imported foreign dynasty; and Belgians plotted against their German prince, and dreamed of the republic the Powers had robbed them of. Spain stirred under the Bourbon despotism. Ireland vented its chronic misery, now augmented by the great famine and for-midable emigrations.

It wanted but a spark to set the smouldering mass aflame, and the spark was given at the beginning of 1848. Once more a French Revolution gave the broadest expression to the movement, but it was really Italy that led in the revolt. Austrians, Bourbons, and Popes had for thirty years savagely repressed every effort of the Italian patriots, and filled the jails of Italy. The Carbonari, an offshoot of Neapolitan Freemasonry, had spread a network of secret rebels over the land, and then Mazzini, from his exile in Marseilles, where he met a certain Captain Garibaldi, organised the younger Italians, and sent his eloquent appeals out from his secret presses. The election of Pius IX relieved the pressure in central Italy for a time, but his liberalism was short-lived. In January 1848 there were revolutionary stirrings in Sicily, Naples, Tuscany, Venice, Lombardy, and Piedmont, Mazzini was at London; and his wide circle of liberal friends, and the wider fringe of radical sympathisers, were still discussing the spurts of rebellion in Italy, when the news came that Paris had once more swept a king from the throne. Louis Blanc had published a formidable indictment of the July monarchy in his *History of Ten Years.* Liberal politicians came at length to denounce its political corruption and despotism with vigour, and the people of Paris, who know little of the subtle distinction between theory and practice, for a third time deposed their king, and put radicals like Louis Blanc and Ledru-Rollin in their provisional government. Further east the Hungarians, whose Diet was busy with demands of financial and social reform, sprang up at the news from France, and Kossuth made the " baptismal speech of the revolution" on March 3rd. It was translated into German, and on the 13th all Europe was amazed to hear that the people of Vienna had risen, forced Metternich, the leading statesman of the reaction for thirty years, to fly, and won concessions from the emperor. Hungary got its constitution, and Bohemia also secured reforms. The King of Prussia was forced to yield after the fall of Met-ternich. And, far out on the wings of Europe, Poland and Ireland stirred into pathetic rebellion.

This is a bald summary of the messages that poured cataractically into London in the first quarter of 1848. It will fall in our sphere to consider later the swift failure of all these movements, when we shall find the fugitives from nearly every State in intercourse with Holyoake at London. For the moment we have only to imagine the effect of the news on the little group of "Democratic Firebrands " at the John Street Institution. It must be borne in mind that these continental agitations were often conducted by moderate liberals, who detested the more advanced agitators almost as much as they hated the despots; but the general lesson of the outbreak seemed to be clear. Cooper had grumbled that " the tone of the foreigners" did not suit him, and when he remonstrated "Moll got up and said: 'Votyou mean? If you Chartists had bought arms instead of talking so mush you vould have been someting like democrats I'" It would be their turn now. George Julian Harney was already an active member of the group, and was firing it with Dantonesque oratory. Feargus O'Connor came to the metropolis in February, and attracted vast crowds. Ernest Jones was inflaming the provinces once more. There are sober historians (as in Traill's *Social England)* who declare that England was "on the verge of revolution." What came of it all, and what part Holyoake played in it, is the next point of importance that we have to consider.

CHAPTER VII FROM CHARTISM TO LIBERALISM

Holyoake himself has severely criticised the ChristianSocialist writers who have exaggerated the Chartist demonstrations of 1848. He ridicules the statements of Canon Kingsley and Dean Stubbs that there was any serious danger of a rising in London that year. He is undoubtedly right in holding that the Government of the country did not run the least risk in 1848. It had at its command forces overwhelmingly superior to any that could have been set in motion against it; so superior, in fact, that a revolution was out of the question, and a rising would have been mere folly. The Chartists probably numbered a million at least of the workers, but there had been none of the secret arming and drilling of 1831 and 1839. The 20,000 of them that are supposed to have been a menace to London were quite unarmed, and were surrounded by an army of at least a hundred thousand soldiers and constables.

The Chartist proceedings of 1848 are only notable historically as the last considerable appearance of that body on the political stage of England, though they have a more direct interest for us. Holyoake had always resisted the physical-force majority, and connected himself rather with the more sober and cultivated leaders. As early as October 1844 we find Bronterre O'Brien writing to him:

"My Dear Holyoake,

"I have had the pleasure to receive your kind note, and was much gratified by your friendly wishes, which I am sure are quite sincere, and which with equal sincerity I cordially reciprocate. Be assured that if I can do anything, through my paper or otherwise, to gratify you, it shall be done...."

O'Brien, a tall, stooping, quiet man, with dignified bearing, was immeasurably superior to his colleagues in ability and knowledge. He and Hetherington, another intelligent and thoughtful politician, though less scholarly, retained their attachment to Holyoake, and appreciated his more sober counsels. But the news of successful revolutions abroad stirred the more violent orators into fresh life. John Frost was still in jail for the futile "rebellion" he had initiated at Monmouth in 1839. But Harney, O'Connor, and Ernest Jones came to London, and held a series of demonstrations.

By the middle of March, when the news of the French Revolution had reached all parts of the kingdom, the authorities began to make those ostentatious preparations that have so impressed historians. On the 13th there was a meeting of 20,000 people on Ken-

nington Common, and the tricolour flag waved boldly over the hustings. Some 4,000 constables were drawn up in readiness, and the gun-sellers in the city were ordered to keep their weapons unscrewed (in case of raids) and their stock of powder out of the way. On the following day the Chartists crowded into the John Street Institution, which they had obtained as their headquarters. Lloyd Jones and Lovett had returned from Paris, where they had been sent as delegates, and they now gave a glowing account of the supremacy of the workers and the opening of the famous national workshops at Paris. Enthusiasm rose to a white heat when, in the next few weeks, the news of the successive revolutions in other parts of the Continent reached England. There were meetings almost daily, and long, defiant processions marched out, often in pouring rain, to Blackheath or Kennington, or some other open space. At their headquarters they set up a National Convention, recalling the First French Revolution, and declared it to be in permanent session until the Charter was granted.

The citizens of London and the Government were undoubtedly alarmed. There was hardly a country in Europe that spring which did not witness a successful rising, and England, with its vast Chartist organisation already formed and able to summon a quarter of a million workers to its red flag in so many parts of the kingdom, seemed a more likely field for their success. Hence, when it was announced that the Chartists were gathering five million signatures to a last petition, and were going to send this to the House on April 10th with the support of a gigantic procession, the crisis was felt to be near. Rumour and the press magnified the matter in their way. It soon became generally believed that 500,000 armed Chartists were to march from Kennington Common to Westminster, and give Parliament its last chance to make peaceful concessions. As, despite Carlyle's optimism, there was no serious hope of the Charter being granted, there seemed to be a grave outlook. Nevertheless, Holyoake is not unjust in his stric-

tures on Wellington and the Government for the formidable preparations that they made, and that have so much misled historians. The most popular Chartist leaders were now urging their followers to abstain from violence, and the London Chartists were destitute even of the crude arms of the provincial iron-workers. The age of pikes was over. Every improvement in the rifle and the gun and in military training made the storming of bastilles more wildly impracticable. Bronterre O'Brien spoke to large meetings in his sensible way. Holyoake addressed an overflowing audience at John Street on the evening of the 9th (Sunday night), and warned them to beware of violence even under grave police provocation. Men like Hetherington assured him that they would die under the truncheons of the police rather than strike a single blow. Even Feargus O'Connor and Ernest Jones now deprecated violence; though their followers, who had so long been fired with their reckless appeals, looked on them with some coldness and suspicion. The Convention actually sent a delegation to assure Earl Grey that their intention was purely pacific.

Yet London trembled with expectation when, on the Monday morning, little bands of Chartists set out, with red banners and tricolours, for the common at Kennington. The most daring of them cannot have gone far before they dropped all idea of physical force for that day. The guns of the Tower were manned and loaded. The employees of the Post Office were supplied with 2,000 rifles. The Bank bristled with artillery, and the sandbag parapets on its roof barely concealed the lines of infantry. The bridges and approaches to Westminster were commanded by an army of 10,000 horse, foot, and artillery, whose red coats and flashing steel peeped out discreetly from every point of vantage. The 6,000 horse and foot police of the metropolis lined the streets with truncheons and cutlasses, and behind them was an army of 170,000 special constables. The slightest show of violence might have led to fearful carnage. Holyoake and forty others constituted themselves reporters for the day, and spread over the route, notebook in hand. The police, not suspecting that they were spies on themselves, took kindly to them, and Holyoake got a good position at Blackfriars Bridge. He saw "a coarse, plethoric alderman" going from man to man, whispering that they must "strike hard to-day." Presently he would see the members of the Convention march across with their great petition on a gaily decorated dray drawn by four horses.

Holyoake says "a million special constables," and Gammage 70,000. It was a day of dreams. Molesworth gives the more credible figures. Holyoake seems to be as far *below* the mark when he says that only 4,000 Chartists marched. Other writers put the number at from 15,000 to 150,000. On the whole, it seems probable that there were about 20,000 Chartists, 10,000 regular troops, and nearly 200,000 constables. Probably 200,000 spectators, more or less in sympathy, lined the route; and all London was on the move at a safe distance. Louis Napoleon was amongst the special constables.

People waited on the idle streets—all vehicles had been withdrawn, lest they should help to form barricades —for the issue, and at last all fear was swept away in laughter. The tiny army of Chartists had been nervously and timidly harangued on the Common by O'Connor, and had then sent off their petition in three cabs to the House. There it was met with a device more cruel than artillery. It was at once handed over to a staff of clerks, and they soon announced that, instead of 5,700,000 signatures, it contained only 1,975,496; and that, as many of these were fictitious (they included the Queen, the Duke of Wellington, and so on), it was wholly discredited. London disbanded its armed protectors, and laughed the unmasked conspirators off its streets. Chartism of the old type was irretrievably ruined in the metropolis. Holyoake did not greatly regret the fiasco. He wrote curtly in his paper that "the Chartist Convention had poked up the Government to growl and stretch them-

selves, as the showman pokes up his lions." The failure had merely discredited the din of physical-force oratory which had so long drowned all the more sober voices. The points of the Charter, it must be remembered, were really moderate political reforms, and could and should be entirely dissociated from revolutionary language. That night some hundred of the moderates met at the Farringdon Hall, and founded the People's Charter Union. Holyoake was elected on the Council.

During the Eastertide that followed vast Chartist meetings were held in the provinces, but the flood had turned and soon began to subside rapidly. Fresh divisions weakened its strength. Feargus O'Connor, who had alienated all the more moderate workers, was now abandoning violence, and drawing nearer to the radicals. Holyoake and his friends sought no help from him, for his power was failing, and in a few years the famous demagogue—sincere and courageous, but ill-balanced and utterly injudicious—would pass into the living grave of an asylum. He was now taken up with a huge land-scheme, or plan of founding a Chartist city (Oconnorville), of which Holyoake foresaw the failure. His late colleagues refused to accept his new guidance, and clung to the old themes as long as revolution triumphed abroad; though that inspiration was destined to fail them before the end of the year. They set up a "National Assembly," and John Street continued to resound with their explosive oratory and Jacobin quarrels. But, as the more violent elements weakened, Holyoake's moderate counsels gained a surer hearing, and the more sagacious Chartists rallied to him. I find him dining with Lloyd Jones in March (1848), and often afterwards. Jones had settled as a tailor in Oxford Street, and a few lines from one of his letters to Holyoake will show his feeling at the time:

"Dear Sir,

"Your vest shall have the pocket put in. It is not only silk velvet, but the very best, having cost me above one guinea per yard. I only give it to special favourites...."

Hetherington, Linton, Collet, O'Brien, and other moderates were wholly with him. A letter from Mr. W. M. Reynolds (of *Reynolds' Miscellany)* runs:

"My Dear Mr. Holyoake,

"I return you many thanks for inserting my circular letter in your excellent periodical, of which I am a reader; and I rejoice to see that your views coincide with mine relative to the necessity of an union among the friends of political progress and social reformation.

"Accept the cordial assurances of friendship which I take this opportunity of proffering to a worker in the good cause, and believe me to remain, etc."

On April 18th W. J. Linton, one of the most cultivated of the London Chartists, sent for him and proposed that they should jointly edit a new Chartist paper. His reply shows an unusual degree of gratification:

"Never since the death of Ryall has any proposal of personal association given me so much pleasure as the one you have made. The presence of that which we can venerate in him whom we esteem makes up the charm of intercourse. I find this in you. No possible literary communism could have been proposed to me which I should value so highly. In him in whom Poetry and Art join with a passion for the liberty and elevation of the common people I find my ideal of that patriotism which is the hope of the great future that lies before us."

But the association proved a very brief one, and Linton afterwards became far from friendly. The first issue of the *Cause of the People*—a title borrowed from the *Cause du Peuple* that George Sand was then editing at Paris—appeared on May 20th. It attracted attention by its soundness and sobriety, and Bronterre O'Brien came to ask Holyoake for a place on it. George Hooper wrote most of the paper, under Holyoake's direction. Unfortunately, Linton's affairs seem to have been involved at the time, and the paper only lasted nine weeks. The *Reasoner* was, of course, maintained all the time, and Holyoake also wrote in a sixpenny weekly (the *Peoples Press)* that was published by Shirrefs in the Isle of Man, and had a brilliant list of contributors.

The legal work of the *Cause* was managed by Mr. Ashurst, whose letters show a warm personal regard for Holyoake. In one letter the aged solicitor asks Holyoake to "take him through the first book of Euclid," and the Sunday evenings are often spent at Ashurst's house at Muswell Hill. One of his daughters became Mme. Venturi, and another Mrs. James (afterwards Lady) Stansfeld; his house was for years one of the gayest radical centres in the metropolis. The American visitor, Mr. Vale, whom Holyoake took there, brought him a surprise in the form of a letter from his lively friend Hollick, who had now a medical practice in New York. Holyoake's reply shows a touch of character:

"If your letter is not written in banter of American manners and sentiment, I must suppose that you have snuffed up, like the war-horse, the air of American hyperbole — for such a 'tarnal' rant was never manufactured by an Englishman before. You say you have 'been in the south buying niggers,' and that 'it was not a good spec' I am glad of it. I am too much your friend to contemplate with satisfaction prosperity cemented by the blood of the negro. But you joke with me. You cannot so have changed. I will not believe that you have sunk into a mere dollar-hunter, till the tones of your own voice assure me of it."

Dr. Hollick afterwards returned to grace, and had pleasant days with him in New York in 1879 and 1882.

From his associates no less than from the tone of his political articles, which we will consider presently, the Chartist workers regarded him with suspicion. He realised this during a provincial tour that he made in June and July, and that gives us some idea of his activity and position. Molesworth speaks of Manchester about this time as "the centre of a district which was regarded as one that was emerging from barbarism," and even to a Birmingham worker it had sinister features. The entrance into it by rail made him recall Dante's descent into the nether regions. Its climate was, and is, a European joke. Holyoake left behind in the rooms he had occupied at a Salford hotel a certain "memorandum for travellers." It bade the stranger " prepare to escape by night" if he wanted to depart in fine weather. His lectures were not very well attended, but he had proof that he was becoming known. One night he missed his way, and asked a policeman. "A very clever fellow is that Holyoake," the man added, when he mentioned the hall he sought. In the neighbouring towns his success was complete. Oldham cheered him with two northern specifics — a brass band and a rousing tea-party. Liverpool, Ashton (where he spoke in Rayner Stephens's chapel), Rochdale, and Staleybridge found him enthusiastic audiences.

At Staleybridge he was drawn for the first time into one of those gladiatorial combats of wit that delighted and thrilled Victorian audiences in the provinces—a public debate. Dr. West challenged him to discuss a religious question, under the novel condition that the debate should continue " until one of us yielded himself as conquered or the meeting terminated the discussion. " Either alternative pointed to infinity, and Holyoake asked amended terms. They debated for two nights, from half-past six to eleven, before 1,000 people. A renewal of the debate was demanded, and a few weeks later he met Dr. West at Rochdale. The *Manchester Guardian* gravely declared that it understood the two were confederates, travelling together to play "some sort of drama" (Holyoake taking the part of "Deist") and sharing the ill-gotten proceeds. Whatever conclusion one may draw from the fact, Dr. West failed to appear on the third night, and sent the excuse that his son had been robbed of his watch at Liverpool!

From Lancashire he passed to Yorkshire, and found the dialect even more formidable. Speaking of the proposing of a vote of thanks to him at one place, he says: "I never heard such an intonation in public before. I thought one of Catlin's Ojibbeway Indians had escaped, and was asking me the way home." He lectured at Stoke on his return to London, and then at Cheltenham, Bristol, Worcester, and Birmingham on his way to the north once more to meet Dr. West. One day his notes were stolen in the train. Another day he was dragged into discussion by a minister in the train, and learned afterwards, from an article by the clergyman, that he was "most amiable and very intellectual," and that, as "deep sighs occasionally escaped him," his conversion was not beyond hope. But his chief adventures were with the Chartists, whom he tried to draw into discussion everywhere. Their organ, the *Northern Star,* was content to call him "the mildest-mannered man in the ranks of public disputants"— a heavy censure in their grim world — and the Chartist workers of the north distrusted his politeness and temperateness. They were heard in places to speculate whether he was not a Whig in disguise, or even "paid by the Government. " He somewhere bought a pike—a relic of the earlier troubles—tipped it prudently with cork, and brought it back to London in his carpetbag as "a sample of Chartist arguments." He wondered what would happen if the police took it into their heads to examine his luggage. The implement was one of the famous Colonel Macerone's spears, and greatly interested Holyoake's visitors in more peaceful days.

He delivered thirty or forty lectures in the provinces that summer, and one notices by the titles how his general social interest is displacing the theological, or reducing it to a co-ordinate position. The *Reasoner* still claimed a large amount of his time; and he continued to give classes to young men and prepare educational works of an original character. It was in the midst of these labours that he set himself the task of learning the elements of the classic tongues and acquiring French. The spectacle of Cato studying Greek in his old age is hardly more heroic than that of Holyoake doing Latin exercises in 1848 and 1849. He was only in his thirty-second year, but his position was remarkable. He had already become, not only one of the leading theological disputants in the country, but a political and social teacher of influence. He was being treated as an important colleague by men like Francis Place, Robert Owen, Thomas Allsop, Francis Newman, Ashurst, Sir Joshua Walmsley, Collet, George Henry Lewes, Thornton Hunt, Louis Blanc, and other men of distinction. He daily entered circles in which the gravest problems of politics and humanity were handled by masters. He had travelled very far since he first set foot in the metropolis, an unknown youth, six years previously.

Yet his political development had been a direct and steady growth. One would not, indeed, think less of him if he had disavowed crude and hasty conclusions to embrace larger views. Consistency, Emerson has said, is a virtue of cowards. In truth, however, he had from the first instinctively grasped the sober principles of the systems in which he began his activity and avoided their excesses. We saw this in regard to Owenism, and now find it in respect of his Chartism. To a modern mind, with a vague knowledge of political history, it seems to be a swift and long stride from Chartism to Liberalism. Yet the transition was an easy one. Chartism, it must be remembered, was a demand for six definite political reforms, three of which have been won, and the other three are now demanded by many Liberals. The question whether they were to be obtained by terrorism or by peaceful agitation lay outside the Charter. Holyoake from the start maintained that they could and should be secured by constitutional work; and the points themselves (except that it became less important in time to have *annual* Parliaments) he never abandoned. On these points the workers and the middle class could easily agree, and his conciliatory nature, as well as his political judgment, sought union of forces wherever it was possible. He thus never ceased to be a Chartist in substance, nor did he desert his own class, on the political issues of that time, in advocating an alliance with the middle class. It was the middle class, we must remember, that had won

the reforms all over the Continent. However, his early colleagues would not admit that it was their violence that had caused the Whigs to use violence, and they distrusted every man who associated with them.

"This dispute," Place wrote to him, referringo to one of his "Ion" letters, "now consists of three of us, you and I and Chambers, all three of us being, in vulgar parlance, philanthropists." The letter is given in full in *Sixty Years,* I, 217, and *Bygones,* I, 100.

It is chiefly in a series of letters over the signature of "Ion " that Holyoake developed his principles and drew ahead of his old associates. Robert Buchanan and Lloyd Jones started a paper called the *Spirit of the Age,* and when it threatened to collapse, in the usual way,

Mr. Ashurst bought it. It began in July (1848), and advocated the points of the Charter (with triennial instead of annual Parliaments) and a number of specific social remedies. Thoroughly Owenite in spirit and phrase, it gave education and industrial co-operation as its leading principles. Owen himself wrote much in it It eschewed all violence, and urged " the gradual introduction into our social arrangements of new principles, in accordance with nature and truth." One is strongly tempted to see Holyoake's phrasing and views in its earliest leaders, which were admirable, but he does not speak of working on it until November. Mr. Ashurst then bought the paper, and gave editorial control to Holyoake. Foreseeing that the editorial change as well as differences of opinion would give trouble, Holyoake advised Ashurst to pay Jones and Buchanan three months' salary, and dismiss them. They were paid, but retained, and soon disclosed their hostility. Holyoake laid down as a principle "fairness towards the middle and the industrious class": they preferred a class-war, in the modern phrase. In his last contribution to the *Spirit* Jones wrote unpleasantly, and Buchanan and he went off to found a rival journal. The division of the small available reading public not only revived the old differences between Holyoake and Lloyd

Jones, but was fatal to the paper. Holyoake made a scrupulous return to Mr. Ashurst every week, and at the beginning of March he was obliged to urge the discontinuance of his journal. He had secured brilliant contributors (including Mazzini and two members of the French Provisional Government), and was furnishing a paper of solid value, but he could not honestly anticipate sufficient support for it, and with his usual straightforwardness he warned the proprietor. Ashurst did not regard the financial loss, but—he, too, had the refined moral sense of a true follower of Owen—he declined to continue the paper on lines that were distasteful to its founders. Lloyd Jones, who soon joined the Christian Socialists, repaid Holyoake with much hostility.

Francis Place thought otherwise of the paper, as the following interesting letter, written to Holyoake before he began to edit the paper, shows:

"My Dear S1r,

"I send you a number of the 'Spirit of the Age'—a misnomer, it should be the ' Folly of the Age.' I send it because it has reference to you. I take advantage of this to say that I hope you have not adopted the cant of the party here and at Paris in the use of the words, 'the right to Labour.' The words are absolute nonsense—but that might pass if they were not injurious. As the words have no meaning in themselves, they serve to mystify the men whom they who use them pretend to serve. I know that some of these have crazed themselves, and, like all crazy people, believe they are profoundly wise when they are egregiously silly. I know too that many among them are sad rogues.

"I hate all mystery, and more than any other the mystery which misleads the working people to their injury, as the words I am commenting upon do. No one can regret more than I do the humbug of the var1ous 'isms which have been and are the greatest impediment to the increase of knowledge among the working people and made them to a great extent unteachable in matters absolutely necessary to the bettering of their condition as well physically as morally.

"Yours truly,

"francls Place." Vol. 1. L

Holyoake began in the paper a series of political letters which he signed " Ion." It was the name of a play by Sergeant Talfourd which he admired. Linton urged him to call his paper the *Matter of the Age,* and sign himself " Iron," in allusion to the practical nature of the journal; though in time, when Linton thought he was losing his inflexibility of principle, he wrote that the *r* was well omitted from the name. The letters were a spirited and readable advocacy of the political principles I have already described. They began with a professed defence of " The symbols of the continental revolutions" —Liberty, Equality, and Fraternity. His first note was defiant. The cry of the '' respectable" press for '' order" as opposed to liberty he takes to mean "that selfish opulence should disport itself with applause, and intelligent mechanics learn to starve with politeness." The workers feel that " Law keeps a stern outlook on labour, while it vouchsafes capital a gracious and courteous license." The second article begins to qualify. Equalisation means to him raising the level of the lower, not pulling down the higher, and must take account of inherent inequalities. The great thing is "to substitute the greatness of man for the littleness of the great." On fraternity he is eloquent and safe, but his divergence from the extremists is made plain in later letters. Writing on "The School-days of Nations," he chides the impatience of reformers. "In the husbandry of reformation, as well as of nature, the ground needs preparation. The reformer forgets this. His expectations are without consideration, measure, or sobriety." Ion's aim is "to arrest the impulsiveness of the public judgment and to suggest sounder rules of political criticism." He has three letters in appreciation of Cobden, whom the Chartists had fiercely opposed. At last, in a letter on "Impediments to Progress," he makes a direct attack. Reformers need more vigilant attention. "Delighted by the completeness of what they promise, men forget to in-

quire what they accomplish." The Chartists are unreasonable in their "war on the middle class." The middle class made free America, and the middle class alone in England can check the higher class for them. "The Radical," he goes on, "forgets that society has a past—the Conservative that it has a future. The Radical ventures upon the unknown without the compass of experience or the chart of history. The Conservative denies freedom and growth to the present: he fetters aspiration and chains improvement. We want the wisdom which will dare, but dare securely." By the " Radical" he clearly means the extreme reformer, and is not using the word in its normal political sense. He was working with the Radicals, and his own position was Radical. A politician who demanded the six points of the Charter—let me, for convenience, repeat them: manhood suffrage, annual (later, triennial) parliaments, the ballot, no property-qualification, payment of members, and equal electoral districts—and fundamental social reforms could not be described otherwise. But I speak of his "Liberalism," partly to indicate that his political development was already complete, and partly because of his persistent wish for union instead of divisions.

Here, in 1849, is the Liberalism of Holyoake's last years fully developed. One cannot be surprised that the letters were fiercely attacked. Lloyd Jones made a fiery reply and abandoned him. Miss Collet, on the other hand, expressed the feeling of many when she wrote him that she found the letters "bracing as quinine." In her biographical sketch she says that the letters were bitterly attacked, and adds: "This is not the first time, and will not be the last, that the severe self-restraint of a passionate soul has been mistaken for coldness, and a life of unceasing renunciation set down as traitorously politic. " She fully approved of Holyoake's final conduct: "You have acted like yourself about the *Spirit.* Lloyd Jones is indeed 'an unfavourable circumstance,' as the Socialists say—and a stupid spoilsport besides." She urged him to trans-

fer the Ion letters to the *Reasoner,* and for a time he tried the experiment, until he found a more suitable medium in the *Leader.*

Though it involves a glance at a few years ahead, we may at once bring to a close Holyoake's connection with Chartism. He remained a member of the Union, and even a member of its executive, until it died in 1852, and his efforts to reform it hastened its end. His aim was to make its methods constitutional and its language polite, and to prove the possibility of political co-operation with the middle class. To such a body as the Chartists, with its long record of imprisonments and its ears attuned to violence, the remedy was impossible. With the middle class they would have no compromise. The historian of the movement, Dr. Gammage, admits that Holyoake's position was never obscure, and underwent no change whatever. He merely complains—as does G. J. Harney, who, however, retained respect and friendship for Holyoake to the end— that Holyoake ought to have left the movement. But, since Holyoake clung to the six points of the Charter as sincerely as any, that is an unreasonable plaint. It was more than honest to remain and seek to turn Chartist energy into more effective channels for reaching its own object. He brought men like Thornton Hunt and Le Blond into the body, and worked steadily, and with growing success, for an alliance with Radicalism. He is first personally distinguished at Chartist meetings in February 1849. In that year the Radicals, under the lead of Joseph Hume, were more than willing to amalgamate with the moderate Chartists. When O'Connor moved the points of the Charter in the House he had the strong support of Hume and W. J. Fox and other radicals, with whom he now worked. The whole year was marked by attempts to bring about an alliance between the middle-class reformers and the right wing of the Chartists, and Holyoake assisted in every attempt. We find him in the short-lived National Reform League that Bronterre O'Brien and Lloyd Jones founded to provide a common ground.

He joined also the League of Social Progress (with L. Jones, Hetherington, Buchanan, etc.) that met for the same purpose at Anderton's Hotel. All this work was necessary and valuable for the redistribution of political forces. A paragraph that Holyoake wrote nearly sixty years later so accurately expresses his attitude at the time that I cannot do better than quote it:

"The enfranchisement of the working class, for which Place worked so unceasingly, could not come—in the ordinary course of things English—until the middle class had succeeded in their contest with their feudal masters. By the possession of the vote in 1832, the middle class became a rival power to the aristocracy; and that power would be greatly augmented if the middle class should favour the extension of the franchise to the working class, as many of them were naturally inclined to do. The Tory policy was then to sow animosity between the middle and the working classes, which might prevent them acting together.... The Irish in England, who thought their chances lay in English difficulty, willingly preached distrust of the middle class, and their eloquent tongues gave them ascendency among the Chartists, many of whom honestly believed that spite was a mode of progress, and, under the impression that passion was patriotism, they took money to express it."

He gives ample proof that E. Jones, T. Cooper, and other Chartist leaders, accepted Tory money to maintain the war with the Whig middle class. Against this war he now used his whole influence. A painful incident of the year shows a notable increase of this influence. Hetherington, one of the bravest and most effective workers in the Chartist and Owenist ranks, died in August (1849). During his last illness (cholerine) he had Holyoake to tend him— he despised medical treatment—and made plain to all his great attachment to the young man. All the advanced workers in London gathered at his graveside, and thousands of spectators, many of them in tears, lined the route. Holyoake was the chief speaker at the grave.

So through 1849 and 1850 he made his way in the decaying movement. In January 1851 he was elected to the executive, securing sixth place out of twenty-one candidates. The one at the head of the list polled 1,805 votes, F. O'Connor 1,314, and Holyoake 1,021. Throughout the year we find him prominent in attempts to maintain dignity of procedure and co-operation with other reformers. In January 1852 he was re-elected to the executive by 336 votes (the first securing only 900). The movement was drawing to a close under stress of this last schism. A few months later Ernest Jones drew off the extremists to Manchester, and formed a new executive. They thus defeated the aim of Holyoake and Hunt: and they ended the great movement that had filled the political stage for ten years. From that time Chartism was the mere shadow of a name. And as, on the Continent, the work of 1848 was being undone in every country, the workers of England wearily dropped the idea of revolution. *Bygones,* I, 109. He admits, looking back, that the middle class "have not shown themselves as solicitous for the political claims of labour as they ought. "

Thus for the second time Holyoake was, on the face of the matter, an important agency in the dissolution of a great organisation that he had joined. His criticisms hastened the death of Owenism, and his insistence precipitated the fall of Chartism. But the injury was only apparent. Both the great democratic movements of the earlier half of the nineteenth century were foredoomed to failure. One had been cast in, and the other assumed, a form that precluded success. In his half-conscious acceleration of their dying he was acting in the spirit of progress. The vital principles of Owenism—industrial co-operation, education of mind and character, and improvement of the conditions of life— had to be entrusted to separate organisations, which should work with all the intensity of specialisation. Owenism had not lived in vain, nor was its death without profit. Chartism, on the other hand,

had lost its original features. The People's Charter had been drawn up by a combination of working men and radical politicians. It seemed to Holyoake all through that the combination should be maintained; Gammage admits that he never concealed his view. But the Feargus O'Connors first instilled into the Union a profound distrust of the middle class, and then proved their own incapacity to run it separately, and it had to die. For the next few decades Radicalism would be the common political ground of action, until a Labour party should arise to reassert the old claim. No one foresaw Socialism in 1850. Holyoake saw the half-century close with no misgiving about social and political progress. And we pass on with him from the heroic to the practical age.

CHAPTER VIII THE 'LEADER AND THE NEW ENVIRONMENT

The years that followed were filled by Holyoake with an intense and very varied activity. His Radical associations brought him political and journalistic occupation, and introduced him to a wider and more distinguished social circle. His sympathy with struggling labour drew his notice at once to the Co-operative ventures that were then inaugurating the great movement of his later life. The triumph of reaction over the Continent was driving the more brilliant and uncompromising democrats to this country, and enlarging his circle with such figures as Kossuth, Pulzsky, Louis Blanc, and Mazzini. And—lest the reader be tempted for a moment to think that the interest and distinction of his new associates had too much to do with his emergence from an unpopular body—he still clung to his anti-theological work, and organised it afresh in face of the bitterest prejudice that then existed in England. All this work fills the next five years with a most interesting and complex activity, and we must ignore chronological order to some extent, and deal separately with his new energies.

It is convenient to take first his action in English politics and the journalistic world, especially as this affords a good opportunity for that more personal consideration of him of which we have seen too little. We can piece together a fairly complete picture of him in 1849, between his editorship of the *Spirit of the Age* and his work on the *Leader,* and it is a rare one. He removed in May from Chelsea (4 Oriel Place) to Tavistock Square, so as to be near both Fleet Street and Gower Street, and from a little flat in Woburn Buildings he turned alternately to his masters at the college and his thousands of admiring pupils in the press and the lecture-hall. He walks home with Louis Blanc at two o'clock one morning, after a night spent in profound discussion of French politics; a day or two afterwards he buys a tyro's copy of "Latin Exercises," and soon notes in his diary, marking the accents like a school-boy, "spes animum implet. " He is turned out of his flat by the landlord for his shady reputation—though the man politely alleges the noise made by the children—and on the same day sits to the painter Merritt for his portrait. On one day in May he visits Francis Place, attends a meeting on the Italian question and a lecture by F. D. Maurice, and has Miss Collet to tea; and the next day he sits on the benches at Gower Street in the "senior Latin class." On the 27th he delivers a great lecture—one that made a deep impression—at John Street, on "Why there has been no revolution in England "; and on the 30th he is "up at five studying Latin," and in the evening "begins to study Blackstone." In August he spends two days whitewashing, for the cholera is about, eschews cigars, and "tries careful experiments in vegetable diet," and has to sell his wife's watch and his own clothes to save his brother from the bailiffs; and meantime he is meeting General Avezzana, dining with George Henry Lewes, discussing American journalism at R. W. Russell's, and burying Hetherington amidst an immense gathering. A quaint mixture of very little problems and very big ones: a drastic condemnation of " self-help" in education!

His home-life ran its happy course under the quiet and tactful rule of Mrs. Holyoake. Three little mouths were now added to his obligations, and he notes in his diary, with some sadness: "The necessities of home compel me to abandon all work that is not remunerative. At last I am a slave, with my own consent, which only death extorts." It was one of the few good resolutions he had to register periodically and trample on habitually. Friends were good to the little ones. "Mrs. Captain Grenfell gives the children 13J." he enters one day. Mrs. Grenfell, "a handsome, dashing Irishwoman of the type of Lady Morgan," was a frequent visitor. She had inherited much of Julian Hibbert's money, and seems to have carried out a wish of his in giving an occasional cheque to impecunious reformers. Two of the children had attained the age of speech, and the diaries reflect the brightness they gave to the home. Some one sent her love to Manfred, and the little utilitarian remarked: "Oh! that's no good to me"; and when they bought a new lamp, that proved refractory, he opined that it "will go when it gets used to us." Holyoake began at this period to grow his beard. "Poor dada! We have made his whiskers grow at last," was the comment of little Evie (now Mrs. Praill). The parents agreed to leave it to their mature years to learn anything about religion, and then form their own judgments. But religious phrases soon dropped on their ears, and one day they were found playing at paying visits, like grown-ups. Manfred was introducing himself to Eveline as "Mr. God." "He understood it was a friend of mine," Holyoake says. The task of training them on rational lines worked well, but had its inconveniences. "Does you let yourself do what you likes?" Manfred asked gravely, when some restriction was laid on him.

It was in the spring of 1849 that he began to attend Gower Street. Some of his friends seem to have regarded his departure with very scant favour, as W. J. Linton (who had not yet quarrelled with him) makes clear:

"Now may I say a word on your communication of the other day? And do not take it unkindly or ungraciously of me. For what are you studying Latin and (I presume) Greek, or attending college? For the social position of a degree? Be sure that LL.D. will in no way serve you. 'Dr. Holyoake' will still be Holyoake the Atheist. The world never forgives: never will allow you any degree of forgiveness. You have but a choice between two things. Either recant, and the greater sin will, of course, make the greater saint's fortune; or work in the teeth of the world. No LL.D. or M.A. can serve *you.*"

Holyoake had, it is clear, expressed some hope of obtaining a degree, but the pressure of political and journalistic work soon crushed his classical studies and they pass into obscurity. His more cultivated and professional friends seem to have felt merely that the methodical culture he would get at Gower Street would be beneficial in a general way. The last entries I find referring to his studies are in November 1849, when he is attending the courses of Francis Newman and Professor De Morgan. After that year he makes long provincial tours.

A letter he received about that time from the editor of the *Weekly News and Financial Economist* (the successor to *Jerrold's)* is interesting as an indication of the current estimate of his culture:

"My Dear S1r,

"Perhaps I am intruding too much on our slight acquaintance to make the following proposition to you: it is simply this. Would it be worth your while to give us *notices* (I could not expect elaborate reviews) of our mental scientific books? I know the subjects are especially yours, and I should be glad of such an opinion."

Mr. Charles Mackay, the song-writer, has an interesting letter to him at the same period:

"Dear Sir,

"I quite agree with your criticism upon the song 'There's a good time coming, boys'—except where you allege that / am not aware of the vulgarity of expression alluded to. On the contrary I feel it, and deplore the bad taste of the public, which permits it in spite of my judgment—in neglecting better things—and lavishing its favours upon that which is worthless. It is humiliating to think that when a man writes *up,* the public will not follow him; but that when he writes *down,* he receives applause. I do not say this is always the case, but in my own case I can truly state that the most inferior of my compositions—the song alluded to— has been made the most popular, and, what is more, that the musician has made it more vulgar than the author.... I wish you would read my new work, 'Egeria. ' I think you will find a higher tone in it, to restore me to your good opinion. I wish men like you to know what I am doing in reality, and to be judged by something better than my failures."

Many who recollect the wide popularity of the song for decades will read the author's opinion with surprise; but Mr. Mackay followed serious reform-movements in London with great conscientiousness, and his song was the opening chorus of many a radical meeting. John Stuart Mill sent Holyoake a copy of his *Political Economy,* arid a cheque for 10 for his Italian fund, as soon as he started it. Ashurst continued his genial hospitality. He notes one night returning late in a cab with Mrs. Stansfeld and Mrs. Hawkes, who enlivened the night-journey with songs. Mr. (afterwards Sir) J. Stansfeld was another constant and very pleasant host of his: he was later Chairman of the Board of Trade. F. Place he visited constantly; and George Lewes invited him to dinner, and formed a close friendship, when he reviewed Lewes's *Robespierre.* W. J. Birch, the Shakespearean scholar, visited him frequently, and offered a large tract of land in America for a fresh communal experiment if Holyoake would take control of it. T. Allsop, an intimate friend of Coleridge and Lamb, and a strenuous political worker in the fifties, had great regard for him. A letter of his begins:

"My Dear Sir,

"Some months ago you made me a promise to spend a long Sunday with me. Now Christians may, relying on the Atonement, break promises with safety, but as you have no such refuge, it behoves you to fulfil your promise. Seriously I hope, now the year has put on its park attire, that you may yourself participate in the benefit you will confer if you will inhale the country air with me at my farm on Sunday next."

Francis Newman, whom he met as a professor at Gower Street, entered into a correspondence with him of which a huge bundle lies before me; a few of the letters may be quoted in a later chapter. On one occasion he entertained Robert Owen, and the company he brought to meet him included W. J. Birch and some students from Gower Street, two of whom were Percy Greg and Michael (afterwards Sir Michael) Foster. At the London Mechanics' Institute he met his old acquaintance George Combe, and had the satisfaction of discussing education with him and W. Ellis on terms of equality. Nor were his older associates deserted. He saw L. Jones and Buchanan constantly until the quarrel, and had many talks with Harney, O'Connor, Cooper, Hooper, O'Brien, Truelove, and the old workers he was now outpacing.

Holyoake never published this fact, but it is entered in his diary (Febr. 1850) after a breakfast with Mr. Birch.

His health suffered constantly under the strain, but he eagerly undertook all useful work that occurred to him, whether or no there was remuneration. He gathered funds for placing a monument on R. Carlile's grave, and spent many days canvassing for Baron Rothschild's election in July. In the summer there was a fearful visitation of cholera, and, as he fell ill (about the time of Hetherington's death), he made a will, which he has nowhere published:

"If this epidemic takes me suddenly I shall be obliged to apologise to my readers and friends for my abrupt and unceremonious departure. Yet, when I think of it, I am so busy that I really have not time to die. My duties and my studies so occupy me that I shall be obliged to treat the cholera with rudeness, as I shall be too much engaged to pay it any attentions. If, however, the cholera should be wilful and not disconcerted by my incivilities, it is necessary that I make a will.

"I bequeath all my property to Eleanor Williams, my wife, for her maintenance and the children's. In case of her demise before mine I leave it to the children equally, and I pray my valued friend, W. H. Ashurst, Esq., who above all others has been my friend, or Mr. Stansfeld, to obtain my policy—discharge my obligations —and entrust the remainder to some one on behalf of my children.

"Geo. Jacob Holyoake.

"Aug. 15, 1849."

At the time he wrote this his health was poor, and cholera was close at hand in ghastly form. It was carrying off 700 people a day in London, and Covent Garden was not at that time a salubrious district. Until the middle of September it had 500 victims a day in the metropolis.

Interesting as were Holyoake's work and associates at this time, events occurred in 1849 that greatly increased his activity and influence. The chief cause of this was the recovery of the reactionary powers on the Continent and the general flight of the revolutionaries of 1848 to England. Holyoake's relation to them and work for their countries demand a separate chapter, but the triumph of reaction was not without effect on English political life. It was felt that a new organ of progressive feeling should be created, and Ashurst once more concerted a plan with Holyoake, and the issue of it was the publication of the first number of the *People's Review.* Ashurst deplored Holyoake's agnostic views in his genial way, but he so much respected his honesty in maintaining his heterodox work in his new surroundings that (the diary relates) he offered to bank 100 in security for the new volume of the *Reasoner,* and he sometimes wrote in it over the pseudonym of " Edward Search." However, they needed a separate social and political organ, and he set Holyoake again to construct it.

The *People's Review* was a novel departure, even for an age that seemed to have exhausted the possibilities of journalism. Speaking somewhere of the monthly apparitions of new journals, and their frantic vicissitudes of form, colour, size, price, etc., he says: "Like flags carried in battle, they were made out of such material as happened to be available in the exigencies of forced marches, and were often shot into tatters by the enemy." The new venture was a small monthly of octavo size, and was sold at a shilling. It was edited by " Friends of Order and Progress," a daring combination that was thought impossible at the time. The "friends of order"— the conventional press—denounced it as another "whole hog" periodical; and the "friends of progress," the Chartists, contemptuously pronounced it "milk and water." Their opposed verdicts would assure Holyoake that he had succeeded in his aim at the golden mean, but unfortunately his philosophic temper was still too rare. The review was born in February (1850) and died in April of the same year, leaving the customary liabilities. Ashurst lost £70 on the three issues.

In the meantime the idea had been taken up by a journalist of great energy and distinction, who had far better opportunities than Holyoake for carrying it out with success. Thornton Hunt, son of Leigh Hunt, has been so generously delineated by Holyoake *Sixty Years,* ch. xlii) that I need say little of his person and character. A man of great nervous energy, generosity, zeal for social advance, and the broadest and most tolerant interests, he early contracted a warm friendship for Holyoake, to whom he was introduced by Lewes. They worked together on the Chartist executive, and in later years Holyoake often drove with him when he called on Palmerston and other high officials. He was on the *Spectator* in 1849, when the need for a more radical organ became apparent. With his close friend George H. Lewes, the Rev. E. R. Larken (a liberal Churchman), Holyoake, and a group of other advanced political students who met at the Whittington Club, he drew up the plans for the new journal. The first number of the *Leader did.* not appear until March 30th, 1850, and a letter of Hunt's to Holyoake, dated Nov. 22nd, 1849, will give some idea at once of the careful preparation made for it and the confidence he placed in Holyoake's as-

sistance:

"My Dear Holyoake,

"I received your letter on my return home last night with the greatest pleasure on every account—the Vol. 1. M assurance of your friendship, the interest which you exhibit in our endeavour, and the possible adhesion of so useful a man as Mr. Ashurst.... I propose next Sunday to adopt the following plan. On the table as you found it in my study will be also a joint of cold meat, and all who like to make their dinner of that may keep with us till we have done work and are ready for tea: this will save the form of dinner for so large a party, which would probably exceed our scanty means of attendance, crockery, and other table munitions. I hope for a good attendance and well-considered counsel. "I shall count upon you as one of the tea-drinkers: am I not right? I write in great haste—the greater because my assistant is ill, which has delayed my answer a few hours.

"Your most sincere and glad friend, "thornton Hunt."

One would like to be able to tell more of that remarkable gathering at Hammersmith, but the documents fail. In December Hunt writes again:

"my Dear Holyoake,

"As a formula we could perhaps have something like the following:

"We are aware that in the case of men who have considered freely and naturally on most subjects of politics, sociology, or religion, they entertain opinions considerably in advance of those which they avow, or are permitted to avow. The tyranny which keeps down the expression of opinion in our time, though less *dangerous* than it has been in times past, is more domesticated, more searching and constraining. The real opinions that exist, therefore, do not come out, bear no fruits, and do not even know their own strength. To fortify them, to enable them to bear their fruits, we propose to bring them together without exposing them to the action of that social tyranny. We therefore invite all who are in such a position, or who desire the development of opinion, to unite with us in that work through

a confidential combination. Some have already done so. Our organisation is very simple; and hitherto the friends who have united have given their co-operation in the frankest and heartiest spirit.

"Very hastily written, this may still serve as the sketch which others may fit to their own language. "Ever yours most truly,

"thornton Hunt."

Hunt's formula was accepted. They issued privately a circular in which the principle of the new journal was laid down as "the right of every opinion to its own free utterance," and a staff was carefully formed. Thornton Hunt was editor. Lewes and W. Savage Landor wrote the literary section, which was a brilliant feature; though Lewes also wrote in the other (unsigned) columns. Herbert Spencer contributed articles on social and scientific matters. Holyoake, who often met him in their gatherings at the Whittington Club (at the "Old Crown and Anchor" in the Strand), says he had "a half-rustic look" and "gave the impression of being a young country gentleman of the sporting farmer type. " He was, for all his ruddy and robust look, a *malade imaginaire,* and the chief proprietor of the paper, Mr. E. Pigott, begged Holyoake to cure him, which he seems to have done by a regime of bluff. Another writer was the Rev. E. R. Larken, who was broad enough to tolerate its anti-clerical note. W. E. Forster, George Eliot, T. Ballantyne (afterwards editor of the *St. James's Gazette),* W. J. Linton, and George Hooper (the hero of the "byway tragedy" in ch. xii of *Sixty Years),* were also contributors. Charles Kingsley wrote a letter in it, but when his friends took alarm he said that their inclusion of his name in the list of writers was "an impudent attempt to involve him in opinions which he utterly disclaimed." This was on account of the inclusion of Holyoake's name, which cost the paper 1,000 to his knowledge, Holyoake says; but we defer that episode for the present.

The first issue of the *Leader* appeared on March 30th, 1850. Its policy and aim were clear from the start. The first sentence in the first issue ran: "If any political party would make way just now out of the stagnant slough of indifference, it must do so by carrying with it the great body of the People." In the vein of the *Westminster Review* it described the Whigs (then in office) as a "do-nothing party," but it went on to say that the Radicals themselves were "not doing enough," and were "minister-infatuated." It had no specific principles or "planks," in the later phrase, but informally it had several consistent aims, such as manhood suffrage, secular and national education, liberalism in religion and reform of the Church, and free trade. It was the programme of the moderate Chartists and bolder Radicals. The Tories lay quite outside its purview, and the clergy soon came to denounce it as an "insidious promulgator of infidel doctrines"; though Holyoake, the only "infidel" on it, reserved his agnostic views entirely for the *Reasoner.* Its quality was excellent, and its columns were packed with information, especially international information, of social value. Lord Goderich (Marquis of Ripon) introduced to them a Parisian correspondent who proved extremely useful. Its correspondence columns were remarkably solid; Francis Newman wrote incessantly, and Froude, R. Owen, Harriet Martineau, S. Smiles, E. V. Neale, and other well-known names occurred.

Holyoake was not only an important member of the The correspondent was Mr. Robert Staunton Ellis. Lord Goderich said: "He is, from his sympathy with the principles of your excellent journal, very desirous of doing so, and I have this day written to him to write to you immediately himself." staff, as we shall see, but had a pleasant relation to the others of a practical kind. It was he who engaged the rooms (in Crane Court, off Wellington Street) and negotiated all the legal arrangements. Throughout February he was busy superintending fixtures and other preparations, and when the work began he took over the "commissariat" of the office. George Eliot, who then lived close at hand in the Strand with Dr. Chapman,

and often joined them at their camp-meal, called him the "Providence of the office," and Lewes named him the *doyen* of the staff. With both he soon formed very cordial relations. Hunt found his genial, practical help of immense service, for he was himself extremely careless in small matters. His notes run:

"My Dear Holyoake,

"Will you cause my inkstand to be provided with some *permanently* blue ink: useful in markings and corrections? Will you cause the casters to be taken off my table and chair? I do not want it for the purpose of lowering the same (though I have no objection to that result) but to prevent their sliding. Faint and weary I vainly pursue the evasive table, the chase lengthening as I go.

"For these blessings Pigott refers me to you, O sacred Parent of the Misletoe.

"Yours ever,

"T. H."

Holyoake was manager of the paper. At the preliminary meeting Ashurst, who took shares in it, said (without warning Holyoake) that he understood Holyoake was to be manager and he "wished to say that he had held a similar appointment under him, and had saved him a thousand pounds by his advice when it was to his interest that he (Mr. Ashurst) should go on expending the money; and that Mr. Holyoake was the only person connected with the ink-pot, with whom he had relations, who had repaid him when he had taken a pecuniary interest in his affairs." Holyoake was too confused to thank him, and Hunt and Lewes came to his relief. They evidently made him manager, for he notes in his diary in the summer: "conjugating *s'abonner,* to subscribe." To his Latin, Greek, logic, history, editing, subediting, lecturing, etc., he had lately added the study of French, under the tuition of a refugee colonel. The management was the least pleasant part of the work, for the journal never paid. Holyoake drew up scrupulous accounts every week. After a few years of loss he warned Mr. Pigott, with whom he was breakfasting, that there was no prospect of it paying, and proposed that all their

salaries (including his own) should be reduced by one half. It was done, and he says that his colleagues bore him no ill feeling; but we shall find one of them turning bitterly against him.

Holyoake was, at the same time, an important member of the editorial staff. Hunt's letters show how much he was consulted as to policy and contributors, and, though most of the writing is anonymous, his own work is often signed "Ion." The *Leader* proclaimed itself "Socialistic," and under pressure of correspondents defined this to mean "the substitution of co-operation for competition." It had no "system" of Socialism, but stood for the general "doctrine." "Equality of capacities" was a chimaera, but "equality of intelligence" was a possible and a very desirable reform; it would give the people "the power to develop a system." The broad principle soon narrowed down to a keen interest in the Co-operative experiments that were being made all over the country, and the work was entrusted to Holyoake. We shall see in the next chapter what he did for Co-operation in those early days. But his work was not confined to these columns. In the first issue he has a letter on "the taxes on knowledge" (an Owenite phrase of earlier date for the press-stamp), and he continued that topic in the *Leader* and the *Reasoner,* as we shall see. He wrote also on education, prison reform, and other particular subjects. His general political attitude was the same as that ot Hunt, with whom he was in cordial agreement. Briefly, they sought a union of all men of progressive temper so as to force the pace of the Whig Government in social reform. A private letter of Hunt's shows very clearly the almost religious character of his zeal for progress. Detained in the country in search of the health that he was ever pursuing, he wrote his feeling apropos of some move of Holyoake's:

"The sight of so many of my fellow men, met under one of the most sacred impulses, labouring against obstructions to the welfare and advance of their kind, must have forced me to utter the feeling of surprise and regret which oppresses me at looking upon those obstructions, upon the political and social mistakes which create them, and upon the unconscious sufferance of the people which prevents that people from striking them off. If the children of the People had faith in themselves and in each other, they might establish the means of coming to a common understanding and a common accord on their condition and its improvement. To every man upon the surface of this planet, by the law of Nature, so far as I can interpret it, are given the elements from which his labour may extract subsistence for himself, his mate, and their progeny; also the faculties to enjoy the bounties poured out before him. I can see that artificial bungling laws repeal that law of Nature, and convert multitudes of the human children of God into what a presumptuous science—a science of *those mistakes* political economy—calls a 'surplus population ': that numbers toil *not* to live: and that to many of us a day ending in ease and happiness, like our Monday Sunday?, is a rarity, not, as it should be, the natural condition—daily rest and recreation after work. But the more I watch the operation of social machinery, the more conscious I become that the depressed condition of the people is a purely artificial state, and that it is one which demands only a common understanding and common accord among themselves for an effective, and not a very remote, self-rescue."

Associated as he now was with many men of this type, Holyoake was confirmed more and more in his opinion of the falseness of the Chartist cry of "war on the middle class." It is well to remember, to the honour of Owen, that it was he who chiefly inspired professional men with this sentiment of justice. Leigh Hunt, as well as Thornton, Ashurst, Allsop, Trevelyan, Birch, and many others were impregnated with the spirit of Owen's social teaching, and looked on him as a master in social principles. Knowing so well their temper, Holyoake returned to his criticisms of the Chartists. In February (1851) he began in the *Leader* a series of Ion "Let-

ters to Chartists." Hunt and he were then, it will be remembered, on the executive of the party. The *Northern Star,* the standard of the extremists, made an exaggerated complaint of "the avalanche of Billingsgate," and he reminded the editor that his own office had been a busy manufactory of that kind of.speech for twelve years, and that " when such coals were shot down at Newcastle they might, if they pleased, complain of error in the delivery, but they had no right to be indignant at the quality of the load." His friends appreciated his discomfiture of the extreme school. "Ion is graphic," Mr. W. J. Fox wrote to him; and "you have rendered good service—' to me, and, what is the real importance—to truth." Sir Joshua Walmsley, as president of the National Parliamentary and Reform Association, wrote: "I thank you heartily for the service you have rendered to the cause"; and in a letter to Hunt refers to "our conversation on Saturday as to enlisting the able pen and sound judgment of our friend Mr. Holyoake in the preparations for the coming conference as one of our Council"—an idea which was carried out.

We have seen the further development on the Chartist side, and need not pursue the political question in detail. One incident that occurred in 1853 will suffice for our purpose. In the spring of 1853 Holyoake severely censured Lloyd Garrison for admitting into the *Liberator* an article on the supporters of slavery that ran into great violence of language. He was rebuking such language in England, and regretted to find it sanctioned by such a man as Garrison in a cause that he fully supported— the abolition of slavery. In the summer a bitter and venomous attack upon himself, in the form of a reply to his criticism,was published in the *English Republican* (Vol. II, p. 257), and he heard with sorrow that it was reproduced by Lloyd Garrison in the *Liberator* (in July). The article was written by his colleague, W. J. Linton, and does not seem to have reached his notice until late in 1853. It was one of those transparently exaggerated attacks that

thoughtful people would dismiss at once; but so many whom Holyoake wished to influence were not thoughtful. He at once published it himself, as a supplement to the *Reasoner* (Nov. 9th, 1853), and made a temperate reply. The reply brought another bitter attack from Linton, who eventually issued his letters as a pamphlet—and Holyoake coolly put the pamphlet in his shop window in Fleet Street, and gave all London an opportunity of reading it. He gave the same publicity to all attacks on himself. There is an interesting entry in the diary for February 27th, 1852. "Breakfasted with Sir Joshua and Lady Walmsley. Offered engagement on the *Daily News. "* His republican candid friend, Linton, put it that he had become "touter in ordinary to the Walmsley incapables," Linton's vigorous effort as *advocatus diaboli* gives us a good estimate of Holyoake's real position at the time, and one point in his arraignment has political interest. Most of the points are frivolous. That Holyoake had deliberately provoked the imprisonment at Cheltenham in order to pose as a martyr we know to be untrue. That he had "shuffled out of atheism when his respectable patrons preferred a less obnoxious title " (Secularism) we have also seen, or shall see, to be an untruth; in fact Linton's own diatribe goes on to complain that Holyoake is *still* debasing England with his "atheistical folly." The gibe at his "affectation of politeness in the advocacy of truth" and at "the delicacy of this smooth-ironed Professor shocked by the rude earnestness of the American Abolitionists " is merely splenetic. More serious, at first,' seems the statement that Holyoake needed a " personal inducement" before he would help to raise funds for Italy. The implication of the phrase is obvious. Yet Linton protested, when it was challenged, that he merely meant that Holyoake had to be asked personally by Mazzini before he would take action! All this is the mere vapouring of jealousy. Holyoake says it arose from the fact that he himself raised much more money for Italy than Linton did, but the jealous feeling probably extended to his whole success and his rapid advance beyond older men like Linton.

Two years before Linton had written a letter to the *Reasoner,* which begins: "I am one of those who, thanks to your teaching, have thrown off the last trammels of superstition, and ceased to believe in a God. Up to this time a belief in God and what I understood as his law served me as some poor sort of ife-guidance. I have done with all that nonsense now." The letter was anonymous, and Holyoake did not betray him. But the original letter lies before me.

The only point on which explanation seems desirable is the statement that Holyoake had "plotted for the liberticide Palmerston and the assassin Graham." Holyoake replied that one person had put to him in 1852 the idea of creating a movement to secure the premiership for Palmerston, and that he had replied that it might be good to replace Lord Derby by Palmerston, if they could then be sure of quickly ousting Palmerston himself. Linton triumphantly and treacherously answered that Joseph Cowen (junior) had told him of the plot, and said that Holyoake, Hunt, and others were in it, and the *Leader* would support it. The betrayal of confidence was fatal to Linton, and did little harm to Holyoake; but I have before me the letters of Hunt to Holyoake that were shown to Cowen, and they vindicate themselves. On June 21st, 1852, Hunt writes:

"My Dear Holyoake,

"I had your scrap this morning. I hope you take care of yourself, and that you will be fit for the work before you.

'' I proceed at once to subject No. 111, and the one which most presses in point of time: and shall delay post until to-morrow, and most probably even longer—namely, until I know that you have this.

"The 'situation' I view in this wise. Everything in the way of movement has become *impossible*—the most we can do is to continue marking time, so as to continue the work when we find the obstructions removed. The great thing is to move *out of this*. The man most probable as uniting eligibility to office and

active getting out of this appears to be Palmerston. Numbers are wishing that 'Palmerston were in office.' He seems to be awaiting an initiative. A number of men acting together, though not ostensibly, could consolidate and stimulate that feeling. Once *begun,* they could communicate with him, and enlarge their own movement. I propose that some score of men, of various circles, meet, and agree to what..." end of the letter missing.

Shortly afterwards he writes again:

"My Dear Holyoake,

"Of adhesions to the *idea* on which I wrote to you I may now mention Toulmin Smith, Lord Dudley Stuart, J. Stansfeld (in a *primd facie* conversation), besides others. I attend a private meeting to-night at Prince's. You are at Newcastle: speak to Cowen. You see the importance of taking *the initiative:* that is effected if we proceed. I shall write again on Monday to Newcastle, if you don't alter the address.

"In speaking to any let it be *few,* Trusty, and CONFIDENTIAL.

"The idea is—An effective minister, able to vindicate national interests at home and abroad, as a means of *getting out of this deadlock.* Special questions placed in abeyance—*not* by special sets of men, but by the general body. I propose to have *no* organisation, but only an understanding. I shall probably have more names on Monday to report. If practicable for George Dawson, we ought to meet him *soon.*

"Yours ever affectionately,

"th. H."

The letters evince a perfectly honourable intention, whatever one may think of the estimate of Palmerston; and where Toulmin Smith and Stansfeld approved, Holyoake could very well cooperate—to whatever extent he did. The Derby ministry was thrown out in December, and a coalition-cabinet, under Lord Aberdeen, succeeded it. It is precisely at this juncture (October 1852) that W. J. Fox strongly praises his "Ion" letters; and Fox had hitherto been a very temperate admirer.

Holyoake's friends deeply resented the attack. Ashurst replied in the *Lib-*

erator, to whose readers he was well known, and wrote to Holyoake:

"I see by your ire for the *Liberator* that I have already spoken the true word of you. I cannot write in tune, for I have no scribe, and I am obliged to be as mute as a fish. You might Linton-ise me without fear—yet, though you are an atheist, and have no apprehension of eternal roasting, I have no fear of injustice from you."

More gratifying still was the intervention of Harriet Martineau. She wrote a letter to the *Liberator* which must have had great weight among the Abolitionists. Holyoake has published it *Bygones,* I, 184-6), but it must be reproduced here.

"Dear Sir,

"I see with much surprise and more concern an attack in your paper upon the character of Mr. G. J. Holyoake, signed by Mr. W. J. Linton. I could have wished, with others of your readers, that you had waited for some evidence, or other testimony, before committing your most respected paper to an attack on such a man from such a quarter. Of Mr. Linton it is not necessary for me to say anything, because what I say of Mr. Holyoake will sufficiently show what I think of his testimony.

"I wish I could give you an idea of the absurdity that it appears to us in this country to charge Mr. Holyoake with sneaking, with desiring to conceal his opinions, and get rid of the word 'Atheism.' His whole life, since he grew up, has been one of public advocacy of the principles he holds, of weekly publication of them under his own signature, and of constant lecturing in public places. One would think that a man who has been tried and imprisoned for Atheism, and has ever since continued to publish the opinions which brought him into that position, might be secure, if any man might, from the charge of sneaking. The adoption of the term Secularism is justified by its including a large number of persons who are not Atheists, and uniting them for action which has Secularism for its object, and not Atheism. On this ground, and because by the adoption of a new term a vast amount of impediment from prejudice is got rid of, the use of the name Secularism is advantageous; but it in no way interferes with Mr. Holyoake's profession of his own unaltered views on the subject of a First Cause. As I am writing this letter, I may just say for myself that I constantly and eagerly read Mr. Holyoake's writings, though many of them are on subjects—or occupied with stages of subjects—that would not otherwise detain me, because I find myself always morally the better for the influence of the noble spirit of the man, for the calm courage, the composed temper, the genuine liberality, and unintermitting justice with which he treats all manner of persons, incidents, and topics. I certainly consider the conspicuous example of Mr. Holyoake's kind of heroism to be one of our popular educational advantages at this time.

"You have printed Mr. Linton's account of Mr. Holyoake. I request you to print mine. I send it simply as an act of justice. My own acquaintance with Mr. Holyoake is on the ground of his public usefulness, based on his private virtues; and I can have no other reason for vindicating him than a desire that a cruel wrong should be as far as possible undone. And I do it myself because I am known to your readers as an Abolitionist of sufficiently long standing not to be likely to be deceived in regard to the conduct and character of any one who speaks on the subject.

"I am, yours very respectfully,
"Harriet Martineau.
"London, November i, 1853."

Lloyd Garrison did not hesitate to insert the letter, and it made the foundation of Holyoake's friendship with distinguished Americans like Wendell Phillips. Thus the first attack on Holyoake by jealous colleagues ended in remarkable honours. Miss Martineau had begged him to visit her some time before. She found some of the The date, 1855, given in *Bygones* is erroneous. It should be 1853.
writers on the *Leader* unsound on the American question, and wanted him to use his influence. He was in the north in July (1853), and went over from New-castle to Ambleside, where she lived. "Glad to have you at last," she said (the diary reports) when he arrived. On the following day, Sunday the 24th, she drove him to Wordsworth's house, and then, at his request, to Brantwood, where W. J. Linton lived (and Ruskin lived later). Curiously enough, I find a note scribbled by Holyoake on the back of a letter that he wrote to a Newcastle correspondent on the 25th. It runs: "I and Miss Martineau drove over to Linton's on Sunday. *He* his italic was very friendly—we had a pleasant visit."

That month Linton's article appeared in the *Liberator.*

But another distinction had come to Holyoake shortly before, and I may close this chapter with a brief account of it. In the early spring he became conscious of whispers about a presentation, and finally he was invited to attend a dinner at the Freemasons' Tavern (off Lincolns Inn Fields) on May 26th. There are only three lines about it in the diary, but the *Leader* affords a fuller account. There were 200 diners, with Thornton Hunt in the chair, and many of his oldest colleagues at table, while Harriet Martineau, R. Owen, Chilton, and G. Dawson wrote to regret their inability to attend. The *leader* states that the purpose was to present a testimonial to Mr. Holyoake "and to his mode of advocating the right of all men to utter their opinions in fearless confidence." It was a singular triumph for him. Hunt and most of the others dissented entirely from his agnostic views, and at the same time made no mention of his political or journalistic services. It was a pure testimonial to character.

When dinner was over the tables were removed, and the room filled with a friendly crowd. Hunt said that the object was "to recognise Mr. Holyoake's services in the free and fearless utterance of opinions. Mr. Holyoake had done a double service in that respect: he had proved that free discussion had become safe, and he had shown that even religious controversy could be conducted with courtesy and mutual forbearance. He had, in fact, contributed to rescue religion itself from the discreditable protection of the tyrant and the policeman. " T. and R. Cooper and Le Blond also spoke, and then the publisher Watson presented him with a purse containing,£250, a portrait, and an engraving. The latter was a private gift, and one reads with some stir of humour that it represented " Exiles on the way to Siberia." Holyoake, who was "very earnest and subdued," read his reply, and his speech "evidently told home to every heart in that immense meeting."

CHAPTER IX EARLY CO-OPERATION AND CHRISTIAN SOCIALISM

During the last few months of Holyoake's life, when a friend and he were one day looking back over the stirring memories of long and useful careers, and comparing the great ideals they had served in the cause of human advance, the friend asked him which of the movements he had wrought in stood highest in his esteem. He answered at once: "The Co-operative Movement." It was assuredly the one amongst his early ideals that sixty years of national experience had the most patently approved. It was a work that he had espoused when it lay under the frown of the press and people of this country; when to advocate it meant to take sides with a few hundred working men against the overwhelming majority in culture and Church; when only one or two social students in England suspected that it differed from the social bubbles that rounded and burst every decade on the agitated surface of national life. He had the distinction to be one of those few, and the pride to live until it was pronounced by a great statesman "a State within a State," and its vast frame could command the respectful attention of the economists.

"I knew Co-operation when it was born. I stood by its cradle. In every journal, newspaper, and review with which I was connected I defended it in its infancy, when no one thought it would live. For years was its sole friend and representative in the press. Vol, i. «77 *m* have lived to see it grow to robust and self-supporting manhood."

How true these words were, and what place Holyoake should hold in the memory of modern Co-operators, we have now to consider. If there is one literary distinction that indubitably belongs to him, it is that of historian of the Co-operative Movement. But his historical works convey only a poor suggestion of the debt the movement owes to himself, and this chapter would be a brief one if it relied on them. Indeed, with all its charm and sparkle of narrative and its industrious massing of facts his *History of Co-operation* is faulty and baffling from the historical point of view. The composition is irregular and the natural sequence of events too violently distorted. When we read the story in its proper continuity we see more clearly his own place in it; though, of course, we must restrict ourselves here to a mere outline of the general story of the movement.

We have already seen, time after time, that the two phrases, "Self-help by the people" and "Co-operation instead of Competition," occur very early and constantly in his teaching in different forms. He lived through the adventurous early phase of Co-operation without contracting the dull despair that fell on older men at its failure. From his earliest years he was familiar with the idea. Birmingham was a strenuous centre of Co-operative interest when he was a boy. Curiously enough, he discovered, when he set out to write the history of the idea, that Birmingham had been the first place to witness a Co-operative experiment, in 1777. At other isolated centres—in Oxfordshire, at Hull, etc.— the idea was roughly embodied before the end of the eighteenth century, but it was the influence of R. Owen, "the originator of Co-operation," as he calls him, that brought it fully on to the plane of social reform. The first journal to advocate it was the Owenite *Economist,* in 1821, which announced a "Co-operative and Economic Society " in its first issue, and declared, in the oracular Owenite way of revealing things: "The secret is out: it is unrestrained Co-operation, on the part of all the members, for every purpose of social life." There was a Co-operative Society at London in 1824, one in remote Devon in 1826,

one at Birmingham in 1829, and so on. There was a *Co-operative Magazine* at London in 1826— the paper that advocated the beginning of the new age by marrying a hundred handsome tailors by ballot—and a *Co-operative Miscellany* in 1830. Julian Hibbert founded a " British Association for the Promotion of Co-operative Knowledge," and made W. Watson a Co-operative apostle. Briefly, there were 266 societies, with 20,000 adherents, and nine journals in support, by 1830; and the number of societies grew to 400 in the next three years. These were by no means all Owenite societies— of the 46 London societies many were attached to Methodist and other congregations— but Owen's teaching gave the great impulse in the " enthusiastic period." Preface to his *Jubilee History of the Leeds Industrial Cooperative Society.*

Throughout the thirties Co-operation was a familiar scheme to every reformer. Most of the Radicals favoured it, and Owen's 100,000 followers were wedded to the principle. But in the course of that decade the tide turned, and when Holyoake came into public life the adventurous vessel of Co-operation seemed to be hopelessly stranded. The Labour Exchanges that the Owenites created in 1832 were conceived as ideal Co-operative stores, where capital had not an inch of footing, and their rapid failure injured the general principle. Owen, too, frowned on all these little experiments in industrial reform. The nation must accept his big scheme at once, and the details would mend themselves. Moreover, the early Co-operative stores were managed by enthusiasts instead of experts. Amateur shopmen, "mostly pale and thin"—they were afraid to get plump and ruddy, lest they incur suspicion of peculation— controlled the businesses, and "there was not a regenerating lunatic at large who did not practise on them." By 1843 "never human movement seemed so very dead as this of Co-operation." Dead movements were common enough in those days. The uncommon thing was a young man trying to restore them to life. And it was in 1843 that Holyoake

lectured on "selfhelp" to a little gathering of weavers at Rochdale; and in the following year they opened the famous Toad Lane Store, which was the cradle of the gigantic Co-operative organisation of modern times.

In 1843 Holyoake was released from Gloucester Jail, and resumed his lecturing. The very lecture he had given at Cheltenham, which led to his imprisonment, was on "Home Colonisation," or the general principle of co-operation. We saw that he quickly discarded the Owenite idea that men should retire from the world to co-operate in model communities; he claimed that sounder principles could be introduced into the actual industrial world. In this spirit he went north in July, and lectured to the Owenite societies that still lingered in Lancashire. It was during this brief tour, which I have recorded in an earlier chapter, that he delivered the fateful lecture at Rochdale that he has described in his *History of Co-operation.* Little did he or any member of his audience dream that within twelve months they would start a movement in Rochdale of which the fame would be carried, through Holyoake, over the whole civilised world. It was a drizzly night in early summer when he went to the little room they had engaged in Yorkshire Street. From the window at the back he watched the tired workers coming over the sodden fields. There had been hard times in Rochdale, and for months men had put their poor brains together to find relief. The distressed flannel-weavers had formed a committee that looked about helplessly for a plan. On Sunday afternoons little groups of them met in the Temperance room or the Chartists' room, and wearily discussed the situation. The Socialists had had to give up their hall in Yorkshire Street, and the Chartists had taken it; and in 1843 it was the debating place of the three small groups that held social theories in Rochdale — the Socialists ("Branch 24" of the Rational Society), the Chartists, and the Temperance folk.

This small combined group—or, more correctly, the Socialist Society, with a sprinkling of the others—formed

Holyoake's audience in 1843. In his *History of Cooperation* he has reproduced at length the address he gave to them. One must take with a certain liberality a lengthy reproduction from memory thirty years after the event, but Holyoake had a wonderful memory. Countess Russell once told me that, when she was a young girl, she was taken to a house where Holyoake was staying. Years afterwards—only a few years ago—she met him again, and he at once reminded her of his seeing her in her early years. But there are many other reasons for accepting implicitly his statement that, amongst other things, he advised them to open a store. There had been a Co-operative store in Rochdale in 1830, and the idea would be revived in their discussions. Further, a few words he wrote in the *Movement* at the time (July 1843) afford an interesting corroboration of his memory:

"All my lectures in the north have been designed to enforce what for two years has been with me a favourite idea—the capability of Socialism to build up individual as well as general character, to serve as a complete body of moral, political, and social philosophy; in fine, in the words of Milton, to enable a man 'to perform justly, skilfully, and magnanimously all the offices, both public and private, of peace and war.' I have been in earnest about this, for seeing the many hindrances that would lie in the way of the wisest of us in carrying out our community-projects, and desiring to induce our friends to regard, as they justly may, Socialism's benign and practical philosophy as something in itself worthy of esteem, even though ulterior intentions should never be realised."

What he meant by "Socialism" we know. Indeed, he wrote in the same paper (p. 315), a week or two later:

"We have only, by the Co-operative views, 'to floor money and Malthus,' then moral and social improvement will have a free hand."

And throughout the whole of that year he is urging the workers to help themselves, for neither their rulers nor the wealthy will help them.

These were seeds of Co-operative enterprise; and when we find the historic store opened at Rochdale a few months afterwards, we have ample justification for his claim that he stood by the cradle of the infant movement. But a little research has shown a more direct connection. Shortly after his visit to Rochdale, Holyoake published the criticism of Cjueenwood that shook the whole attenuated frame of Owenism. The " A 1 Branch" (at London) passed a vote of censure on him, while several provincial branches voted their thanks to him. Amongst the latter was the little group at Rochdale that he had addressed in 1843. Mr. James Daly, of Rochdale, wrote a letter of support to the *Movement,* but I need only quote its postscript:

"P.S.—Some of the members of the Rochdale Branch, hearing that I was about writing on this subject, and thinking that he who gives expression to truth without mystery should not be paid with votes of censure by Rational Philosophers, requested leave to attach their names to this letter.

"But I wish it to be understood that I have neither canvassed for signatures nor made this letter public with a view of forming a party—had I done so I could have sent a longer list of names.

"chas. Howorth, *President ofBranch* 24. "Wm. M'malim, *late President.* "john Jenkinson, *Secretary. "*Wm. Cooper, Robert Kershaw, John Crannis, John Garside, Samuel Tweedale, John Bent, Malcolm Kincaid, *Members of Branch* 24."

This document is interesting. It shows that the chief members of the Rational Society were among the chief founders of the Pioneers' Society. Daly was its first secretary, Howorth one of the first trustees and the originator of the idea of profit-sharing, Tweedale one of the first directors, Cooper "the principal organiser of the Pioneers' Society" (as Holyoake is told in a letter in 1866), and Bent an original member. Two other Owenites, Smithies and Greenwood, Holyoake's constant hosts afterwards, were amongst the chief workers. Alderman Lister, who helped to arrange the

lecture, was an Owenite, and greatly aided the store. The Pioneers met for their preliminary meetings in the Socialists' room, and they borrowed some of their rules from the laws of the Rational Sick and Benefit Society. And amongst their rules was the unmistakably Owenite resolution: "That as soon as practicable this Society shall proceed to arrange the powers of production, distribution, education, and government: or, in other words, to establish a self-supporting home-colony of united interests, and assist other societies in establishing such colonies."

It seemed interesting to establish more fully than Holyoake himself would have been justified in doing the connection of the Rochdale store with Owenism and its young apostle. The rest of the story need not detain us. How the Socialists and Chartists took the idea of a store to the Weavers' Committee and secured their co-operation: how they put their twopences together and purchased a stock of plain and necessary articles: how they timidly opened their shutters one Saturday night and exposed their flour, butter, sugar, and oatmeal, and plodded on through every peril and discouragement, and their 28 members became 1,500 in ten years, and the "grim, despairing, sloppy hole of a town" put new life into the Co-operative ideal—all these things are familiar history. The characteristic of their experiment was that they distributed profits according to the amount of purchases made. This had been done at a Co-operative mill in Yorkshire for many years, though it was original at Rochdale. The earlier societies, which failed, had shared profits on a basis of capital invested in them. Rochdale, adopting the new basis of division, and rigorously setting aside a part of the profits for educational purposes, opened the new era in Co-operation. They were ever mindful of the counsels of Holyoake. Year after year he came again to address them, and there were always one or two of the Pioneers to meet him at the station with a "Tha mun coom and see t' Store." His letters were always addressed there.

Slowly the story of Rochdale's democratic work moved over the country, and Co-operative societies began to dot the map once more. Leeds, which now has the greatest of all the stores, heard of the Pioneers in 1847, and followed their example. Derby heard of it in 1850, and set up a society that has prospered beyond all its dreams. Bingley and Oldham (the Industrial Society) were founded in the same year; and the Oldham Equitable and Halifax (for which Holyoake obtained encouraging letters from Mazzini and Francis Newman) followed in 1851. Manchester already had an Industrial Society (with shops in Ashton Old Road and Ardwick), founded by the Owenites, but its great modern Co-operative institution dates more directly from a religious effort in 1859. By that year Holyoake had written the history of the Rochdale Pioneers, and its inspiration brought societies into being all over the country. In 1846 the Friendly Societies Act extended some protection to their funds and facilitated their trade, and in 1852, largely through the activity of the Christian Socialists, the Industrial and Provident Societies Act gave them complete legal security.

It would be tedious and difficult to attempt to trace Holyoake's personal relations with the Societies that were formed in these years. His service to the movement lay chiefly in his persistent advocacy of the Co-operative idea in the journals he controlled. The *New Moral World,* the last Owenite journal, came to an end early in 1846. After a brief interval of the *Herald of Progress,* Holyoake started the *Reasoner* in June of the same year. In the first issue he included his maxim of "Co-operation instead of Competition " amongst its leading principles, and he consistently advocated it. For two years his was the only journal in England that wrote in the interest of the new movement. In 1848 he established the *Spirit of the Age,* and declared that its chief object was "the organisation of labour." In that year the cause of Cooperation obtained new and powerful friends. John Stuart Mill spoke of it in his *Political Economy* as

"a noble ideal," and said that "there was no more certain incident of the progressive change taking place in society than the continual growth of the principle and practice of Co-operation." In spite of his plea for the retention of competition, these and similar passages in Mill's work gave weighty economic sanction to the struggling efforts. He sent a copy of his work to Holyoake, for whom he already had esteem and respect. Miss Martineau and Lord Brougham also could soon be quoted in support of Co-operation.

The other auxiliary that the movement found at this time was Christian Socialism, and Holyoake's relations to this body merit a fuller investigation. Two points in those relations may be indicated at once. The first is that the movement was set up explicitly in opposition to Owenite or Secularist Co-operation, and cordiality between them is not to be expected. Since the only journal in England that advocated Co-operation was an "atheistic" journal, the establishment of an organisation and a journal under a distinct Christian ensign was inevitable; and some aloofness on Holyoake's part was equally inevitable. But the second point is that Holyoake has appraised very highly in his history their influence on the development of the Co-operative movement. They had a useful "idealist" action on the societies, besides their spreading of the idea of Co-operation, and their influence was "the most fortunate which has befallen the movement." The time came when their separative colours were hauled down, and they worked together. The last time Kingsley saw Holyoake he said: "The world is very different now from what it was when you and I commenced trying to improve it twenty-five years ago."

Christian Socialism had its rise in the intense and informed zeal of Frederick Denison Maurice, the historian of philosophy and distinguished social student. Teaching at King's College, Maurice gathered about him a group of religious students and professional men who caught his ardour for social service. The revelation of the sufferings of

the London poor in one of the dailies and the eruption of similar suffering all over the country in Chartist agitation gave keen edge to his zeal, and he summoned Kingsley, from his rectory at Eversley, to help him in the metropolis. Kingsley had conceived an equal zeal at sight of the sufferings of the rural workers. With their band of religious followers they tried to turn Chartist violence and despair into more peaceful channels in 1848, and posted a placard on the walls that drew the attention of the workers to them. In May Maurice and Ludlow (a young barrister) edited *Politics for the People,* which soon failed, and they afterwards issued a series of tracts, including Kingsley's famous essay on "Cheap clothes and nasty." In 1850 they issued the *Christian Socialist,* and opened a Co-operative tailoring shop on the model of the French *Associations Ouvrieres.* Edward Vansittart Neale and T. Hughes (afterwards Judge Hughes) were now working with them, and they held a conspicuous position in the progressive life of the metropolis. Other workshops followed, and a "Society for Promoting Working Men's Associations" was founded. Further they gave valuable legal assistance to the Trade Unions, and helped in the passing of Acts that protected industrial organisations; and they were the founders of the "Working Men's College."

This is a bald summary of the work done by the Christian Socialist party from 1850 to 1855. Their workshops failed, from unskilful control and other causes. The "Society" broke up in 1854, and afier that time (Woodworth says in his historical sketch of the movement) there was no *party* calling itself Christian Socialist; though we shall find the men in the van *o* progress long afterwards. The modern Co-operator knows what he owes to E. V. Neale, Judge Hughes, and J. M. Ludlow. But we cannot well understand some later episodes, and some of Holyoake's literary references to them, unless we glance at the friction between them.

The Christian Socialist party had the aim of propagating Co-operation, which was what they chiefly meant by Socialism, and at the same time defending religion. Holyoake says that their work was, in Maurice's own words, "to Christianise Socialism"; and we saw that this was very far from being Christian. Woodworth, a sympathetic writer on the Christian Socialists, says that there was much confusion about their aim, but it was "primarily religious." We cannot be surprised, therefore, to find Maurice writing to Kingsley (January 15th, 1851) that "Holyoake has declared war" and "you young men must fight." Holyoake would naturally oppose any attempt to associate a broad social reform with theology. He was at that time, as we shall see, conducting the Co-operative columns in the *Leader* without the least tincture of anti-theological spirit. It was a secular issue; and he resented the suggestion that social zeal needed a theological base. So far it had been mainly the people without a definite theology—the Socialists and Chartists—who had shown any such zeal. But F. D. Maurice (like his son and biographer) exaggerates the friction that naturally arose. The copy of the *Reasoner* that fell into his hands on January 15th contained this editorial passage, which he calls a "declaration of war":

"From various parts of the country inquiries have come, 'What are we to do with the Christian Socialists? Are we to debate with them, or hear without dispute what we feel to be incorrect?' My advice has been, and is: 'Open your halls to them whenever asked; give them the hand of generous fellowship, till time furnishes the proper opportunity of remonstrating without damaging the efforts after practical good which they are making.' Those of our readers who were with us in the former Socialist agitation will remember that many among us committed the same fault on the other hand. First enthusiasm is seldom reflective, and where men mean well, all may be rectified when the time of consideration comes. When doctrinal error is allied to excellent practice, such as that presented in the Cooperative exertions of the Christian Socialists, we will leave their doctrinal error alone till we can find an opportunity of disproving it, without appearing at the same time as the opponents of their good works. For the present we can find plenty of opponents whose doctrines and practices are open to our animadversion. These we will seek out first. The position taken by the Christian Socialists is both illogical and ungracious; but we do not despair that appeals to their good sense and good will will lead to some improvement in these respects."

Never was there so humane and dignified a " declaration of war "! Professor Maurice's son, General F. Maurice, is very unhappy and misleading in his whole account of their relations. He says that "the stock agitators were afraid of the working men being drawn from them by Co-operation," and that "Ernest Jones and Holyoake fought hard to warn off working men from Christian Socialism," which he identifies with the cause of Cooperation. The truth is that, whereas Ernest Jones *did* resent the new interest in Co-operation as a distraction from the Charter, Holyoake was wholly opposed to E. Jones, and was doing at that time more valuable propagandist work for Co-operation than any man in England. There are only two episodes that call for particular notice. The first was the trouble that Maurice incurred at King's College, the supporters of which were generally wealthy and religious. Dr. Jelf, the principal, wrote to Maurice in November (1851) to say that the authorities were concerned about his position. He is known to be a friend of Kingsley's (whom Jelf detested), and Kingsley was identified with Holyoake, who was identified with "Tom Paine." The letter does little credit to Jelf. Paine was as convinced a theist as he, and much more convinced than Kingsley (according to what Sir Leslie Stephen told me of conversation with Kingsley on the subject). On the other hand, the only association between Kingsley and Holyoake was that the names of both were included in the list of contributors to the *Leader*, a political and social journal. However, Maurice secured from Kingsley a violent repudiation of the *Leader* and its "impudent attempt to involve him in opinions which he utterly disclaimed and hated."

Jelf was pleased, but went on to say that their uneasiness remained. Maurice's personal orthodoxy was not quite clear, and his social opinions were suspicious. For the time Maurice quieted their concern with a vehement rejection of "communism," but he was superseded two years later. General Maurice says that on that occasion Holyoake inserted in the *Reasoner* "a warm eulogy on Dr. Jelf," and gives point to it by referring to the *Inquirer's* "less savage terms." Holyoake says that he again was the innocent occasion of the trouble. An address that he delivered at the grave of Mrs. Emma Martin was published in the *Leader,* and revived Dr. Jelfs concern. But to speak of his comments as "savage" is most improper. His article (December 21st, 1853) is headed, "A word on behalf of the Rev. Principal Jelf." He premises that he has often joined in the appreciation of Prof. Maurice, and will now say a word for Dr. Jelf. But the article is mainly ironical. He applauds Jelfs action in expelling "an able minister" from the Church, on the humorous ground that the more of its abler ministers are expelled the better—from the Secularist point of view; and because Jelf, in pinning the Church to the "repulsive dogma of hell," makes the attack easier. There is not one word of attack on Maurice; and the only serious word of praise for Jelf is that he has shown "manliness" in deposing an influential cleric when he thought it his duty to do so.

The second point, of greater interest, is that Holyoake worked to some extent in their Co-operative schemes, and was brought into relations with a very curious member of the group. In setting up their workshops they engaged the help of a French refugee, who professed advanced views. This "J. L. St. Andre" was a St. Simonian, "handsome, literally smooth-faced, and mellow; he was quite globular, and when he moved he vibrated like a locomotive jelly." Having " large commercial views of an indefinite outline " and some knowledge of the recent French national workshops, he was associated with Lloyd

Jones in establishing their Cooperative tailoring house, and afterwards in the "London Co-operative Store and General Agency," at 76 Charlotte Street. In the autumn of 1851 the manager of the Stores writes to congratulate Holyoake on his notices of their house in the *Leader*—" the best I have seen "—and begs to see him. A second letter appoints him agent of the business during his tours in the provinces. Holyoake's report declares: "Whether your agency be ostensibly based on Christian grounds, or avowedly on Secular principle, I would alike aid it, because its object would be good; but when represented as strictly commercial I can do it without exposing myself to an ambiguous judgment." This is in complete accord with his article in the *Reasoner*. The reply to his report thanks him for his " discretion " and his " able and useful notices" in the *Leader,* but regrets that "from the strong objection which many of our best friends and persons with whom we are publicly connected feel to the opinions identified in popular apprehension with your name, we think that on the whole it will be desirable that the formal connection between us should be brought to a close, though we have no desire to change the pecuniary arrangement into which we entered with you, as to any orders you may be able privately to obtain for us." This document is signed by E. V. Neale and Thos. Hughes.

Holyoake remained friendly with the globular Frenchman. When the Christian Socialist Co-operative schemes failed one after the other, and they concentrated their energy on the Working Men's College, St. Andre" set up a business as "Universal Purveyor," which was to "undertake an Equitable Arbitration between Producers and Consumers, etc." He had secured the aid and patronage of the Dean of Oriel (the Rev. C. Marriott), and took Holyoake to Oxford on a pleasant visit to the Dean. His business failed, and he returned to France. After 1870, when the secret documents of Napoleon III were exposed, it was discovered that St. Andre had been all the time a paid spy of the Imperial

Government!

Holyoake's further relations with the principal workers in the brilliant episode of Christian Socialism in the early fifties will fall under our notice later. For the moment we may revert to his journalistic activity on behalf of Cooperation. There are frequent appeals for Co-operative action in the *Reasoner* in the course of 1849. On April nth a lengthy " Ion" letter, the first of the new series, occupying the first four pages, deals with ". First Steps to Association. " He pleads that, as there is so grave a reaction against Socialism, its friends should " in the meantime work for Association, and thus prepare the public for the next wave of opinion." He criticises Mill's defence of competition, and holds that " it brings neither Justice, Harmony, nor Satisfaction." There are no specific suggestions, but the general principle is advocated: "As property is accumulated, let it be distributed more among its creators than now." He does not attack " Property." "So far from assailing riches, I would that all men were rich." But point is given to the principle a few weeks later when he announces: "We have received the Laws of the Rochdale Society of Equitable Pioneers. Those persons forming Co-operative Stores in any locality would be advantaged by procuring a copy of these Laws from the secretary, James Daly, of Rochdale." In the following year he again visited Rochdale, and, in describing his tour, observed: "This town presents the most instructive example extant of a Co-operative experiment. Those who are curious upon this subject may see in the Associative department of the *Leader* some explanatory papers embodying the principal facts." He also visited Leeds and Derby, where stores had already been opened. But with the beginning of 1850 he had begun propagandist work on behalf of Co-operation that it is impossible and needless to pursue at any length. In the first issue of the *Leader,* Alexander Somerville— the Scots Grey who had dropped anonymous letters to the people on the streets of Birmingham in 1832—had a letter urging " association on reproductive

principles." Holyoake criticised his remarks on the " moral sentimentality" of the Socialists, but otherwise supported him. In June Holyoake gave an account of the progress of Co-operation in Lancashire. A number of Co-operators from various parts had held a joint meeting at Middleton, to compare Vol. 1. o views and measures. He added: '' Let the operatives follow the advice here given to them: let them have confidence in each other, let them act so as to preserve confidence, and they cannot fail to elevate themselves. If they want help from the middle classes, they may rest satisfied that the surest way to obtain that help is by showing how much they can do for themselves and each other." In the same issue a letter appeared urging the formation of "Joint Stock Co-operative Societies," and a leader was written in support of it.

The notices multiply, and at last, in August (1850), Holyoake is entrusted with a special department of the journal, consisting of from two to four columns, under the heading of "Associative Progress." "It is very gratifying," he says, "to find the Co-operative-store plans, which have been ignored for so long a time— which promised such useful results eighteen years ago— reviving and bearing fruit in late season." For several years Holyoake kept this unique record of Co-operative progress in the columns of the *Leader,* and gave great prominence to the reports from the distributive stores. His columns furnish a valuable record of progress in that first decade of the modern movement. The network of stores was now slowly spreading over the map, and at the older centres the work had got beyond the experimental stage. A weekly and ample record of all that was being done must have been of incalculable service to the cause at such a period; and not only was the *Leader* a journal of far wider and greater influence than any slight distinctive organ could be, but it was once more the only paper explicitly furthering the Co-operative movement.

From this time onward, until Holyoake takes a more important part in the constructive work of the movement, it is unnecessary to recount every occasion on which he comes into direct touch with the new centres. In May, during a provincial tour, he "spent an agreeable day with Mr. David Green, Dr. Lees, Mr. West, and the founders and promoters of the Redemption Society," the earliest Co-operative venture in the Leeds district, and the germ of the great Leeds Society of our time. In October he opened a new Socialist hall in Manchester (Garratt's Road). The event is not without interest in itself, as one of the latest spurts of Owenite activity, bringing together audiences of six or seven hundred people. But when we learn that this Society went on to form a "Manchester Co-operative Manufacturing, Trading, and Agricultural Association," the interest is increased. On the Monday he lectured at the Miles Platting Mechanics' Institution, and was elected as their delegate to the Educational Conference summoned by the Lancashire League, at which Cobden and other educationists spoke. From Manchester he revisited Rochdale, and on his return he wrote in the *Leader* a sketch of the history of the Rochdale Pioneers—the germ of the little work of 1857 that would carry the account of their adventures all over the world. Rochdale became one of his favourite centres in Lancashire— his favourite county for lecturing—and he knew it well when he began his history. A letter written to him a few years ago by Mr. P. A. Lister, son of the Alderman Lister who aided in the formation of the Society, has recollections of him about the time we are considering:

"Dear Mr. Holyoake,

"I read your letter in the *Daily News.* I thought it may interest you to know that I always read your name and all you have to say with much interest.

"I recollect you well when you used to visit my father, George Lister. I have often thought of the time when you came there, and were unwell—had weak eyes, and I used to fetch cold water from the pond whilst you bathed your eyes in the shade of the yew bushes on the lawn. That was about fifty years ago. You were a man of about 35,

and I a boy of about seven. I have never forgotten it....

"You must be a wonderfully strong man for your years, and yet, as I recollect you, you seemed anything but robust in those days...."

The son in turn founded a Co-operative store at Dursley, where he settled as an agricultural engineer. Holyoake had by this time many friends in Lancashire, who made absence from home more tolerable. An anonymous letter to him from Manchester about this time begins:

"dearly Beloved And Much-honoured Master, "If it should seem fit to you to grant to your disciple the honour of being your host during your Manchester visit, the which he much covets, desires, and seeks earnestly to obtain: write to him forthwith and inform him when you will make your appearance in his abode in No. — Rusholme Road, to which he removes on Monday.

"I must drop the third person—damn it: it is no go....

The writer seems to have been Mr. Percy Greg. From Derby a friend (Hetty Jackson) wrote:

"Dear Friend,

"Brevity may be the soul of wit, but it is sometimes adverse to social enjoyment. May I trouble you to inform us whether you can stay in Derby one evening besides the one on which you lecture?... A few Unitarian reformers with Dr. Hutton, their minister, have requested the pleasure of meeting you here."

One of his older friends, T. Cooper, who changed the views he had once shared with Holyoake, wrote him that amidst his "opulence of new ties" they could afford to part. "Go on in your polite way," Cooper said; "my old rugged path suits me better. We need not jostle: the world is wide enough for both of us." But Cooper renewed his friendship and took part in the presentation to him at the Freemasons' Tavern.

His father died in May 1853, and he went home to spend the last day or two with him. In an entry in the diary shortly before that date he says: "Breakfasted at Muswell Hill. Mr. Home made a mag-

netic calculation of my head. Cautiousness as 16. Home 79." If the ratio of Holyoake's domestic feeling to his cautiousness were really 79 to 16, it would be phenomenally high for a public man. In fact, however, it was high. His sister, now living in America, gives me some recollections of him at this period. When he came to visit them, she says, he would

"open his valise and give me sixpence to go and buy him a large pear for his dinner, and mother would say: 'He is just like his father, very fussy what he would eat.' Mother often talked to us younger children, and told us what a dear son he was to her. She could always depend on him for the truth, from a boy to a man, and a more affectionate son and brother never existed.... When my father died in 1852 1853 I was twelve years old, the youngest of the family, and we were all round his bed. He took my hand and put it in George's hand, and said: 'George, you are the oldest son. Take care of your dear mother all you can, and this your youngest sister.' And if any son or brother kept the promise as he did, I am sure they would be, like me, very proud of their brother."

Austin and he went down to Birmingham on the Sunday, and found their father dying. "Smoked a cigar with him," the diary notes. The next day the entry runs: "Found father anxious to see me. Died while I was at Baker's and looking for a pipe for him. Smoked a cigar with him previously. Left five pounds to buy black." He returned for the funeral, and on the following Sunday took his mother to church. From that time he constantly sent money to Birmingham.

We will take up again later the thread of his Cooperative work, and see how he passes from propagandist and counsellor to constructive statesman. But his work from 1844 to 1854 had great influence on the fortunes of the movement. Through him men like Mazzini and Saffi became interested in it, and took the idea with them into the new Italy of a later year. Through him, through his articles in the *Reasoner* and columns in the *Leader,* scores of social students and thousands of workers were reminded constantly of the Co-operative idea and its growing success, until they at length stirred themselves to give it a fresh embodiment.

CHAPTER X THE FOUNDING OF SECULARISM

Throughout these early years of the more distinguished and more pleasant part of Holyoake's career we have found his older friends frequently suggesting that he had been unworthily lured away from them. To them, as they observed his advancing fortune, it brought some consolation to reflect that he had left them on the rugged paths up the hillside to mingle with easy folk on the plains. Nor was their memory of his career an impediment to their thinking this with some sincerity. Atheists recalled phrases he had used in the *Oracle,* and frowned when they now heard of his taking tea with Brooke Herford or the Dean of Oriel. Chartists and Socialists looked back over their copies of his flamboyant *Cause of the People,* and felt that to share the hospitality of a Lady Walmsley or Lady Beaumont was apostasy. It seemed to them that he was now firing shot into the faded flags he had once borne with them.

Certainly there had been a change. To us who look back on the whole social history of the nineteenth century, and see how Chartism and Socialism had played their parts and must make way for new actors, the change offers no difficulty in the interpretation of his character: to them, having no glimpse of the greater movements to come, the change was treachery. We must, indeed, be careful not to exaggerate the change in him or the charge against him. As late as April 13th, 1853, I find him at a "Tea Party and Public Meeting" in honour of " the Incorruptible Robespierre," with half the firebrands of Europe—Louis Blanc, Nadaud, Saffi, Kossuth, Ledru Rollin, Dawson, Harney, E. Jones, Linton, R. Moore, and other pyrotechnic orators. Yet there had been a change— a more fixed habit of walking in "the polite way" that Cooper deprecated, and a clearer conviction that even peers, priests, and politicians might become

sincere co-workers in the cause of the people. Such changes are peculiarly apt to bring the word "compromise" to the lips of the captious. Compromise may mean wise idealism: when you take as much as you can get of a good thing, and wait impatiently for more. But the suggestion that one has surrendered or modified an ideal with an eye to comfort is a different thing.

Any such suspicion in connection with Holyoake's development at this stage is wholly precluded by the story of the present chapter. Most of his ideals were repugnant to some or other body of his neighbours. One ideal—that of the outspoken criticism of religious beliefs—was repugnant to the vast majority in the country, and was deeply regretted by almost all his new political associates. It had conducted him to a jail, with every circumstance of ignominy and discomfort, when he stood on the steps of manhood; it gave pain throughout his career to the men and women he respected most; and it was the one shade that lay upon his memory for the majority of those who came to honour him in death. Yet he maintained that ideal without swerving to his last year. He knew well all that it would mean to him if he would desist from his critical work; and he not only did not desist, but he spent large sums of money and great stores of energy in pursuing it. Whether or no one can understand *why* it was a matter of conscience with him, the fact that he held duty before comfort remains. Nor can it be without interest, even to the religious, to see how the first organic body for the criticism of religious beliefs arose in this country, and what design of its structure and activity took shape in the mind of "the mildest-mannered man in the ranks of public disputants."

Until 1853 there was no free-thinking organisation in England. How far the Rational Religion should be entitled to that name we need not stay to consider. There was a large amount of criticism effected through its machinery, but its chiefs repudiated the description and their followers were divided. The attempt to reject the description altogeth-

er split a large fragment from it, and for a time Holyoake and his colleagues led something of a party. A nearer approach to organisation came with the establishment of the *Reasoner,* which at first professedly succeeded the *Oracle* and the *Movement* as an "atheistical " journal. But Holyoake was never happy under the name "atheist." In the minds of most people it connoted dogmatism of statement and hardness, if not coarseness, of character. He saw, too, how a narrow concentration of interest into critical channels was consistent with poor types of character. One needed to be clever for the work, but moral quality could—he observed—be dispensed with. He saw that it would be folly to dissipate, or to divert to selfish purposes, the great stream of energy and devotion that had been associated with religion. It should be directed to tangible human interests. On these considerations he created Secularism, in which the criticism of theology should be balanced by a concern for culture, character, and social progress. It was bound to fail—the aim now was too broad—but it became for some years the chief interest of his life.

On March 21st, 1849, he notes in his diary: "Issued the first 'Secular' number of the *Reasoner."* There is really no perceptible change in the paper at that time; possibly articles on social matters begin to occupy more space. From the first the *Reasoner* had maintained a good tone, and he wished to give the paper solidity. Once he tried to draw Dr. Martineau into its columns, but the distinguished Unitarian replied:

"sir,

"I am obliged by your attention in sending me a copy of the *Reasoner* with the article by ' Aliquis' on the question at issue between the theist and the atheist. I willingly acknowledge the duty of persons who have anything new to advance on this question to communicate it, where there is a fair chance of an unprejudiced hearing. But I also esteem it the duty of those who have *nothing* new to advance, to hold their peace and be content with their private convictions. Agreeably to this rule, as I think,

Aliquis would have done wisely not to write his paper, so must I decline the invitation to answer it. Moreover, those who fancy they have any fresh truth to state must really choose their own time and mode of stating it; and Aliquis is less of a workman than I if, on a chance invitation, he can stand up and find time for a game of theological battledore and shuttlecock. In this noisy world we must get our matters said as the pauses may allow.

"Meanwhile I freely confess my opinion that the course of speculation on which Aliquis has entered has no tendency to settle the question at issue, one way or the other. And I could feel no interest in becoming party to an argument, apparently holding in suspense a grand truth, which in reality is quite independent of its whole scope.

"I remain, Sir, yours with respect,

"james Martineau."

Holyoake answered with courtesy, and embraced the "opportunity of thanking him for the several charming things he had said elsewhere from which he had derived infinite gratification." The *Reasoner* was, of course, far below the intellectual level of Martineau. It was "a work of vulgarisation," in the pregnant French phrase. Holyoake's articles were always shrewd, and often thoughtful and helpful, but he had neither time nor equipment for philosophy. Ashurst wrote occasionally in it over the name of " Edward Search," and MissS. D. Collet over that of "Panthea." Her brother wrote in it, in 1848, a long series of articles on "The Rise and Progress of the Swiss Republics," and for some time made it the organ of their campaign on the press-stamp. "Aliquis," whose identity was so carefully concealed, was a wealthy Teignmouth gentleman, Mr. Gwynne, a strong supporter of Holyoake and his journal. "Eugene" was George Hooper. "Lionel Holdreth" was Mr. Percy Greg. W. Chilton, who was evidently well acquainted with the theories of Lamarck and the contemporary discussions of Cuvier and Agassiz, wrote scientific articles, and brought the new batteries of geology to bear on *Ge-*

nesis, Paleyism, etc. When we remember that the paper was bound, from the very nature of its political and social articles, to seek a circulation mainly amongst the workers, its quality and competence cannot be disputed. We have seen how the *Daily News* singled it out as one of especial capability amongst the rebellious journals of the time. A Unitarian clergyman, Mr. Layhe, wrote in his *Report:* "The chief merit of the editor is the improved moral tone which he has introduced into the literature of unbelief.... It is greatly to be regretted that a man of so much nobility of nature has no faith in God." But its circulation was always small; it had to appeal constantly for what the editor lightly called " Reasources," and even with that help he drew only about fifty pounds a year from it.

Several other letters passed between them, of which a sentence or two are interesting. In declining Holyoake's challenge to a public discussion, Dr. Martineau said:

"I do not think that the theistical doctrine is one which can be proved or disproved by any mere scientific reasoning at all, but is a higher certainty than any that can come under this description.. .. As to books in confutation of your views, it is not in my power to mention any: simply because I do not see that you *have* any views, beyond critical objections to other people's arguments; and I do not think much better of those arguments than you do."

The condition of anti-Christian feeling in the country at that time—about 1850—will have been gathered from what has preceded. The writings of Paine, Shelley, and Gibbon had engendered a good deal of revolt against the Churches, but the free-thinkers were still generally deists. The lectures of R. Owen and his disciples, of R. Carlile, and of most of the Chartists, had stimulated and spread the feeling—once more generally within the limits of theism. But the Secularist theories of Bentham, now enforced by the two Mills, the translation of Strauss—I find the Chapmans consulting Holyoake as to a popular edition of the *Life of Jesus*—

and other advanced Germans, the opening of the scientific controversy over *Genesis,* the pantheism of Coleridge and Carlyle and Emerson (which obliterated the God of Deists and Christians, and offered no substitute that the artisan-mind could fix and retain), and the prolonged and intense fight over secular issues, greatly promoted the spread of what was vaguely called "infidelity." When Southwell, Ryall, Chilton, and Holyoake began their atheistic campaign, for the first time in our history, they found a comparatively large body of followers. This body was scattered again at the closing of the Owenite halls, and by 1846 there were not sufficient followers in the country to pay for the mere printing of the one small weekly (the *Reasoner)* that criticised theology. By 1848 Holyoake and his friends had half a dozen lecturing centres in London, and that number was maintained for some years.

The condition of the provincial towns in this regard can be seen most vividly in Holyoake's lengthy account of his tours in 1850. He had a week in Scotland in March. In the following month he had a debate with the Rev. John Bowes at Bradford, in whom he found "the two worst qualities a man can have to contend with in debate—prudence and dulness." But 1,500 people crushed into the hall, and hundreds were turned away nightly. His thin voice was at a disadvantage, for "a Methodist junto " was trying some refractory preachers in the next room, and the friends of the accused gathered at the doors and sang hymns for three hours to intimidate the judges; until a burly Yorkshireman in Holyoake's audience arose and said: "Mr. Chairman, I move as how some on us go out and move yon singers away. " The motion was hailed with delight, but Holyoake, who feared they would " put an end to the melodists as well as the melodies," dissuaded the men and endured the pipers." Of the 1,500 auditors he calculated that 1,000 agreed with himself. The *Bradford Observer* made comments on "the religious boxing match," which you paid *1d., 2d.,* or *3d.* to witness, but Holyoake interviewed the editor, and he became more polite. The *Leeds Times* called them a couple of " noisy wind-bags," and hinted at a "wind-fall" of profit. During his week in Bradford, he was invited to speak at an education meeting, at which the vicar took the chair with great courtesy and Mr. Forster also spoke. From Bradford he went to Keighley. He had full but perplexed audiences. They could not tell "what yon man wur loike: he wanna loike a Christian." Bingley and Heckmondwike also were visited.

After visits to Leeds, Manchester, and Liverpool, he went up to Sunderland and Newcastle, where the clergy appeared and challenged him to "a six nights' debate." Before it could be arranged he had to keep engagements at Ipswich and Norwich, and return to London for *Leader* work and classes. At Ipswich, where the local clergy had attacked him, the Quaker-proprietor of the only hall refused to let it to him, as a Quaker had done at Northampton. He hired the bowling-green of the Freemason's Tavern. The audience numbered more than four hundred. It happened to be a fine evening, and he went on answering questions far into the dark hours; and as the people could not be seen in the dark by their pastor, who was present and militant, they gave him an anxious time. The meeting ended with three cheers for the lecturer. At Norwich he spoke in the Maid's Head Inn, to large audiences. The *Norfolk News* says that the address was distinguished by good feeling and "great clearness and simplicity of style," and that the answers to objections "appeared to give general satisfaction." The meeting lasted three hours.

There was another set debate (with Dr. King) in London on his return. Remembering that this was the first year of the *Leader,* we feel that he must have worked hard. On October 16th he took the chair at the Temperance Hall in Commercial Road, when a tall, vigorous youth of seventeen discussed the "Past, Present, and Future of Theology," and took the collection, because he was "the victim " of a neighbouring clergyman. It was Holyoake's first acquaintance with Charles Bradlaugh. A week later he was opening the new Socialist hall at Manchester, and attending the Educational Conference there with Cobden and others. He had lively meetings at Rochdale ("that tea-cup of Huddersfield"). One clergyman "began a speech, the melancholy burden of which was the number of persons who had been murdered by the atheists during the French Revolution: one million seven hundred and fifty-four were, I think, the number." He was a muscular Christian, dancing about frantically from seat to seat, and at last precipitating himself at a window which he took to be a door. He was followed by a preacher "of sanguinous temperament, and of somewhat sanguinous speech," and the long string of orators concluded with an old "hard-working hard-looking man " who assured them that "at the bottom of all things is a globulic principle, round and circular." From Lancashire he went further north, gave two lectures at Newcastle and two at Sunderland, and finished with a three-nights' debate at Newcastle before 500 people. A clergyman who wished to debate with him was held back by his apprehensive congregation, and he could only secure a lay Unitarian speaker for what the papers were calling " gladiatorship." The debate was polite, though the *Gateshead Observer* called it "a revival of the savagery and bigotry of the fifth of November." The *Newcastle Journal* thought it a "shameful exhibition," and wanted to know where the magistrates were that they did not suppress this "cockney atheist" and his "sham opponent." Holyoake generally bearded these editors in their dens, and generally disarmed them. He remained in the town for the local "reply," which gave him a fresh audience of 1,000. When Holyoake had gone, the *Newcastle Journal* wrote: It may not be without interest to note that these audiences in 1851 were larger than any lecturer on the same lines can get in the same towns to-day.

"The town of Newcastle-upon-Tyne has been for some time past infested with a succession of low, scurrilous vagabonds, too lazy to work and too illiterate to earn an honourable livelihood—creatures who appear to be proficient in nothing but in spouting blasphemy and infidelity. It would seem as if there were to be no end of this abomination—that the inexhaustible channels of vice and immorality in the metropolis were to be distributed in innumerable streams over the provinces, and that this town was destined to receive considerably more than its proportionate share."

Fresh lectures at Norwich, and at Diss, Derby, Longton, Leeds, and other places occur in the same year, and the tours are repeated each succeeding year with infinite variety of adventure and ever-increasing audiences. We have seen sufficient to form an opinion of the state of feeling in the provinces. The residue of Owenite agitation, with the new stirring caused by the religious movements of the time, gave the elements for an organic body, and Holyoake began to frame his plans in the beginning of 1852. The first difficulty lay in the choice of a name. Atheism he was now determined to supersede, for reasons I have explained. At one time he suggested " Netheism," but a clerical critic promptly pointed out that *ne* was merely the Latin for the Greek *a*. "Limitationism" also occurred to him. But all these titles were negative, and what he really sought was positive culture, to which the correction of errors should be incidental. The word "secular" had been used by him several times as a good description of the interests he sought to promote—the interests of this world—and "Secularism" was an obvious appellation for a system that aimed at concentrating attention on mundane affairs. "Giving an account of ourselves in the whole extent of opinion," he says, when he uses the word for the first time (December 3rd, 1851), "we should use the word 'Secularist' as best indicating that province of human duty which belongs to this life." From the first he thought so little of including atheism necessarily in it that he asked Miss Collet to join; but from the first the tendency was plain enough, and she refused to join. Her comments on him and his views at the time (published in her biographical sketch) are interesting:

"In attempting to estimate Mr. Holyoake's character as a public teacher, the chief characteristic thereof that attracts the attention appears to be this—that in theological criticism, which is usually abandoned to the keenest, coldest exercise of the mere intellect, he is remarkable for the pre-eminence of his moral development. He is not a systematic thinker. Though endowed with manly good sense, and frequently flashing forth striking and eloquent thoughts, he is remarkably ! deficient in speculative genius. His literary culture is also very imperfect—a circumstance which frequently leads him into awkward blunders.... The inspiration which for thirteen tireless years has urged on his steps is the resolution to conquer a free field for the human conscience, where, unfettered by harsh creeds and unjust laws, it may develop into its true proportions."

Another contemporary estimate of some value is that of the Rev. W. N. Molesworth, the historian. Writing under the year 1846—the paragraph is a little antedated —he says:

"In the course of this year a 'system of ethics' to which its author gave the name of Secularism was widely propagated by Mr. G. J. Holyoake, a London bookseller. We place before the reader the description of the system as given by its founder... long description in Holyoake's words. Secularism is, in fact, the religion of doubt. It does not necessarily clash with other religions; it does not deny the existence of a God or even the truth of Christianity, but it does not profess to believe in either the one or the other. Nay, most of its advocates have often and strongly assailed both. It differs little, if at all, in substance from the opinions of the freethinkers of the last century, but it differs widely from them in the manner of its propagation and the persons by whom it was embraced. The old freethinkers made few converts, and these chiefly, if not exclusively, among the upper class; but Secularism was embraced by thousands and tens of thousands of the working classes. The success which attended the at-tempts made to propagate it was due partly to the fact that great masses of the working classes, especially in the large manufacturing towns, were already lost to Christianity, and had, in many cases, almost unconsciously adopted the ideas which Mr. Holyoake fixed and shaped into distinct doctrines, but which are in fact the views that naturally replace Christianity in the minds of those who have practically renounced it; partly to the zeal, activity, ability, and boldness with which Secularism was propagated and defended; and in no small degree also to the qualities of Mr. Holyoake, who had assiduously cultivated great natural gifts, who delivered his opinions with a calm, quiet, and persuasive earnestness, and had won the favourable attention of the working classes by the enlightened interest he had on many occasions taken in their welfare, and the thorough mastery he displayed of many social problems in the solution of which they were deeply interested." *George Jacob Holyoake,* p. 24. VOL. I. p

Thus it was well understood from the first that Holyoake aimed at a positive culture. He did not think the system should take its name from its inconsistency with certain religious views any more than from its inconsistency with certain political or social views, to which it was equally opposed. We shall see how his aim was frustrated, and how this broad expansion of his principles put too severe a strain on them. From 1851 to 1853 he worked slowly at the organisation of the movement. A handbill announces, for December 29th, 1851, "the first Free Discussion Festival in connection with the Secular Society" at the Hall of Science, City Road, with tea, songs, and speeches on the provincial plan. At this meeting Holyoake gave an account of "the present position of Secularism in the provinces." Other speakers were Mr. W. J. Birch (an Oxford M.A., and writer on Shakespeare), T. Cooper, Dr. Brooks, and Mr. Eb. Syme (Unitarian minister). In March, at another of these quaint "festivals," and an "aggregate meeting of London Freethinkers," Holyoake was to "state the constitution of the Society of Seculars, being the model proposed for the organisation of Freethinkers." The list of lectures he offered to provincial societies contained only six on theology to thirteen on political and social subjects, and in October he visited Oldham, Manchester, Stockport, Accrington, Rochdale, Lincoln, and Middlesborough. At Manchester he convened a conference in the new hall—now the "Secular Institute"—to which delegates came from all parts of Lancashire, as well as Scotland. A remarkable number of familiar Co-operative names appear amongst them. From that date the adoption of the name Secularist became general amongst freethinking societies, and Holyoake was recognised as the leader. T. Cooper found the movement too sceptical, and withdrew. Southwell first criticised its mildness, then imitated it, and finally emigrated to New Zealand, where, for want of better employment, he edited a Wesleyan journal, and horrified his employers by a death-bed avowal of atheism after having controlled their paper for several years. *History of England 1830-1874,* II, 235. The reader who desires further information may consult Holyoake's *Origin and Nature of Secularism* and Chambers' *Encyclopedia,* in which the article on Secularism is by Holyoake. Mr. Molesworth writes with knowledge. He lived near Rochdale, and was cpnnected with Co-operation.

In 1853 Holyoake was presented with £250, as we have previously described. With £p he had founded a paper: with 250 he determined to found an institution. Money was scarce enough at 17 Woburn Buildings, where there were now school-bills for the children. But not a penny of the presentation, which was a purely personal gift, went to personal use. The movement he was interested in needed a habitation in the metropolis, a centre of crystallisation, and the whole of the money was used in creating one.

The first step, and the first error, was to buy the publishing business and the stock of his friend James Watson in Paternoster Row. Watson was a brave and earnest man. He had served in R.

Carlile's shop, and had then for years sold prohibited literature himself. He was well known to the police. But his conduct at this juncture was not pleasant, probably from some tincture of jealousy. His business was worth very little, and his entire dusty stock did not realise 50, but he claimed £350, and pressed Holyoake hard for the payments. Mr. Ashurst, who acted legally for them, clearly thought Holyoake quixotically generous, and Watson rather mean. Holyoake gave him 100 down, and was to pay the rest within five years; but he one day saw Watson looking hungrily at his shop, and he sent Austin over with the balance due to him—the whole of the money they had. The whole of his presentation had gone in an act of excessive generosity. The little shop in Queen's Head Passage proved quite unsuitable, and he had, towards the end of 1853, to buy the lease of 147 Fleet Street (now the "Press Restaurant"). This cost him 570, and he had to find 150 for fittings, etc. He had won the citizenship of Fleet Street for his organisation, but had sown a crop of debts and troubles.

Mr. Birch, Mr. Ashurst, and other friends, had advanced money, but he had insisted on affording proper security, and had even pledged his life-insurance policy. At first he felt little anxiety, but the clouds quickly began to show. A friend who had promised him 1,000 had losses in business, and could not pay it. I fancy this was Le Blond. Presently a graver disappointment came. His chief source of content was that he had in his care the will of an elderly admirer, Mr. Fletcher, which bequeathed him 30,000 on that gentleman's decease. One day Mr. Fletcher asked him to tea, and begged him to bring the will. His rival, Robert Cooper, was present. Fletcher took the will from him, destroyed it, and assigned his money to Robert Cooper.

The sequel to this disastrous experience is one of the most striking illustrations of Holyoake's chivalry. It was not long before he discovered that Mr. Fletcher had been told by one of his own shopmen that he had hindered the sale of Cooper's pamphlets and other

literature of the fiery order, which Fletcher esteemed. This man, Mr. F. R. Young, had been a clerk and a Wesleyan local preacher at Ipswich, when he made Holyoake's acquaintance in 1853. His early letters are repellent in their mixture of piety and adulation of Holyoake. At his appeal Holyoake paid his debts, amounting to some twenty pounds, and gave him the management of his shop, though he remained a Christian. Within a year or two he partly borrowed and partly appropriated 101 of Holyoake's money, and was dismissed but not prosecuted. It was then that he made the charge against Holyoake, and Cooper retailed it to Fletcher. When Holyoake threatened action he withdrew his many calumnies of freethinkers, and merely claimed that Holyoake did not press the sale of Cooper's works. That will seem plausible enough to any one who reads the *Infidel's Text-book* and Cooper's other writings. In 1857 Young applied for admission into the Unitarian ministry, and, on the application of Mr. Kenrick, Holyoake accepted *£50* and gave Young a clean bill. His letter to Mr. Kenrick, which was not published, runs:

"Dear S1r,

"My position is this. The loans obtained from me by the Rev. F. R. Young, and monies used by him while in my employ, were, as he was aware from the first, Trust-money. *The whole I have to repay,* and I do not see that I ought to accept less than 50 os. in settlement of my claim of.£101. By doing so I am undertaking to pay the other 50 os. myself. Those to whom I am debtor forbear and acquit me morally while I place the full claim in their hands. Not wishing any harm to Mr. Young, and not desiring to take a course which may appear to his present colleagues as personal hostility to him on account of his ministerial position, I have forebore all mention of his name in this matter publicly. By such a step I could obtain the *whole* by public subscription—to make good a loss sustained by such a person in such a way. By giving the facts of the case at the point I mark in the *History of the Fleet St. House,* where the loss

is mentioned but the name concealed, I might have had the whole money before this. My personal regard for so many gentlemen of the Unitarian body with whom I have friendly relations makes me unwilling to take this course, and, though I cannot hope to be credited with such a feeling, *it* alone has restrained me, and has induced me to repeat the offer previously made to Mr. Young. I write after having consulted with Mr. Shaen.

"Yours very respectfully,

"G. J. Holyoake."

Another unforeseen tribulation that befell the Fleet Street House was that the Vicar of St. Bride's demanded his tithes. When Holyoake hinted that tithes on the profits of infidel works seemed a little incongruous, he declared that the right had been sold to a layman two centuries before, and they collected them for his descendants. Holyoake demurred in principle to paying tax to the clergy—the profit of the earlier transaction was still theirs—and every half year they made a descent on his shop, and carried off the clock, rolls of paper, or the more innocent-looking books they could find. At last Holyoake told the officers he would pay, and send the tithe to the vicar. The clergyman received from him "payment in kind"—three or four volumes of the *Reasoner,* "that being the 'kind' of property produced on my farm." That put an end to the persecution.

But friends were generous, and the Fleet Street House was maintained for eight years. Mr. Ross, the famous optician, came to him in one of his darkest hours, and gave him 250. Mr. Birch regarded as a gift, when things went badly, his loan of 200. All this, with the initial 250 and 500 more that was given him, was swallowed up in the " British Secular Institute of Communism and Propagandism." Robert Owen, Harriet Martineau, J. Cowen, Major Evans Bell, Mr. Ashurst, Mr. Lister, Mr. Trevelyan, and others, had shares in it, and were generous. Malicious colleagues brought charges against him, of course, and we will consider them later; but when he showed Southwell the real nature of his transactions (with Watson, etc.) that critic changed his censures into: "Jacob, you're a damned fool!" He allotted only 75 a year to his brother, who was secretary and took his place when he was absent. He himself drew only 200 a year, as Director and Lecturer and Editor of the *Reasoner;* and he now assigned the net proceeds of all his lectures to the Institute.

The work of the Institute and the stirring part it took in English and even European life during its short career fully rewarded him for his losses and labours. "We do but reap where you have sown," Professor Tyndall once said to him at a meeting of the British Association. But criticism of theology was only a part of its work. The front parlour over the shop was turned into a "Political Exchange," and became the "rendezvous" of political, social, and religious heretics of every nationality. If the walls of the "Press Restaurant" could speak, they would tell us many a secret that has gone to the grave with the last of the insurgents who plotted in it. French, Italian, German, and Polish refugees loosed their torrents of grievances in it. Defiant flags waved from its windows, and literature of every shade of defiance covered its tables. The campaign on the press-stamp was largely framed in it. The destruction of the Conspiracy Bill was plotted in it. The Garibaldian Legion was partly organised in it. But all these things, so far as we know them, will be considered in due order. For the moment I return to Secularism.

History of the Fleet Strut House, by Holyoake, published in 1856 (20 pp., price 6d.).

In addition to his lectures, debates, and journalistic articles, Holyoake wrote a number of small works at this period that were intended to correct misconceptions of his system. A complete list of his writings will be found at the end of this work, and I will not attempt to notice each pamphlet as it appears. In 1848 he wrote his *Hints toward a Logic of Facts,* an "unceremonious endeavour to enlarge the province and abbreviate the details of logic." He deals with it as

he had dealt with grammar, and the little work (of 92 pages) is bright, sententious, and helpful to young men. *Douglas Jerrold's Weekly* thought it "a bold and able treatise," and the *Critic* said it was " invaluable to the learner." In 1847 he published his *Life and Character of H. Hetherington* (his address at the funeral) and his *Rudiments of Public Speaking and Debate.* The shrewd hints and bright, terse style of the latter won a long popularity for it. It ran through many editions, and was published in America. Wendell Phillips, the great Abolitionist orator, "studied it faithfully," he told Holyoake, until his "well-thumbed copy" was detained by a friend. He also wrote a sixpenny *Life of Carlile.* In 1851 he announced a " Cabinet of Reason." The first volume was the *Task of To-day,* by Major Bell; the second, Holyoake's *Why do the Clergy avoid Discussion?* which was at least successful in bringing debates; the third was his *Organisation, not of Arms, but of Ideas,* a criticism of Chartism, and appeal for his new organisation. For the secular education of children he issued four elementary spelling and reading books, based on his experience at Sheffield. Other little works of that period are his *Logic of Death* (an able and eloquent lecture, which had a very wide circulation and has been recently republished), *Literary Institutions, Catholicism the Religion of Fear* (a censure of *Hell Opened to Christians), Philosophic Type of Christianity* (an examination of F. W. Newman's work, *The Soul),* and other small and unimportant pamphlets that are given in the appendix. Much more important and effective was his *Last Trial by Jury for Atheism in England,* an ample and temperate account of his trial (with the nine hours' speech) and imprisonment Amongst the congratulatory letters on it I find one from Mr. Reynolds (of *Reynolds Weekly)* saying that it was he who began the agitation for Holyoake in the *Weekly Dispatch* in 1843, and he had become proud of introducing Holyoake to public notice. Further small works—*The Constitution and Obligations of Secular Societies* (1852), *Secularism the Prac-*

tical Philosophy of the People (1853), *Secularism Distinguished from Unitarianism* (1855), and *The Principles of Secularism* (1859)—discussed various aspects of his system.

As his views found clearer expression his theistic friends evinced less displeasure. Miss Collet wrote:

"I feel increasingly persuaded that you are doing a great work in the reformation of ' matters pertaining to religion.' Though I demur to the definitions you have hitherto given of Secularism, I have a strong sympathy with that which, I believe, forms the main idea of what you mean by Secularism— /'. e., with that development and culture of free humanity trained by disciplined conscience."

She merely quarrelled with him for claiming only a "tolerable morality" for his system. He must and could claim a lofty one. On the other hand, Thornton Hunt wrote him that "in insisting upon 'moral' conduct on the part of persons aiding such movements he might commit against persons who are heterodox in morals or politics exactly the same kind of injustice that is committed in religion upon persons in his own position." Brooke Herford had a very cordial correspondence with him. The distinguished Unitarian minister had noticed the growing movement, and begged that he should be allowed to plead for theism to the Secular audiences. He wrote to Holyoake:

"My Dear Sir,

"Great press of work and absence from home have hitherto prevented me from fitly acknowledging your kind insertion of my letter and advertisement in the *Reasoner* and your very fair and friendly remarks thereon. I do *now* most cordially thank you, and believe me your readiness herein has done much to confirm into a permanent respect the feeling of friendship which I have felt for the Secularists as far as I know them.

"You will, I know, be glad to learn that my appeal to the Secularist Societies has not been in vain; already in the few days since it appeared I have received applications from Halifax, Sheffield, and Keighley, besides the particularly kind and pressing one from London of which you may probably be aware. You will see by my letter to Mr. Adams my reason for declining to deliver the lectures *first* in London. I have not confidence enough in myself, and shall be better able to do justice to my own and your arguments after a few lectures to people, to some extent familiar with me, as those at Halifax are. You would, I am sure, desire that London should be the scene of the most thorough rather than the first investigation of our conflicting ideas.... "For the present, my dear friend, farewell. Don't forget our little den when you come by this way. "Your affectionate friend,

"brooke Herford."

Other cordial letters were exchanged, and Holyoake stayed some days with Brooke Herford at Todmorden, and then entertained his friend in London.

Another Unitarian clergyman who ventured to express friendship was Mr. W. H. Crosskey, who later attained some distinction in geology. In 1851 he dedicated his *Defence of Religion* to Holyoake, causing a great commotion in the Unitarian body. The dedication ran:

"To George Jacob Holyoake, a man who, notwithstanding his inability to share the theist's faith, must permit a theist to regard his brave sincerity and reverence for truth and justice as acceptable worship at the altar of the Holy of Holies, this brief essay is affectionately inscribed."

The book had importance, as it appeared in a series (Chapman's *Library for the People*) that included works by Emerson, Newman, Froude, H. Spencer, etc., and Crosskey was violently assailed. The British and Foreign Unitarian Association declined to sell some of his pamphlets. Dr. Martineau wrote to him:

"I do confess that, while I would stoutly resist any illusage of such a man as Holyoake, or any attempt to gag him, I could hardly dedicate a book to him, this act seeming to imply a special sympathy and admiration directed upon that which distinctively characterises the man.... However, it is a generous im-

pulse to appear as the advocate of a man whom intolerance unjustly reviles." Mr. Crosskey may have replied that he meant precisely to show his admiration of "that which distinctively characterised" Holyoake. When he took the Unitarian Church at Glasgow in 1852, he placed it at Holyoake's service one week evening—as he did to Mazzini, Louis Blanc, and others—and greatly embittered his religious neighbours. Holyoake had a high admiration for such clergymen, and treasured their friendship. His *Secularist's Catechism,* (a penny catechism for Secularist children, of admirable spirit and contents) is based on a catechism written by Mr. Crosskey.

The Rev. H. N. Barnett (editor of the *Advocate)* and other clergymen wrote friendly letters to him, and this cordial correspondence with the clergy, which grew so much in later years, distinguishes—in both senses of the word—Holyoake amongst militant Freethinkers. It is hardly less instructive to consider his relations with laymen of culture and refinement who dissented strongly from his agnostic views. Most of his cultivated friends were of this class, and we have seen many of their letters. There is an interesting letter to him about this date from Leigh Hunt:

"My Dear Sir,

"Accept my best thanks for your kind letter and notice. The more we differ on some points, the more glad I must needs be at our agreement on others, for I have long esteemed your abilities and integrity. Do not measure the amount of my thanks by the brevity of this acknowledgment. I am not well, and am very busy, and so cannot write as much as I could wish. But I could not let another day pass without saying how great a pleasure you have given to

"Your obliged fellow-seeker of what is best, Leigh Hunt."

With Francis Newman, brother of the Cardinal, professor of Latin at University College and ultimately Vice-President of the British and Foreign Unitarian Association, he had life-long friendship and a voluminous correspondence. The three Newmans—John Henry,

Francis, and Charles—represent three types of mind so utterly diverse that they offer a problem in heredity. Francis had far more scholarship and philosophic ability than the Cardinal, but little of his brilliant utterance and subtlety of mind. He was also a keen and liberal student of politics and social questions. Throughout life he stood outside the pale of Christianity, but was an intense theist; in the end he surrendered his conviction of a future life. He had referred plainly enough, without naming him, to Holyoake in his work *The Soul,* which he published in 1847. He protested (p. 87) that some were carried into atheism

"not from any want of religious susceptibility, but, just as others his brother, etc. into Romanism, from an inability to disentangle sophistical arguments and from a desire to be honest in sacrificing their instinctive convictions to their technically erroneous reasoning. Those professors of Atheism who retain pure moral sympathies do, perhaps, under other names, such as Veneration of the Infinite and of Eternal Law, nourish within themselves some nucleus of religion. On no account let us exaggerate the real difference between them and us, though real it is and must be."

These are the phrases he uses in his letters to Holyoake, and indeed Holyoake was the only atheist of that type he knew of in 1847. The studies at Gower Street College brought them closer together, and the founding of Secularism, the stir in European politics, and the rise "I have not changed towards them: they have moved towards me," he wrote Holyoake in 1876. of Co-operation led to a remarkably busy correspondence. It is impossible to give more than a few sentences from these letters, but one of June 8th, 1853, may be reproduced:

Dear Sir,

"I was late in seeing a notice of the very gratifying social meeting at which a well-deserved testimonial the purse of 250 was presented to you, at which I heartily rejoice. Much as I (physically) dislike such meetings, I should have felt it a duty and honour to attend, if I had been invited. This I say, not as though /

ought to have been, but merely to vent my own feelings. However, it causes me the less regret that I had not this opportunity of adding my public testimony to your honour, since in my now forthcoming edition of the *Phases of Faith* I am naturally led to contrast your conduct to the coarse and profane attacks made on me by a Christian (!) opponent. I rejoice to feel that *we* (' atheists' and 'infidels') are really—in no small measure through your aid—winning a higher moral place in controversies than our effete opponents. "Believe me, Dear Sir, "Sincerely yours,

"Francis W. Newman."

A letter of June 13th (1853) puts Professor Newman's attitude to Dr. Martineau in an unusual light:

"While I have an exceedingly high love for him and estimate of him, mentally and morally, I feel my differences from him instructive. He has misunderstood and perverted my *Phases* almost as badly as my most inveterate calumniators."

Newman altered the new edition of his *Soul* to meet Holyoake's objections, and when Secularism was formally presented he wrote:

"I think that such a society ought to exist: I am glad that it does; J see services to be performed by it, and I hope they will be performed—the more perfectly the better. But I desire a Moral Union less sharply limited than Secularism; and I hope to see a wider union of which Secularism shall be one branch."

When Holyoake criticises his theistic position, he makes an interesting rejoinder:

"You appear to me to treat it as something bold and strange and unreliable in me (though frank and manly) to avow that I have no *logical proof* oof my first principles. But this is a mere axiomatic truism. If a principle *had* a logical proof, it would be only a secondary or tertiary, and not a first principle.... So: that the infinite fitness of Animated to Inanimate nature indicates Mind acting on a vast scale in the universe:—that human intelligence is a result of other intelligence higher than itself—is not a source, or a result, of what is unintel-ligent:—this conviction, which is the foundation of all religion, is in my opinion incapable of proof, because all proof presupposes earlier principles, and this is the earliest."

Holyoake's point was, of course, that this was *not* a first principle, and so should be proved. He came to Holyoake's house to meet Brooke Herford, and Holyoake often visited him. But Mrs. Newman was a devout follower of the Plymouth Brethren, and he says: "I think I shall consult for the tranquillity of another's mind by requesting you to give your name to my servant as Mr. George Jacob." A woman who would walk out of the room when Dr. Martineau was announced— "Mr. Jacob " being already there—would have shuddered at the name of Holyoake.

Politically, Newman was a Republican, and had warm sympathy with the foreign refugees. "I think it is now manifest," he writes in 1851, "that Republicanism is the only form in which for the future any portion of Truth, Right, Freedom, Intellect, can advance in Europe." But we shall meet him again in connection with political questions, and must pass over the wide range of subjects—finance, philology, marriage, population (on which he differs violently from J. S. Mill, though Mill's later conduct in Parliament swept away all his resentment), metaphysics, ethics, etc.—on which he corresponded with Holyoake. Francis Newman, who was a competent judge, would apparently have quite agreed with Dr. Flint, when he says: "There is an impression in some quarters that Atheism is advocated in a weak and unskilful manner by the chiefs of Secularism. It is an impression which I do not share."

The correspondence with Charles Newman, the youngest brother, belongs to a later date. We may conclude with a glance at the formal debates with the clergy that Holyoake held at this period. The chief gladiator on the Christian side to step out, when Holyoake published his *Why do the Clergy avoid Discussion?* was the Rev. Brewin Grant, a Congregationalist minister of "fine disputative faculty." As discussion was the main thing that Mr. Grant sought, he very soon responded to the challenge, and a debate took place in the Cowper Street School-rooms (London) on six Thursday evenings in January and February, 1853. These duels were arranged and conducted with great elaborateness, each disputant having a committee, that met and discussed for weeks in advance, and a chairman; and there was a more or less impartial umpire. At the Cowper Street Debate Mr. Samuel Morley was chairman for Mr. Grant, and the Rev. Ebenezer Syme, an ex-Unitarian minister, for Holyoake. The umpire was a Congregationalist clergyman, the Rev. Howard Hinton. It is interesting to find that all the clergymen taking active part, and Mr. S. Morley, had friendly relations with Holyoake afterwards, except Mr. Grant. Holyoake says of his opponent:

"He boasted that he should talk three times as fast as I should, and so have three times more pages in the report... . He was the nimblest opponent I ever met, but he never bit your arguments; he only nibbled at them. He was rabbit-minded, with a scavenger's eye for the refuse of old theological controversy. With him epithets were arguments."

Frankly, Mr. Grant was too loud, arrogant, and vituperative for a debater like Holyoake. He should have met Southwell. He was already boasting that he had "silenced Cardinal Newman," and his little world rang with his crushing victory over Holyoake. I do not intend to analyse the debate, which may still be read by the curious. The subject was: '' What advantages would accrue to mankind generally and the working classes in particular by the removal of Christianity and the substitution of Secularism in its place." The arguments used on both sides are familiar.

Mr. Grant was generous enough to say that "if they were to search England through they could not find one who was better fitted to defend their views "; but as he sank into mere bombast and abuse, and rarely followed an argument out, Holyoake was at a disadvantage. Grant had diligently read through all the preceding volumes of the *Rea-*

soner, Movement, and *Oracle,* for lurid quotations that would suit his style of attack. Miss Collet describes his conduct as "disgraceful," and says that he had recourse to "the meanest insinuations and grossest abuse," his purpose being to weaken Holyoake's personal authority. The Rev. H. N. Barnett, editor of the *Advocate,* and understood to be a friend of Grant's, wrote to Holyoake: "Brewin is as great a miracle, and quite as great a folly, as the winking virgin: he may awaken Vol. 1. Q contempt, but never convictions." But Mr. Barnett was another who was seduced from the ministry. Mr. Syme wrote even stronger language about Grant. They had a further debate at Glasgow in 1854 before 3,200 people (in the City Hall) on the subject: "Is Secularism inconsistent with reason and the moral sense, and condemned by experience?" This debate also was published. "The first striking point in the debate," wrote Miss Collet, after reading it, "is the almost superhuman blackguardism of Grant." As Mr. Grant afterwards left the Nonconformists and became a Churchman, and turned his power of invective upon his old friends, they became willing to acknowledge it. He wrote a book about them, which the *Athenceum.* described as overflowing with "spite, vanity, insolence, and coarse derision." A Glasgow paper said that the casual visitor would take Holyoake to be the Christian and Grant the infidel.

Holyoake's quality as a debater is seen better in a public discussion he held at Newcastle on August 1st, 3rd, and 5th, 1853, with the Rev. J. H. Rutherford. They dealt with the truth of Christianity and the teaching of Christ. The tone is much better, but the arguments are too familiar now for me to dwell on them. The duellists afterwards breakfasted together, and their correspondence shows mutual respect. In the following year Holyoake had a public discussion with a young minister "of whom the world has not yet heard, but of whom it will hear pleasing things some day," the *Christian Weekly News* said. The world did hear of him later as the Rev. Dr. J. Parker. The local press said that "the proceedings were conducted with good temper on both sides," but qualified this by censuring Dr. Parker for "that vituperative style of oratory he exhibited on Monday evening to the disgust of all persons who heard him. " His admirers appealed to Holyoake in a friendly way to rebut this, and he did so at once. Dr. Parker was added to the growing number of his clerical friends. In declining a public discussion with Holyoake in 1855 Dr. Parker, after stating the impediments, said: "Otherwise it would have given me pleasure to have spent a few evenings with Mr. Holyoake in thoughtful and earnest debate. Any man who conducts himself properly would have much satisfaction in meeting such an opponent." The great preacher was not less respected by Holyoake.

CHAPTER XI RELATIONS WITH MAZZINI AND OTHER REFUGEES

We turn now to another work that occupied much of Holyoake's time in the busy years of the early fifties. His political life, it will be remembered, had been quickened in 1848 by that glare of continental revolution which had given a last impulse to the revolutionary Chartists of England. The reaction that followed on the Continent gave weight to the sober counsels he was urging upon English workers. Within a few months the structure that had been raised with—apparently— such brilliant success by the revolutionaries of France and Italy began to tumble into ruin; in less than two years it was almost wholly obliterated from the map of Europe, and despotic thrones were set up with more solidity than ever. All this gave ample confirmation to Holyoake's ideal of political action in England. His "organisation, not of arms, but of ideas" was fully accredited. If in countries where the burden of despotism pressed so heavily on the people violent action brought so little relief, it was futile to dream of resorting to it in England.

But, conversely, the difference in political condition justified him in setting up, or countenancing, a different mode of political action for the Continent. In the Papal States, Hungary, or Poland, no constitutional action was possible, because there was no constitution that allowed action. In France the power was taken from the people once more by the manoeuvres of a Napoleon who had not the redeeming glamour of his great predecessor. Hence, when the radical leaders from these countries fled to London, and associated with or sought the help of Holyoake, he was willing to go to a length that the most fiery Chartist had never asked of him. His action was consistent enough, and the documents at my disposal show it to have been even more romantic than has been suspected. To older readers, whose memory almost reaches back to those stirring days, some of these documents will have the character of revelations. But our generation has, on the whole, only a dim knowledge of the events of the fifties, and I must, as usual, give a brief outline of the historical development.

In February 1848 Holyoake listened at the John Street Institution to the report of their delegates on the French Revolution, and heard with enthusiasm of the prominence at Paris of democrats like Louis Blanc. In December of the same year he notes that he has been dining with Louis Blanc at Mr. Birch's house. Within six months Louis Blanc had fallen from his pinnacle, and been driven into exile. No sooner had the royal family disappeared than a breach steadily opened between the middle class and the workers. Ledru Rollin and Louis Blanc, representing the workers, at once pressed the question of the unemployed, and Rollin secured the erection of " National Workshops." Workers and idlers flocked to Paris from all parts, and the crowd of applicants seems to have utterly disordered the new machinery. By the month of May 120,000 men were being paid "wages" out of national funds. The National Workshops could employ only 14,000, and, as men left the private shops and clamoured for admission to those of the Provisional Government,

Paris was soon irritated and intimidated by an army of 100,000 paid idlers. The middle class became deeply hostile. The radicals, fearing an electoral decision on their work while the confusion lasted, secured a postponement of the elections, but they took place on April 23rd, and gave overwhelming power to Lamartine and the Liberals. The Government, seeing that the Socialists were really a small minority of the 8,000,000 voters, began to undo the obnoxious arrangements in regard to labour. They refused Louis Blanc's plea for a ministry of labour, put down riots with the aid of the National Guard, and at length closed the workshops and ordered the dispersal of the superfluous workers from Paris. For three days the two parties fought on the streets. On June 26th the troops crushed the rebellious workers, and the first refugees from the Continent began to appear in London.

Louis Blanc, who fled to escape a trial for implication in the riots, became a friend of Holyoake's and introduced him more deeply into French politics. He was then only in his thirty-fifth year, and with his small stature—he was less than five feet high—his smooth face and youthful features, looked even much younger. He had not favoured the opening of National Workshops, but he had been the chief representative of the workers on the Provisional Government, and he knew that the trial he was menaced with could have only one result. From him, very largely, Holyoake took his view of the events that followed in France. He was once described by the *Times* as '' the greatest historian of his age and country." Louis Napoleon, the ex-Socialist, working his way upward with great astuteness and hereditary ambition, secured the Presidency of the Republic before the end of 1848, and the title of Emperor at the beginning of 1852.

Meantime, Austria was recovering its despotic sway in Italy and South Germany, and throwing fresh waves of refugees on our shores. We saw that the Italians successfully rose against Austria at the beginning of 1848, and inaugurated the continental movement. By August of the same year Austria had driven the Piedmontese army back to its own territory, and overrun most of northern Italy once more. At Rome, however, there was a rising against the government of Pius IX. His prime minister, Rossi, was assassinated, and the Pope fled to Gaeta. Mazzini and his friends at once went to Rome, declared the papal power abolished, and set up the Roman Republic on February 7th, 1849. Charles Albert set his troops in motion against Austria once more, and was completely defeated; and Austria and Naples concerted action to restore the papal power. Louis Napoleon, however, forestalled them. To gain the support of the Catholics and counteract the advance of Austria, he sent an army to Rome. By July 1850 the Republic was at an end. Mazzini was flying to Switzerland, and on to London; and Garibaldi was leading his heroic 4,000 to the hills. English republicans had now an Italian as well as a French question to deal with.

Austria brought her victorious armies back to Vienna, and prepared to tear up the constitutions she had granted in the revolutionary spring of 1848. The racial animosities of her various provinces soon split the rebellion into fragments, and she could bring them separately to her feet once more. First in Bohemia the quarrel of Germans and Czechs, and the riots that ensued, made an opening for her troops, and enabled her to recover her despotic power. In Hungary the Serbs, Croats, etc., rose against the dominant Magyars, and their scattered forces could not withstand the imperial troops. After a stubborn war, with varying fortune, Hungary was brought again under the yoke of Austria, and Kossuth, Pulzsky, and others, joined the group of the proscribed at London. The Emperor of Russia had joined his forces with those of Austria to stamp out the last sparks of revolution. In Prussia, where concessions had been made solely in view of the impotence of Austria, the return of that Empire to triumphant despotism undid all the work of the radicals, and sent more extremists to London. By 1851 Europe was under the heels of the monarchs once more. Haynau was bespattering Hungary with its own blood: Napoleon III was expelling or transporting from France 10,000 of the best workers in the people's cause: Pope Pius IX and Francis Joseph of Austria were seeing to the extinction of all democratic aspiration in Italy and Austria. It was in 1851 that Mr. Gladstone wrote the famous letters on the bloody methods of Neapolitan despotism that made England shudder.

This very meagre outline of the course of events on the Continent will enable the reader to understand the work in which Holyoake now engaged at London. Broadly speaking, that work was to raise funds for the political or military operations of the continental insurgents, procure friends for them in this country, and use the press as much as possible in their interests. From 1850 to 1860 London was a huge anarchist club, in the eyes of European monarchs. German, Polish, Hungarian, Italian, and French conspirators not only abounded, but were at times greeted with the most enthusiastic demonstrations. Societies for aiding them were openly formed, and collections made all over the country; and in the end it saw the manufacture at Birmingham of bombs for the destruction of Louis Napoleon and the thinly-disguised enrolment of a regiment of Garibaldian soldiers in the heart of London. In all this work, and particularly in the last and most audacious performances, Holyoake was prominently engaged. It would be wearisome to follow in detail his extraordinary activity during those years. Reserving his relations with Garibaldi for a later chapter, I will give some account of his connection with the more famous of the refugees, and the chief points of his activity on their behalf.

With the Hungarian leader, Louis Kossuth, his intercourse was rarely personal, and was several times interrupted. After the defeat of Hungary, Kossuth fled to Turkey. Russia and Austria demanded his surrender, but the British fleet sailed to the support of the Sultan, and his name became popular with British crowds long before he arrived at Southampton. For a month he made a triumphal march over England, addressing vast crowds and receiving civic honours at London and Manchester and elsewhere. It was the speeches he delivered on these occasions that led to a misunderstanding with Holyoake. Kossuth had gone to America, and Holyoake had worked diligently for his cause. When he opened his Fleet Street shop he engaged some of the artists among the refugees to make busts and pictures of their leaders, and he sold copies or casts of these to the public. A Hungarian sculptor made for him a bust of Kossuth. He then made a collection of Kossuth's English speeches, and intended to issue them in a popular edition. When Kossuth returned from America, he sent him a proofcopy, through Francis Newman, and was astonished to hear that Kossuth was much annoyed with him.

The correspondence with Newman shows that Kossuth was not only piqued that the crudities of his English delivery were reproduced, but he had looked forward to making a little money by publishing an edition himself. He was living on a fragment saved from his wife's fortune, and needed to earn money. When several publishers had his speeches reported, and published them, he said to Newman that "it might be lawful, but it was not the deed of gentlemen." Newman only partly removed his irritation. He took a strict view of his proprietorship of a speech, whoever reported it. Holyoake was, of course, unaware of any other intention to publish, and had acted mainly in zeal for the cause of Hungary. As Kossuth in time also had differences with Mazzini, apparently from some little jealousy of the greater help given to the Italian cause, there was a further hindrance to good feeling. It is largely on these grounds, which he has not published, that Holyoake represents Kossuth as never obtaining the understanding of English ways and character that Mazzini and Louis Blanc evinced.

With Pulzsky, who had been Prime Minister of Hungary during its brief independence, he had very friendly intercourse. Pulzsky had settled in Kentish Town (afterwards at Highgate), where he kept the royal jewels and crown of Hungary in half a dozen ironclasped chests in a bed-room. Holyoake dined with the family several times, and contrasted the humanity of the revolutionaries in 1848 with the savagery of their repressors. To his confusion Mme. Pulzsky, a gentle little lady, assured him that if ever they recovered power in Hungary they "would cut all the throats they had spared before." Pulzsky took great interest in his sale of busts and pictures of the refugees, and Holyoake had his own picture painted by one of the Hungarian artists, Hahn.

His relations with Mazzini were more important and cordial, but it is well to remember that there were impediments to anything like intimacy between them. Mazzini was an intense and devout theist, and habitually looked with extreme dislike on atheists. He once spoke of them in Garibaldi's presence with his usual vehemence, and the General had to remind him that he was an atheist himself. With all his recognition of Holyoake's services to Italy this seems to have imposed some restraint on him for a long time. Atheists like A. Trevelyan retorted, in letters to Holyoake, that Mazzini's thirst for war was not consistent with his professions, and after a time Mazzini offended many of his helpers by his strictures on Socialism. Sir James (then Mr.) Stansfeld writes to beg Holyoake to overlook them.

But Mazzini showed appreciation of the work and character of Holyoake. They met for the first time that I can trace in September 1850, when he returned in deep sorrow after the fall of his Roman Republic. He had lived in England since 1837, when his political ardour first brought exile upon him, and he was quite at home in our tongue and our ways; though the dull, gray face of London oppressed him after the radiance of Italy, and he lived in poverty and self-denial. Dante had long been a connecting-link between English culture and Italy, and Mazzini, an industrious and distinguished literary man, made many friends. When the Government opened his letters in the interest of Austria, he became more widely known and respected. As his friends, such as Ashurst and Stansfeld, were to a great extent Holyoake's friends, it is possible that they met earlier. In 1847 they founded the Society of Friends of Italy, and in the following year, when the news of the Pope's flight reached London, Mazzini set off exultantly for Rome. In six months his Republic fell, owing to the treachery of Louis Napoleon, and he was back in London. Holyoake met him in September. He was then in his forty-fifth year: a tall, slender man, with high forehead, and large black eyes flashing on you unexpectedly from his grave, scholarly features—features now worn to gray sadness.

The Friends of Italy gathered about him once more, and Holyoake met him frequently. Before long he mastered his instinctive and ill-informed repugnance to know a "materialist." "To my friend, G. J. Holyoake, with a very faint hope," he wrote in a copy of his *Duties of Man* that he gave to him. His mind was of so spiritual a texture that he was literally unable to understand such an attitude as Holyoake's on religious matters. He even hinted to him one day, with perfect delicacy, that "a public man is often bound by his past." It is a common failing of minds of his refined type to set up theoretically a certain low standard of character in connection with minds of a more concrete and logical order, and, when they meet these characters and find them different, declare that they are inconsistent. In the spring of 1852, and afterwards, we often find Holyoake breakfasting with him, or dining with him at Stansfeld's (in Fulham) or Ashurst's, or sharing his one luxury—his cigars. Mazzini never wrote an insincere word; and the "my dear sir" of his earlier letters to Holyoake was exchanged in time for "my dear friend."

So many desperate causes besides that of Italy now pleaded for aid in London that a " People's International League" was substituted for the "Friends of Italy." An engraved card was issued, signed by Mazzini for Italy and Kossuth for Hungary, and thousands of working men all over the country gladly gave their shillings to the common fund in return for the treasured signatures. Holyoake was already on the committee of the League, with Cowen, Froude, Forster, Viscount Goderich, D. Masson, Linton, Lewes, W. S. Landor, Miall, F. Newman, and others. But Mazzini felt his personal action to be of great importance, and appealed to him to open the columns of the *Reasoner* for subscriptions. This is the letter that Linton so unfortunately misrepresented. That Holyoake should wait for an appeal is intelligible enough. Mazzini's constant strictures on Atheism and Socialism were well known to readers of the *Reasoner,* and it could not be assumed that either they or Mazzini would welcome the use of the *Reasoner* in this way. Mazzini conquered his scruples, and Holyoake had none to conquer. He inserted the letter in the *Reasoner,* and then had it neatly printed and circulated at his own expense amongst likely supporters. The letter reproduced in *Bygones* (I, 209) is only a part of the original, and it will be read with interest in full:

"My Dear S1r,

"You have once, for the Taxes on Knowledge question, collected a very large sum by dint of Sixpences. Could you not do the same, if your conscience approve the scheme, for the Shilling Subscription? Could you not at least insert the enclosed statement, with a few words of appeal, in the *Reasoner?* "I have never made any appeal for material help to the English public; but, once the scheme started, I cannot conceal that I feel a great interest in its success. The state of Europe, and the dispositions of the *active* party everywhere, are such as to make us foresee that a supreme struggle will take place between Right and Might before a long time has elapsed, and every additional strength imparted to militant Democracy for that time is not to be despised. Still, the *moral* motive is even more powerful with me. The scheme is known in Italy, and will be known in Hungary; and it would be extremely important for me to be able to tell my countrymen that it has not proved a failure. Ten or twenty thousand working men, standing up in England and bearing witness to their sympathy for our cause, would constitute a *vital* fact, equally strengthening for us and honourable for you. And I think this Shilling Subscription one of the best and most undeniable practical means for that end. Look at the Rothschilds' loans to absolutism! Is it too much for European Democracy to oppose a voluntary tax of One Shilling?

Holyoake observes in a foot-note: "Our opinions of Mr. Mazzini's views on Socialism we have before given in the *Reasoner,* and we shall re-discuss the subject in the same place." Mazzini, I may remark, wrote with even more scorn of the "individualistic age." His objection to Socialism (as then understood) was rather based on spiritual grounds, and directed against what he regarded as the mechanical theories of the French Socialists.

"I know the prejudices that are creeping up amongst a portion of the working classes since the attack of the French Socialist leaders. It is because these prejudices are an unjust thing, and a pernicious one to the general movement, that I address myself to you, as one who is influential among the deluded working men. Though blaming what you call the violence of some of my expressions, you have felt that I might in the end be right. I think I am. I think the time has arrived to stand up for the great, free, collective, progressive, European Social Thought, against narrow, despotic, individual, stereotyping, French, Socialistic crotchets and formulae. Many Frenchmen thought so, silently. I was bold and careless of the results—that's all. Since then my influence amongst the Parisian working men—and I quote it as an excellent symptom—has increased in a measure astonishing even for me; there is a transformation going on in that element which in a short time will show itself. All this has very little to do with the object of my note, but I take gladly the opportunity of adverting to it. Your working men, and some of you, seem to be lying under a strange delusion. What is it that you value so much in Louis Blanc, Cabet, and others? Their own individual solutions or systems? No. The first must be, if read and understood, unsatisfactory to an Englishman, more than to any other man. You are, above all, Apostles of Liberty. The second is unknown, I dare say, to almost all who complain of my attack. Let them read, from the first to the last page, the *Icarie* and judge. Is it their love for the cause of the People? And are we not fighting for it these twentyfour years, and now more actively than they do? Ask our common enemy whom they fear the most. Is it their influence on France? They have none. They are 200,000, divided in six or seven schools, in a population of 35,000,000. Depend upon it, my dear sir, there is no danger done to the cause in telling the French people to bury their dead, and march on with us to the highway of Humanity. I have never in my life yielded to an impulse, and on this occasion I have tried to fulfil a great duty.

"At all events, do the English working men believe we are honest—that we are trying to put down for ever the two heads of European despotism, Pope and Emperor? That we shall not do that for the benefit of aristocracy, but of the people at large? If so, let them be consistent, and show by some external act that they side with us. Should you approve, you may ask cards and statements, either from Sidney Hawkes or from myself. We have, too, large bills.

"Ever faithfully yours,

"joseph Mazzini.

"15, Radnor St., King's Rd., Chelsea. "June 12, 1852."

The letter was imprudent—thoroughly Mazzinian. To remind English Socialists of the fatal rift in the revolutionary movement—the division of liberals and radicals—and to discredit Holyoake's chief friend, Louis Blanc, was a bad introduction of an appeal. Many of Holyoake's wealthier supporters resented it on one or other ground. W. J. Birch declined to look upon Kossuth's cause as parallel to Mazzini's: Trevelyan grumbled at Mazzini's transcendentalism. But Holyoake worked earnestly, and in a few months collected

9,000 shillings. Mazzini thanked him for his "noble appeal in the *Reasoner*. " It was not, as Linton suggested, his first appeal for Italy. In 1849 he notes in his diary a collection of seven pounds he made after one of his lectures on the Italian question, and the receipt of a ten pound note from J. S. Mill for the same cause. On Christmas Eve (1852) he writes in the diary:

"Went to Stansfeld's and Hawkes's at 9, Beaufort St., Chelsea. Mazzini came in at 11. Shook hands with me without noticing me. But having lighted a cigar he came to me, when I found that he did recognise me, for turning to the company, he said: 'Mr. Holyoake is the most practical man in England.'"

It is the longest entry he ever made. But Mazzini came to esteem him for other qualities than his practical capacity. From Mazzini's numerous and cordial letters to him I will quote only one more. It is quoted in *Bygones*, but in a curtailed form. Holyoake had asked, in 1855, if he might publish some of Mazzini's work, and the reply was:

"Dear Sir,

"You are welcome to any writing or fragment of mine which you may wish to reprint in the *Reasoner*. Thought, according to me, is, as soon as publicly uttered, the property of *all*, not an individual one. In this special case, it is with true pleasure that I give the consentment you ask for. The deep esteem I entertain for your personal character, for your sincere love of truth, perseverance, and nobly tolerant habits, makes me wish to do more; and, time and events allowing, I shall.

"But, whilst gladly granting your kind request, I feel bound in my turn to address one to you; and it is to grant me the selection of the two first fragments. They will shield my own individuality against all possible misinterpretation, and state at once the limits within which we do commune. These limits are political and moral, not philosophical. We pursue the same end— progressive improvement, association, transformation of the corrupted medium in which we are now living, overthrow of all idolatries, shams, lies, and conventionalities.

We both want man to be, not the poor, passive, cowardly, phantasmagoric unreality of the actual time, thinking in one way and acting in another, bending to powers which he hates or despises, carrying empty popish or thirty-nine article formulas *on* his breast and none within; but a fragment of the living truth, a real individual being linked to collective Humanity, the bold seeker of things to come, the gentle, mild, loving, yet firm, uncompromising, inexorable apostle of all that is Just and Heroic, the Priest, the Poet, and the Prophet.

"We widely differ as to the *how* and *why*. You, sir, are a Secularist: I can scarcely understand the word: everything seems to me meaningless, worthless, unintelligible, unless it be a step to something higher *usque ad infinitum*, a line of the everlasting Poem which extends from the depths of creation to God. You find before yourself a form of creed spurning earth, and you answer by spurning heaven. Heaven and earth are to me the two poles of the axis: I spurn neither: I want to relink them both. You reject God as a mystery: I feel myself surrounded by mysteries, *life* being the first of all. I do not pretend to solve them, but I cannot deny them. They are to me like rays coming down from far distant stars which neither naked eye nor telescope can now discover. You do not understand Immortality: I do not understand Death. Life and Death are to me what vigil and sleep are in this terrestrial period of existence—a successive renewal and transformation. I find within myself an incessant aspiration towards an ideal which I cannot realise here, vol. 1. R

I own; I *must* therefore realise it somewhere else; and philosophy, science, the continuous life of collective humanity, everything around me, appears to me like a symbolic confirmation of this intuition of my heart.

"You say with me that the right thing is a Religion of Humanity; it is, but because Humanity is God-like, the progressive expounder of God's law, the realisation of God's scheme, the successive embodiment of a higher Divine ideal, of which, from epoch to epoch, we

discover a new fragment. You believe that religion is dying; I believe that *a* religion, or, rather, a form of religion, is dying; that a higher conception of the Ideal is dawning; that, once reached, it will shape itself religiously, as well as politically and scientifically. Religion the high covenant of humanity agreeing about its own origin, and duty cannot but, as we get a clearer insight of these things, develop, modify, and transform itself. We are going to substitute for the old doctrine of the Fall the doctrine of Progression; is there not in this new advancing step through the sphere of the Ideal the germ of a whole religious manifestation, if not a new definition of life, the foundation of a collective creed? I perceive through history undeniable traces of a Divine educational scheme, of an intelligent providential *law*. Am I not to acknowledge, love, and worship the lawgiver? Or can I admit Providence and limit its action to one single aspect of life, to the *collective*, and not to the *individual*, to *mankind*, and not to *man*? God, Immortality, Progression, Religion, are, in my mind, inseparable terms. On these is grounded my knowledge of a law of duty and self-sacrifice, of man's mission on earth: on these my right to *educate*: without these I could only appeal to force, and establish or accept the worship of the established fact. It is what our irreligious society, issued from the negative work of the nineteenth century, tottering between a degrading theory of utility and a forlorn hope of temporal happiness, between Bentham and Volney, has come to.

"I do firmly believe that all that we are now struggling, hoping, discussing, and fighting for, is a religious question. We want a new intellect of life; we long to tear off one more veil from the Ideal and to realise as much as we can of it; we thirst after a deeper knowledge of what we are and of the *why* we are. We want a new heaven and a new earth. We may not all be now conscious of this; but the whole history of mankind bears witness to the inseparable union of these two terms. The clouds which are now floating between our heads and God's sky will soon vanish, and a brighter sun shine on high. We may have to pull down the *despot,* the arbitrary dispenser of *grace* and *damnation;* but it will only be to make room for the Father and the Educator.

"The two fragments which I send will point out the view I take of the actual state of our European society and some glimpses of the future, such as it appears to me to be forthcoming. After these you will freely choose which will best suit you and the *Reasoner.* "Ever faithfully yours,

"joseph Mazzini."

Mazzini's patient and affectionate effort so far miscarried that, in reproducing his letter, Holyoake has omitted the most beautiful passages. War and political intrigue and Co-operation were, in Holyoake's view, best dissociated from mystic speculations.

When the Fleet Street shop was opened, and the upper room turned into a "Political Exchange," Holyoake found himself a centre of insurgent activity. Anarchists, Socialists, Radicals, and progressive Liberals—Poles, Germans, Italians, Austrians, French, and Irish— enlivened it with polyglot rhetoric. It had a bad name amongst its respectable neighbours. When they decorated for war, it remained drab: when they illuminated for peace, it put up defiant mottoes. Most of the "stormy petrels" of Europe visited it at one or other period. Holyoake had met Dornbusch and Weitling, fugitive German communists, years before. With Weitling he had a publishing experience analogous to that with Kossuth; and when he had engaged the German, who followed the sober occupation of dressmaker, to make a dress for Mrs. Holyoake, Weitling disconcerted her by asking her to take off her dress so that he could make the measurements. Dr. Arnold Ruge, a refugee from the Frankfort Parliament, who settled at Brighton, was another sensitive German, for whom he published and met difficulties. In 1854, however, Ruge wrote him: "Your kindness in publishing my little pamphlet and your friendly way in appreciating that condensed result of a life's working will be a great help to me." Prater was another German refugee who incurred, and finely expressed, indebtedness to him. The secretary of the Polish Central Democratic Committee, Worcell, wrote: "I am instructed to express to you our gratitude and the weight which in our eyes such a help as yours in the present European and especially Polish crisis has for the welfare of our cause... your generous heart and enlightened mind were aware of it the importance of the crisis when you, so generously, offered us your co-operation." Ledru Rollin (member of the Provisional Government in 1848) and Victor Schoelcher (afterwards member of the Senate) were French fugitives who often visited 147 Fleet Street. Of Russian insurgents Heinzen, Herzen, and Bakounin were seen there; and later Krapotkin, Elie Reclus, and Karl Blind were added to the "roll-call of imprisoned friends." Aurelio Saffi, one of the Triumvirs of the Roman Republic, was another friend and visitor; and we shall see presently a much closer relationship to Dr. Bernard and Garibaldi. Mme. Mario, the English wife (J. Merriton White) of Alberto Mario, was a frequent visitor at the shop, and wrote many friendly letters.

Beyond this picturesque circle, and often invading it, was another group of interesting foreigners. These were the spies who came from the Continent to watch the conspirators. Napoleon III, especially, had a large number of spies in London in the fifties. We have seen how one who obtained Holyoake's friendship, St. Andre, turned out in the end to be a paid spy of the French Emperor. Another—" in whom I had more trust," he curiously observes—was an Italian major, who often came to talk with Holyoake, and bring him little presents. Holyoake noticed that he spent money rather freely for a fugitive, at the Cafe d'litoile, where foreigners met, but he acknowledges that he was "very much surprised" when the major's name was eventually discovered, with Andre's, on the list of the Emperor's spies. A third, who seems to have belonged to the same fraternity, was a young Italian, calling himself " Count Carlo di Rudio.

" Like the wounds that the "major" received in the Italian cause, Di Rudio's title was more than doubtful. He was one of the three who took bombs to blow up Napoleon, but he "did not get near enough" to throw it, and escaped from the French prison with suspicious ease. They could prove nothing against him, and they eventually paid his passage to America. He tried to disarm Holyoake with open confessions that he had been tempted. "Many a day we have been without anything to eat," he wrote, "without coal to warm us: twice some propositions very brilliant has been offered to me, but them was brilliant to those that have another heart than mine. " But this was in 1861, when they knew something of traitors, and they held Di Rudio in suspicion.

In 1857 a young Italian found four spies in a restaurant in Panton Street, and stabbed the whole of them, with patriotic vigour, before they could escape. Holyoake was asked to shelter the Italian from the police for a time. He calculated that his premises (1 Woburn Buildings) would be suitable, and offered to do so; but, as there was illness in the house, he wanted an assurance that there should be no more stabbing if the police held the young man up, and the plan had to be abandoned. He had had some experience of spies and their ways in the Chartist days. One of them came to a house he was staying at with a mixture that could be poured into the sewers of London and blow up the whole city. He discovered afterwards that they tried the compound in the cellar while he was taking tea in the parlour above.

This chapter would run to an inordinate length if we attempted to follow Holyoake through all his journalistic work and his lecturing on behalf of Poland, Italy, and Hungary during the fifties. The general indications of his work that we have given must suffice. But in 1857 he was induced to do a service of a remarkable kind— one dangerous in itself, and that would have brought him into more serious collision with the law, if it had transpired, than his impetuous speech at Cheltenham.

He was persuaded to give certain assistance in the preparation of bombs. They were, it is clear, part of the consignment of bombs that were afterwards used in an attempt on the life of Napoleon III, and the experiments that Holyoake made with them were of use to the conspirators. Further, it is now clear, from documents I will quote, that those for whom Holyoake acted were quite aware of, and in sympathy with, the purpose of the bombs; and he would have found it difficult to persuade a jury, knowing all the facts, that he himself was not involved in the terrible occurrence at Paris.

The "affair of the Rue Lepelletier" will be no more than a brief line of history in the minds of most readers of this work, and a few introductory remarks will, I think, be welcomed. By the year 1857 the feelings of all who worked for the unification of Italy and the republican cause in France were concentrated in a bitter hostility to Napoleon III. Louis Napoleon, a rebel, Socialist, and Carbonaro in his youth, had, by a series of cunning appeals, ending in a *coup cTitat* (December 1851), obtained despotic power in France, and had expelled 1,545 and deported 9,769 of his most active opponents. In November 1852 he was chosen Emperor of the French. Fugitive republicans hated him with all the hate that such a career naturally engendered. Further, his army alone kept the papal power intact at Rome, and frustrated the work of Mazzini. As it was agreed that the cause of Hungary must wait upon that of Italy, it will be understood how fiercely attention was focussed on Napoleon. Men talked freely of tyrannicide. W. Savage Landor offered his last £100 in a London journal (the *Atlas)* for the family of any man who would strike him down.

At this juncture a handsome, fiery young Italian escaped from his Austrian dungeon in Italy, and came to London. Like so many others, he found the way to 147 Fleet Street, and asked Holyoake to publish the vivid narrative of his experiences. Holyoake directed him to a publisher who could pay him better, but he did not lose sight of the dark and elo-

quent Italian. Felice Orsini lectured to enthusiastic audiences everywhere, but was discouraged when there seemed to be no prospect of a public action on the part of England following upon the applause. He concluded, like many others, that the influence of Napoleon, who visited Osborne at the time, obsessed England, just as his army guarded the Pope. He quitted England at the end of 1857, and on January 14th, 1858, as the Emperor and Empress were driving along the Rue Lepelletier to the opera, three bombs were thrown at them. They escaped, but ten people were killed and 156 wounded. The assailants were Orsini, Pieri, Gomez, and Di Rudio. Orsini and Pieri were executed. Dr. Bernard, a French physician living at London and active in insurgent circles, a friend 01 Holyoake's, was tried for complicity, but escaped conviction. T. Allsop, another friend of Holyoake's, was sought by the police, and a reward of £200 offered for his apprehension.

In 1855 Napoleon visited London, and drove through the City. Holyoake begged his more violent friends to refrain from making a demonstration on the ground that he was "the Queen's guest." But he put up an eight-feet long placard before his shop, announcing the *Reasoner,* with articles by Mazzini and others. The Emperor put his head out of his carriage and read it. Truelove got into trouble with the police again through the visit. "The course of Truelove never did run smooth," said Holyoake.

That is a brief outline of the occurrence, and I am now able to fill it in with details, some of which could not be made public while any of those concerned still lived. Allsop deliberately co-operated in Orsini's plot. Dr. Bernard co-operated still more intimately. Hodge was perfectly cognisant of, and active in, the plot. And Holyoake, though he was not in their explicit counsels, co-operated in a lesser degree.

In one of the most amusing chapters of his *Sixty Years* (ch. lx) he tells how he took loaded bombs to various parts of the country to test them. They were round shells, four or five inches in diameter, with little nipples sticking out

"like porcupine quills" all over them, percussion caps on the nipples, and an explosive of fearful repute inside the shells. He took them to his home, carrying one in each side-pocket, "lest coming into collision with each other they might give me premature trouble." He packed them in a brief-bag at home, and Mrs. Holyoake—one wonders how much she knew—found a safe place for it. He had to travel to Sheffield for a lecture on the following day, and he took them with him. He carried _his bag cautiously to the station, where he transferred the shells to his pockets, and sat with eyes very alert during the long, slow journey north. One bump against a hard substance would have ended his story prematurely. He watched his bag carefully in his lodging, took it with him morning and evening to the lectures, and kept it on the table before him. If he put it down, one chance kick might have dispatched them all. Was ever lecture given under such circumstances before?

But his adventures may be read in his own account. On the Monday he left one bomb under the mattress, and took the other into the country for experiment. He wandered all day without finding a suitable road, but on the Tuesday he found a disused quarry and flung it from the top. When an inquisitive person appeared, at the roar, he drew him in a different direction, to see if they could find "cannon" anywhere; and at night, when he returned to look for fragments, he found that the explosion had been drastic enough to leave no trace of the shells. He wrote an unsigned note to London:

"My two companions behaved as well as could be expected. One has said nothing; perhaps through not having an opportunity. The other, being put upon his mettle, went off in high dudgeon. He was heard of immediately after, but has not since been seen." He returned warily to town with the second bomb, and was requested to take it to Devonshire for a trial. In a house, known as "The Den," in Devon, he says, there "dwelt one who had the courage for any affair advancing the war of liberty." They found a solitary road, and Holyoake flung it from behind a stone wall, but it stuck in the soil, and a wayfarer nearly found him gingerly extracting it. Eventually they fired two bombs, and he reported to town:

"Leniency of treatment was quite thrown away upon our two companions. As a man makes his bed, so he must lie upon it; still, out of consideration, we wished it to be not absolutely hard. But that did just no good whatever. The harder treatment had to be tried; and I am glad to say it proved entirely successful. But nothing otherwise would do."

The point of these experiments was to ascertain the degree of hardness necessary in the ground on which they were to be thrown. Holyoake says that he was told that they were to be used in the warfare in Italy. Whatever we may think of his own suspicions, we have his word that neither he nor Mazzini was told the real destination of the bombs. But he acknowledges that he received them from Dr. Bernard at Ginger's Hotel, near Westminster Bridge. He had been asked, as one with mechanical knowledge, to examine their construction. A letter that the police obtained showed that Thomas Allsop had ordered the making of the bombs at Birmingham, alleging that they were parts of some new gas-fittings; and as the letter was dated from Ginger's Hotel, we know that Allsop was there with Bernard and Holyoake. The evidence in regard to Bernard I will give presently, but will first run through Allsop's letters to Holyoake in 1858 which have never been published.

Allsop, a cultivated business man with whom Coleridge dined every Sunday for many years, is one of those execrable penmen whom Holyoake describes as "the natural and ready-made secretaries of secret societies." As he, in addition, often used the thinnest paper, crossed his letters like a lady of the last generation, rarely dated them, and spoke a cryptic dialect on this dangerous subject, one does not follow him easily. But there are passages enough, and plain enough, to show that he was

wholly with Orsini in his enterprise. "The Den," at Teignmouth, Devonshire, was a house taken by Allsop. An early letter to Holyoake runs:

"This is a delightful place. You should come here— though, to judge from the sledge-hammer force exhibited in your whole bearing when I last saw you on the Birmingham platform, you would better bear reducing than invigorating. However, it is very beautiful, and I do not see why the Devil should not have moments of enjoyment."

In a letter dated 24th December (apparently 1857), he says: "Many thanks for your remembrance. I am glad that the visits to our *hills* and *moors* has resulted satisfactorily." This seems to refer to the Sheffield experiment. A fragment cut from another letter asks: "Can I do anything for you at Exeter? Can I confirm the out-and-outer at Starcross? I sadly miss your horrid atheism." And on December 25th: "Can I facilitate your advent here? *i.e.* at Exeter or at Plymouth. Remember I am interested."

However, the letters that follow are more decisive. Orsini's attempt was made on January 14th, 1858. As it was known that he came from London, a storm of indignation raged in the French press. Colonels of regiments wrote demanding an invasion of " the land of impurity which contains the haunts of the monsters who are sheltered by its laws," and the French minister made an official request for some Government action. Dr. Bernard was put on his trial, and inquiry at Birmingham put the police in possession of the letter in which Allsop ordered the bombs to be made by an engineer whom he knew. Allsop fled, and the Government offered £200 (not £500, as stated in the *Dictionary of National Biography)* for information of his whereabouts.

Allsop had gone to New Mexico (Santa Fe), and he wrote from there to Holyoake on March 1st and for some months. In these letters, sent through a friend and delivered by hand to Holyoake, he makes no secret of his interest in Orsini's action. He speaks with scorn of "that arrogant and insolent Lord Derby" and of Clarendon, and

those who pressed the analogy of a possible attempt on the life of the Queen. "The essential difference is that little Vicky has never had the opportunity to play the tyrant, and therefore is safe from all attacks which are reserved for the evildoer. I need not say that if it were possible that she should ape his rascality, she would be exposed to his fate." He is delighted that "Joseph" Mazzini? has "justified Orsini." It makes amends for "all his mysticism. " "Do not," he says, in another letter, "think, speak, or act as though Orsini's attempt was a failure. It was, is, and will be, a mighty success." In June he writes: "The not merely possible but probable consequences of Orsini's attempt bid fair to make the 14th of January more celebrated than the 2nd of December. If I were amongst you, I would get up a celebration of that day by means of an anniversary meeting to celebrate his *birth* day.... What a glorious opportunity for Mazzini to preside and to address the meeting in honour of the unintelligible and martyr." He begs Holyoake to publish discreet quotations in his journals in favour of tyrannicide. "I suppose the people who keep gigs look upon tyrannicide as a dreadful crime." Holyoake is to quote Brutus on tyranny from Gibbon. "It is *wholly applicable"* he says; and he asks "Is the assassin yet alive, and, if so, why?" In another letter he says that he is sending a pamphlet which shows that to kill a tyrant, who is also an atrocious traitor, is not only "moral" but an "absolute duty"; and there are frequent references to "the midnight-murderer of December 2nd," "miscreant," and so forth.

There is no mention of innocent "gas-fittings," or even of " Italian warfare," in this secret correspondence. The bombs were meant to kill Napoleon III, and Allsop only regrets that they failed. Holyoake knew this at least from March 1848, and has never denied it. Mrs. Allsop wrote to Holyoake asking his help to remove the "stigma" from the family. "The shells, we all know, were intended for a very different purpose," she says, and "it is a monstrous thing to be accused of." She was allowed to retain her impression. But from the first All-sop declared that he was willing to face a trial, if he were secured against heavy expense. Holyoake and another friend (B. Langley), therefore, audaciously of-fered to give up Allsop, if the Govern-ment would promise them the 200 for use in his defence. On June 16th Mr. Secretary Walpole wrote them that "the Two hundred pounds offered by the Government in the case referred to in your letter has not been withdrawn." They set themselves vigorously to fan the popular feeling that the British Government was " truckling to a for-eigner," a tyrant, etc., and on July 12th they received another letter:

"Gentlemen,

"I am directed by Mr. Secretary Wal-pole to inform you that since the date of my answer to your application of the 9th ult. the Law Officers of the Crown have been consulted, and have expressed an opinion that it is not advisable to take any further steps in the prosecution against Mr. Allsop. The Government have consequently determined to put an end to the proceedings against that gen-tleman, and to withdraw the offer of a reward for his apprehension."

Allsop returned, on September 17th, grateful and unrepentant. "Many and heartfelt thanks from the poor *proscrit* to the horrid atheist for his genial, gen-tle, and most gracious consideration," he wrote. He talked of the "blood now shed, and yet to be shed," and said: "It is useless to disguise the truth: we are about to enter into a crusade compared to which all that has gone before is child's play. The next man to devote himself will succeed." Holyoake seems to have reminded him of the loss of in-nocent lives (which he never notices), as he writes playfully: "After all, you are the worst. What is the evil done by an assassin who only kills the body compared to that inflicted by a horrid atheist who kills the soul?" He retained a deep affection for Holyoake; and Mrs. Allsop, whose hospitality was famous, often entertained Mrs. Holyoake.

With Dr. Bernard we must deal more briefly. A careful reader of Holyoake's chapters on the affair will see that he

never acquits Allsop and Bernard. He pointedly disclaims knowledge on the part of Mazzini and himself alone, and says that, "if there was any thought of operating in Paris," at the time when he received the bombs, "the design was on-ly known to the six persons ultimately concerned." There certainly was such a design; and the six persons seem to have been Allsop, Bernard, Hodge (whom Allsop describes as "secreted in Devon-shire or Somersetshire"), Orsini, Pieri, and Di Rudio. Allsop's letters often mention Bernard, but never suggest that he is wrongly charged. There is, how-ever, an anonymous French work on the subject, *La Veritd sur Orsini,* which, al-though its pages generally have a reck-less and undiscriminating aspect, de-scribes the preparations for the outrage in terms that engender a feeling of au-thenticity. Holyoake is curiously wrong in saying *(Sixty Years,* II, 73) that Allsop was in exile two years. He left England in February 1858, and was back in September of the same year.

The work was published shortly after the fall of Napoleon III, and is, more-over, a fierce attack on (he Emperor; it has no French bias against Bernard.

The author says that Orsini saw some bombs in a Belgian museum, and got a carpenter to make him a model of them. On this he designed additional nipples, and then gave it to Allsop, who ordered five to be made by Taylor, of Birming-ham. They were in two sizes, so that no difficulty arises from Holyoake's say-ing that he saw fragments of the Paris shells—very tiny fragments they must have been, when three bombs inflicted 516 wounds—and they were not the same as those entrusted to him. The five bombs were delivered to Allsop at the beginning of November. Orsini went to Brussels with Allsop's passport, and a Swiss waiter, Georgi, followed him with the upper halves of the shells. Bernard made a solemn declaration at his trial that the shells taken by Georgi to Brussels were not the ones used by Orsini, and that he knew nothing of Orsini's intention. From Allsop's letters and Holyoake's reticence we must con-clude that Bernard *was* in the plot, and

the dates alone show that the bombs were the same. We may therefore fol-low with interest the French writer's cir-cumstantial account. Bernard first se-cured that arms should be available for Orsini at Paris, by an astute arrange-ment with a Parisian merchant. Then he went to Brussels himself with the upper halves of the bombs—Holyoake says they were in sections at Ginger's Ho-tel—and the explosive. Orsini put them together on the way to Paris. Bernard, an able physician, was also an experi-enced conspirator. He had faced eight prosecutions before he came to Eng-land, and this was not his first prosecu-tion in England. But his advocate, Ed-win James, made an impassioned ap-peal to the jury to—in a word—give a defiant British answer to the French Government, and they acquitted Bernard. He was fortunate. It will be noticed that Holyoake speaks coldly of him. Possibly he remembered that amongst his correspondence are letters from the north accusing Dr. Bernard and his lecture-agent of systematic swindling.

The second Englishman in the plot was Mr. Hodge, a republican politician of the time. One fact will be sufficient to indicate his complicity, and it confirms the case in regard to Allsop and Bernard. In 1860 Hodge (as we shall see) lent Holyoake and a London Com-mittee one thousand pounds to meet pressing expenses in regard to the Garibaldi Legion. It was publicly noti-fied as a loan from "a friend of Orsini." But in the letter before me Hodge care-lessly asks to have it notified as coming from " a member of the old firm of Jan-uary 14th."

Other adventures that arose out of this remarkable experience of Holyoake's must be Referred for the present. We must turn now to a more constitutional fight that he was conduct-ing simultaneously with those described in this and the preceding chapter. This was the struggle for the abolition of the press-stamp, in which he played a prominent and even hazardous part.

CHAPTER XII THE FIGHT FOR A CHEAP PRESS

The first plea that Holyoake made when he found at his disposal a journal of wider influence than his own sectarian organ was a plea for the abolition of the pressstamp. In the first issue of the *Leader,* on March 30th, 1850, he wrote:

"When I was working in a factory I first heard that phrase, indigenous, I believe, to political economy, a 'glut in the market.' Neither myself nor my co-workers understood it beyond this—that it meant having nothing to do at the beginning of the week and nothing to eat at the end. Naturally stimulated to correct at least the culinary part of the defalcation, we had recourse to combination, and, as wages fell, we sought to raise them by strikes. These were as fruitless in effect as they were fallacious in theory. Knowing no better, we still went on sowing anxiety and reaping disappointment. All this time, as I have since learned, many newspapers were writing wise words for our enlightenment, but their cost kept them from us."

This passage clearly expresses the motive that informed his vigorous share in the struggle for the abolition of the newspaper-stamp. There is, perhaps, no other part of his work on which a more general verdict of utility would be passed to-day. No one now regrets that taxation has ceased to hamper the free development of the press. Holyoake enlisted his pen in its cause at a time when few men in the country saw the iniquity Vol. 1. 257 s and the social evil of the stamp; and in the tensest hours of the struggle he was engaged by his colleagues to undertake for it perilous duties that few dared to assume. The readers of the cheap journals of our time should follow with some interest the brilliant and adventurous campaign by which the field was won for them fifty years ago.

The " taxes on knowledge "—to use the effective phrase that Leigh Hunt so happily invented—were a very serious hindrance to the enlightenment of the people when Holyoake first entered public life. The gross illiteracy of the workers was being reduced by the spread of elementary schools; but books were dear and comparatively scarce, and the press, on which they must mainly depend for political and social guidance, was hampered by three heavy taxes. A considerable duty was laid on the paper before a single type was impressed on it; a tax of three shillings and sixpence (shortly reduced to one shilling and sixpence) was levied on each advertisement; and a further tax of fourpence was exacted on every issue of a periodical publication. Sixpence-halfpenny was the lowest price at which a paper could be legally and profitably issued, and the force of this disability will be appreciated when we remember the low wage of the workers for several decades after Waterloo. The papers of the gentry might pass tardily through the servants' halls into the hands of the artisans or peasants, or they might club their farthings to buy a two or three days' old paper from town. But it was only the novelty of being able to read at all and the fierce political life of the time that sustained their interest under such conditions. It is, in fact, maintained by the secretary and historian of the movement, C. D. Collet, that these taxes were largely imposed, or at least augmented, for the express purpose of withholding knowledge from the workers. Devised originally in the reign of Anne as a war-tax, the paperstamp was raised from one halfpenny to fourpence by the Georges, and the most drastic penalties were imposed for infringement or evasion of the law. Any person could arrest a hawker who sold unstamped papers, and would gain a reward of twenty shillings, while a fine of £2.0 for each copy of the paper was imposed on those who printed, published, or merely had in their possession, unstamped periodicals. Newspaper-proprietors had to provide heavy securities of good behaviour, and the makers of type had to furnish the Government with rigid lists of their customers.

Happily there were from the first men of spirit and courage who scorned the penalties, and through these Holyoake was initiated to the "holy war." The most famous of these rebels were Richard Carlile and Henry Hetherington, who had great influence on Holyoake. Moved by the conviction of an unstamped paper in 1831, Hetherington at once announced a penny weekly with the title of the *Poor Man's Guardian.* Popular publishers had hitherto been content to evade the law. The rugged spirit of Hetherington gave open defiance. "Established contrary to law" he boldly inscribed on his paper; and in the place of the red Government stamp he put a black one. The widespread interest in the passing of the Reform Bill gave importance to his efforts, and hundreds of poor men risked their liberty in the collision with the police. Twice in six months the authorities sent smiths to break up Hetherington's press and strip his shop. The *Times* described him as one " familiar with the inside of every jail in the kingdom "; and his manoeuvres to keep his paper in circulation—his disguises, his sending out of bogus parcels by the front door, while the precious *Guardian* left by the back, and so on—make a diverting story of heroism. For three years he fought the Board of Revenue; 500 men went to jail for selling his paper; and the battle only ended with a jury's verdict—a quite illegal verdict—that the *Guardian* was not liable to the tax.

In 1836 the stamp was reduced to one penny by the reformed Parliament, and from that and other causes the agitation subsided until 1849. During this period Holyoake entered upon his journalistic work. The *Oracle, Movement,* and *Reasoner bore* no stamp, but ran no serious risk. The Board of Inland Revenue, with the elusive task before it of denning what was or was not a newspaper, and the still more difficult task of crushing impecunious rebels who regarded committal as an honour, had dropped into a pleasant torpor as far as popular propagandist weeklies were concerned. The paper-duty alone brought in three-quarters of a million yearly, and the large dailies paid another 300,000 in stamp-fees, besides the tithe on advertisements. The officials were content to protect these honest traders of the journalistic world from serious competition, and were not disposed to notice small journals, with scanty fragments of sectarian news, like the *Reasoner*. The average price of a daily newspaper was now fivepence, and the proprietors still had to find security against indulgence in political libel or blasphemy.

The active campaign was renewed in 1848, when a fresh wave of political interest poured over the country. In 1846, when the Corn Laws were abolished, Cobden and the other orators of the League were free to turn to new work. Financial reform appealed to Cobden, and in 1848 he framed an ideal budget, which abolished the paper-duty and advertisement-tax, but left the penny stamp untouched. The advertisement-tax had been the subject of attack from a different quarter for many years. Mr. John Francis, editor of the *Athenceum* (father of the present editor), had formed an association for the repeal of the still heavy tax of *is. 6d.* on each advertisement, and led the agitation with great judgment and public spirit for more than twenty years. But the omission of the stamp-tax from Cobden's ideal budget was discussed by Holyoake and his friends on the Chartist Council, and in January 1849 they put themselves in communication with him. Mr. Collet, from whose *History of the Taxes on Knowledge* I take the outline of the story, confesses that the Chartists were anxious that middleclass agitators like Cobden, Bright, and Fox should not secure another great victory independently of the workers. Holyoake, we saw, was at this time eager for the cooperation of the middle class with the more sober of the workers, and the new scheme was entirely to his mood.

He had himself edited a paper in 1848 in evasion of the stamp-law. In the actual state of the law the stamp carried with it the privilege of free postage—hence, largely, the reluctance of some enlightened statesmen to see a grievance in it—and the postal regulations of 1840 had extended the privilege of free transmission to journals published in the Channel Islands or the Isle of Man, which escaped the stamp-law. Linton and Holyoake therefore brought out their *Cause of the People* at Douglas, as we saw. But its career was brief,

and the growth of similar publications led to an alteration of the postal regulations.

With the year 1850 the campaign entered on the brilliant and entertaining stage that was to lead to victory. Cobden complied with the Chartist appeal to include the abolition of the stamp. Indeed, the rest of his budget soon fell out of notice, and the fight raged about the " taxes on knowledge." The Chartist Council supplied men like Collet, Watson, and Moore, of long experience in defying unjust laws; and these, with veteran tacticians like Francis Place and spokesmen like Cobden, formed a "Newspaper-stamp Abolition Committee." A few months after its formation Holyoake, J. Stansfeld, and George Dawson were added, and in a short time its crowded list of speakers included J. Bright, W. J. Fox, Milner Gibson, J. Hume, and most of the famous orators of the Corn Law agitation and the Radical party. Their tireless secretary, Collet, took a two-roomed attic in Essex Street—one room to sleep in and one for an office—and opened the siege of Somerset House. No secretary was ever more fertile in devices; and few secretaries have had so judicious and experienced a Council to control and improve their devices. But I must restrict myself to Holyoake's adventurous share in their spirited campaign.

As we saw in regard to the Co-operative movement, his journalistic service here also was incessant and important. Few papers—the *Athenaum* and the *Daily News* were honourable exceptions—had a sufficiently clear judgment of the situation, or sufficient trust in an educated people, to assist in the work of breaking their own fetters. Holyoake's insistence in the *Reasoner* and the *Leader* was felt to be of value. '' The most encouraging event recorded," says Mr. Collet, in the first year of the campaign, "was that the *Reasoner,* always animated by G. J. Holyoake's genial personality, combined with its editorial support of the cause the collection of expenses to the amount of nearly *£ii,* afterwards made up to 25, for our funds." But the concerting of plans with Collet

for the irritation of the Commissioners of Stamps was a more fruitful service. The easy and indulgent inconsistency of the officials was soon shaken with pitiless onslaughts. The Committee would discover some provincial newspaper, whose sin of omitting the stamp had been genially overlooked, and force it on the attention of the officials. Then, when the heavy penalties of the law were fulminated against the provincial editor, Collet and his friends would put up one of their members to ask in the House why *Punch,* or the *Athenaum,* or the *Builder,* was suffered to evade the law, and insignificant papers were visited so severely. At another time they would induce friendly editors to ask the Board why they were compelled to stamp their whole issues, while 51 journals on the enclosed list— supplied by Collet—published news in stampless impunity, or stamped only the part of their issues that was to go by post. Then they would write of the perplexities and inconsistencies of the Board in every available medium, until they had generated a feeling of contempt for the tax. When, at the close of 1850, they forced the Board to take action against Dickens's *Household Narrative of Current Events,* which was unstamped, they excited indignation in its vast circle of readers.

History of the Taxes on Knowledge, I, 99. The work has a preface by Holyoake, and was published in 1899.

At the beginning of 1851 Holyoake was selected by the Council to defeat the plan of a rival association for the prior repeal of the paper-duty. John Bright, though personally friendly to Holyoake, thought the selection impolitic. "We might be described by the enemy as a society of atheists," he said. But Cobden said he was ready to "accept the assistance of the devil in a justifiable enterprise," and Collet hints that they thought Holyoake particularly qualified in tact and amiability to move a hostile resolution without the semblance of hostility. The meeting, which was held at the London Tavern on January 2nd (1851), was chiefly supported by paper-manufacturers and newspaper-proprietors.

Borthwick of the *Morning Post* and other editors and proprietors had formed an association for the repeal of the paper-duty, and the opponents of the stamp were unwilling to wait until this very heavy impost was remitted by the Government. Holyoake's work was, therefore, to propose an amendment to their resolution, and make arrangements for its success.

To the extreme discomfiture of the conveners of the meeting he secured his object. "In an uncompromising speech," says Mr. Collet, "he declared that the question should not appear as one affecting a trade, but should rest on the dignity of a public principle." Collet and Milner Gibson followed him, and the feeling of the audience was made very apparent; Holyoake and Collet had, in fact, whipped up their Chartist and Socialist followers for that express purpose. The chairman saw that his friends were defeated. He took Holyoake's amendment as a rider to the original resolution, and it was carried with one dissentient. The cause of the separate paper-duty was killed at one blow. It had been intended that this should be the first of a series of meetings. It was the first and the last. Holyoake merely notices that Francis Place declared his speech "capital," and even the *Times* praised it. The *Times* (Jan. 3rd) stated that he moved his amendment in "a speech of some ability."

The rest of the year 1851 was spent in propaganda and in reorganising the Association. It reappeared in May as the "Association for Promoting the Repeal of the Taxes on Knowledge," with Milner Gibson as president, Francis Place treasurer, and Cobden, Bright, Cassell, Passmore Edwards, W. Ewart, Holyoake, J. Hume, Thornton Hunt, Larken, Lewes, and other brilliant workers, on its Council, and the agitation rippled over the country. We do not find any prominent action of Holyoake's until 1854, though he was assiduous on the Council and in the press. No doubt he was mainly instrumental in one of their chief ventures in 1852, when they induced a friend and contributor of his, Frank Grant, to run a defiant journal in the Midlands. Grant, the son of a clergyman, confined to his couch by paralysis, was a young fellow of remarkable spirit and rebellious temper. In December (1851) the long-delayed trial of Dickens's *Household Narrative* had taken place, and the jury had increased the confusion of the revenue officials by acquitting the paper. A conviction would have better pleased the conspirators, but they soon found a way to profit by the acquittal. Within two months of the Dickens verdict Mr. Timm, the solicitor to the Board of Inland Revenue, received from his tormentors a copy of the *Stoke-on-Trent Narrative of Current Events,* edited by Frank Grant. It not only copied Dickens's title, but boldly declared itself published "by authority of the Dickens verdict." Mr. Timm tried his usual threat of the heavy penalties incurred, which generally ended such affairs with a small payment and a hasty retreat, but the paralysed youth defied him. Mr. Timm decided to overlook the matter, and could not be drawn, even when they sent their solicitor, Mr. Ashurst, to accept service of any writ he cared to issue. More questions in Parliament and more ridicule in the press increased the discomfort of Mr. Timm. At last (February 1853) they arranged with Grant to issue a still more defiant weekly, the *Potteries Free Press,* and the Commissioners took action. They summoned the London publisher, Truelove, for selling a copy of it. The Association had the case taken up in the Court of Exchequer, and the verdict was given for the Crown. It served their purpose, as it put Somerset House once more in a ridiculous position.

It is well to note that, whereas Holyoake says the paper was suspended during the long' interval, and Dickens lost £4,000 a year, Collet makes a point of the fact that it was *not* suspended; whereas other periodicals were. Holyoake had a " thousand threepences " subscription for Grant in the *Reasoner.*

In the spring of 1853 the first victory was won by the repeal of the advertisement-tax. Milner Gibson, the Parliamentary leader of the movement, a "debonnaire country squire" working cordially with Chartists and Radicals, made a vain effort to repeal it in April. He wrote to Holyoake on the morning of his motion in the House:

"My Dear Sir,

"I intended to have written to you a few days since to have expressed the pleasure I had experienced in reading your two letters in the *Leader.* I have not seen the last *Leader* to know whether you have inserted a third. We must make up our minds now to strike while the iron is hot while Gladstone's budget was in preparation, and to worry them out of that stamp. It may be done, I am persuaded, in that way, and the Board of Inland Revenue, from what I hear, begin to show decided symptoms of 'punishment.'

"I dread the proposal to-night of a reduction instead of a repeal of the advertisement-duty. However, we may perhaps hear what is to be taken off after the vote of the House on Thursday.

"Yours ever faithfully,

"thos. Milner Gibson."

Gibson was defeated, and Mr. Gladstone carried his reduction of the advertisement-tax from *is. 6d.* to *6d.* on July 21st. Contented ministers and their followers went home to dine, and then there ensued one of those dramatic episodes that enliven the history of the House of Commons. Mr. E. H. J. Crawfurd, member for the Ayr Burghs, seeing that the Government's supporters were now in a minority in the House, moved that a cipher be substituted for the figure 6 in the Budget. It was put to the vote and carried, and, to the laughter of London and the wrath of the Government, the Budget was passed with a tax of " *£0 or. od."* on advertisements. "See the conquering zero comes," men chanted at Crawfurd's club when he came in. Collet says that Milner Gibson was the real deviser of this famous piece of parliamentary strategy.

The war on the press-stamp was now prosecuted with greater vigour and resource than ever. Gladstone had relieved monthlies from the tax, and the Association induced the editors of four monthlies at Wigan and four at Dunfermline to bring out their papers in successive weeks, so as to make a virtual weekly. The Lord Mayor of London issued a large placard on the Crimean war, which had then broken out, and the Association threatened to draw legal penalties on him if he issued a second within a month, because he was publishing news. They induced Mr. Novello, now their treasurer and a colleague of great value, to bring out his *Musical Times* fortnightly, and send Mr. Timm a copy; and when the secretary of the Board kept silent, Mr. Novello sent persistent inquiries about his position, saying that his friends were anxious about the risks he ran. But the year 1854 was chiefly occupied with an enterprise in which Holyoake played a leading part, and we must be content to consider this.

The Council of the Association felt that a more drastic irritation of the Board was needed, and Holyoake offered his services. First he worried the authorities with his little *Reasoner,* which they had found it convenient to overlook. He applied for the stamp for the *Reasoner,* and was told that it was not a newspaper. His solicitors then applied to the Post Office to know if the *Rea.oner* could be transmitted in the ordinary way of journals by post, and were told that it could do so if it bore the newspaper-stamp, which the Postmaster-General suggested they could obtain by making a simple declaration that it was a newspaper. Holyoake then made a dignified appeal to the Treasury for advice. Was it possible that he could only secure justice by making a false declaration that the *Reasoner* was a newspaper, when the officials had assured him it was not? He enclosed a list of seventeen trade-circulars and papers—three of them ecclesiastical journals, quite analogous to his own from the legal point of view—which made this false declaration and secured the postal privilege. The indignity of the whole proceedings must have impressed a man like Gladstone, who was then Chancellor of the Exchequer; but this particular difficulty was met by fresh postal regulations. Meantime, Holyoake was taunting Mr. Timm with his failure to pros-

ecute the *Reasoner,* which he was now willing to stamp for postal purposes, and action was promised; though when it was found that Holyoake, having the freedom of the City, must be brought before the Lord Mayor (who was opposed to press-prosecutions) the matter had to be dropped.

But a more crucial test was needed, and, Mr. Collet says, "we got our friend Mr. Holyoake to publish a weekly paper with the object of testing the blank-space question." To leave a page or more of a newspaper blank was one of the familiar devices for evading the complicated regulations of the Board, and a provincial proprietor had been mulcted by the Board for using it. The *Fleet Street Advertiser,* which Holyoake brought out to test it, was a humorous production. It consisted of two pages, one of which was blank, and the other contained the same news week by week in varied order. Its only customer was the Revenue officer, who bought six copies every Saturday morning. But it was allowed to run from June to December without consequences, and served to illustrate the ridiculous plight of Somerset House.

Then came the decisive experiment. The Crimean War had broken out, and the demand for news evoked a crop of illegitimate newspapers. These were dispersed by a shower of writs from Somerset House, and the Association took up the challenge. It was decided to issue four monthly chronicles in four successive weeks of the month, and Holyoake undertook to publish them. Pigott, the proprietor of the *Leader,* and other men of means refused—very naturally—to expose their fortunes to the very obvious risk involved in an experiment of this kind, and Holyoake was willing to make the sacrifice of his liberty and stock. A 20 fine on every copy of a paper would soon reach a ruinous sum, and imprisonment, with the loss of whatever he possessed, seemed the inevitable penalty. With lively recollections of his former prison experience he kept a warm cloak and some refreshments under his counter, and took his place as salesman of the dangerous pa-

pers. Austin Holyoake was ready to take his place when he was removed by the police. In December 1854 he began with the issue of *Collets War Chronicle,* and this was followed on successive Saturdays by *Moore's War Chronicle, Hoppey's War Chronicle,* and *The War Chronicle.* He would not allow any of his assistants to sell the papers, and his solicitors obtained a reluctant promise from the Government that they would not prosecute any other person until Holyoake himself was put on trial in the Court of Exchequer. Gladstone, whom they interviewed, said that " he knew Mr. Holyoake's intention was to try the law, not to break it." In addition to these nominal monthlies, Holyoake issued a halfpenny *War Fly Sheet,* and bombarded Somerset House with defiant declarations. During the weeks that these papers were issued Holyoake was liable to the penalties that Hetherington had so often incurred. His presses might be broken up, all his books taken away, and he himself incur a long term of imprisonment. It was not twelve months since he had opened his " Fleet Street House," and there were heavy liabilities attached to it. Every penny of his money had gone into the business, and his wife and four children depended wholly on his weekly income. I stress these considerations, because the light and entertaining way in which he has written of these things in his autobiographic chapters tends to hide from us the gravity of his position. He was prepared to make a great sacrifice, without any guarantee of indemnity from the Association. Yet it seems that even in the midst of his danger he kept a light and mirthful pen. Before many weeks a writ came summoning him before the Court of Exchequer on January 31st (1855), and threatening him with the full penalty of £20 for each number of the *War Chronicle* and *War Fly Sheet* he issued. It was computed in the end that he issued 30,000 copies, so that the penalties on this count alone amounted to 600,000; while he had incurred fines of 2,280 on the copies of the *Fleet Street Advertiser,* sold to the Revenue officer, and a good million on the *Reasoner,* if they cared to prosecute that journal. The solicitors to the Association took up the writ, but no case was entered. There was clearly trouble at Somerset House and Westminster. Collet says that the authorities had "too much good sense to take advantage of Mr. Holyoake's courage and public spirit." Elsewhere he relates that when they interviewed Gladstone and the Attorney General on the subject of the trial, Sir Alexander Cockburn was heard to say: "God forbid that my name should be connected with the prosecution of any newspaper." On the other hand, Mr. Timm was now complaining bitterly of a tax that only brought in 300,000 a year, yet cost more trouble to collect than all the rest of the revenue.

Holyoake pushed on the campaign with spirit as he noted the enfeeblement of the enemy. He put a large and conspicuous placard in front of his shop, headed: "Sham war against the unstamped press," and setting forth that, "though diplomatic relations between Fleet Street and Downing Street were suspended," he doubted if there would be an effective "blockade." The atmosphere, it must be remembered, was full of military phrases on account of the Crimean War. Gladstone announced in January that he would repeal the stamp-tax, and Collet and his friends ceased to issue their *Chronicles;* though Holyoake continued to print his weekly *Fly Sheet* until the royal assent to the repeal was given. His policy was right, as the ministry was defeated in February, and Gladstone's successor, Sir George Cornewall Lewis, was disposed to alter the measure that Gladstone had introduced, and insisted on retaining the Securities-system. Holyoake wrote to the Treasury that, as it was impossible for him and many other editors to declare themselves worth.£400, as the Securities-system demanded, he considered the Bill that had been introduced for his relief to be abandoned, and would take action against some of the papers that evaded or transgressed the law. His solicitors (always Mr. Ashurst's firm) drew up an indictment and procured ample evidence, but the Grand Jury concluded that these papers evaded the

law with the connivance of the Government, and ought not to be penalised.

At the same time, however, the new Chancellor of the Exchequer promised to modify his restrictions. Involved in a maze of petitions, threats, and suggestions, with a clear prospect of renewed fighting on the part of the Association, he abandoned his obnoxious amendments. Holyoake was in the House from four in the afternoon of March 25th, when the Bill was passed, until one the following morning. Tory after Tory arose to defend the ancient restrictions on demotic journalism. Each member had received a circular containing extracts from the *Reasoner,* to show the lurid horrors of a free press. Suddenly an "elegant-looking lounger" flung down his hat, and, catching the Speaker's eye, poured out an eloquent appeal for the complete freedom of the press. It was, he learned, Sir Edward Bulwer Lytton. Waverers were won over by his stirring speech, and the Bill was passed. But Holyoake would not lower his flag until the Queen's signature was on it. Disraeli had contributed to the debate an after-dinner speech in which he defined "news" as " what came from the North, East, West, and Sfouth." The next issue of the *War Fly Sheet* announced that it "consisted exclusively of intelligence from the seat of war in the *East,* and was published in accordance with the recorded and mature judgment of the Right Honourable Benjamin Disraeli, formerly Chancellor of the Exchequer, that intelligence from only one point of the compass is not news." On June 15th the Bill for the Repeal of the Newspaper-Stamp received the royal assent. On June 27th Holyoake issued the last number of his triumphant *Fly Sheet.* He had been to the end one of the most prominent and courageous workers in what few will now question to be a great reform.

There remained, not only the Securities-system, but the formidable paper-duty, the third of the taxes on knowledge. The Securities-system was, Mr. Collet says, "deprived of all meaning by the repeal of the stamp, and might be left to die a natural death." But the pa-

per-duty still laid a very heavy tax on journalistic enterprise, and, as it brought a million a year to the Treasury, its abolition would entail a long and severe struggle. With the details of that struggle we are not concerned, as Holyoake's share in the work was little more than that of an industrious member of the Council. The day after the repeal of the stamp-tax the Association issued a number of its *Gazette,* announcing at once the abolition of the second tax on knowledge, and its determination to continue its work until the third had disappeared. It said:

"Talk of the difficulty of making paper out of common vegetable matter, why, the hornet makes brown paper of field herbs, and so would Englishmen, if the Inland Revenue gentlemen would let them alone; that Board forbids that they shall, like the hornet, make brown paper, but when forcing the hornet to be idle, it cannot deprive it of its sting; the paper-makers should build a hornets' nest in Somerset House—the achievement will not be a difficult one. "

The wearied officials knew well that to Collet and Holyoake and their colleagues the achievement would *not* be a difficult one, but the Revenue Board had a far larger sum at stake in the paper-duty, and resisted for six years. We have only to see how Holyoake took his part in the congenial work of constructing the hornets' nest.

There was the usual relaxation of interest when the stamp was abolished, and, as the Association showed a considerable deficit, it was proposed that it be dissolved. At the next meeting Cobden proposed, and Holyoake seconded, that the debt be cleared off, and the Association take up the work of abolishing the paper-duty. The task of gathering material—in a new field—and organising a campaign in and out of Parliament had to be recommenced. The paper-maker, they soon found, was caught in an elaborate network of regulations, to each of which was attached a penalty, rising in cases to 300 for a single omission. To take one curious instance, he was liable to a fine of 200 if he opened a stationer's shop within a mile of his mill; and the duty was so high that Vol. 1. 1

Mr. Charles Knight found he had paid,£50,000 in twenty years, more than half what he had paid for copyrights and editorial work. The Association set to work to make public facts of this kind, and detect flaws, and openings for provocation, in the irregular working of the complex Act. Holyoake conducted one of these pieces of vexation on his own account. As the law still stood, newspapers and pamphlets that were published periodically had to be registered. But the Board had fallen into one of its easy ways in regard to pamphlets, and on this Holyoake fastened. He sent a copy of a pamphlet he had published without registration, and asked Mr. Timm if he would prosecute it. The usual irritable letters were sent in reply to his staid and polite inquiries. Mr. Timm was known to have begged the Chancellor of the Exchequer to "sweep away" all the restrictions on newspapers. Holyoake was really liable to a penalty of;£ioo for not registering, but in the eighth letter of the correspondence they had to admit that it would be a departure from their practice to prosecute. Once more he had exposed their irregularities and the cumbrousness of the old Act.

But it is unnecessary to enter into details. They so effectually worried the Board of Revenue that by the end of 1860 it confessed that the paper-duty was "rapidly becoming untenable," and they instanced as difficulties that "converted" them, as J. S. Mill said, the very devices which Collet and his friends had initiated. In 1861 the duty was repealed, after a severe struggle with the Lords, and the last of the "taxes on knowledge" was swept away, thirty years after Leigh Hunt had invented that militant phrase. The Securities-system followed in 1869. The last mention of Holyoake's name in connection with the reform is in 1861, when it was decided to make a presentation to Mr. Milner Gibson. Mr. John Francis announced that Holyoake collected £200 towards this presentation.

The campaign on behalf of a free press has led us to advance somewhat rapidly in the story of Holyoake's life, and we shall have to retrace our steps to 1855, to consider other important incidents in his career. But we may take the opportunity to reflect briefly on his journalistic activity at this early period. The list of journals in which he wrote between 1840 and 1905 would fill pages. His terse, bright, entertaining manner of writing was particularly suitable for the daily and weekly press, and, in spite of the shudder that his familiar name provoked in religious readers, he had many invitations. When his contributions were to be signed, he was not unwilling to assume a fictitious name like "Ion," "Landor Praed," "Disque," and so on. The disguise was not worn to protect himself, but to obtain a hearing; though he always advised professional men to protect themselves with a pseudonym when they wrote in his own journal. In some cases no one but Holyoake himself knew the identity of his contributor or supporter.

In the course of the fifties Holyoake had a good deal of journalistic experience. He not only had the editing and managing of his own small weekly, and the managing and control of an important department of the *Leader,* but he wrote for several other papers, projected new ones, and negotiated the sale or purchase of others. In 1850 he suggested the title and framed the early plan of *Public Opinion* for Mr. Ashurst, who gave it in charge of Robert Buchanan. The title occurred to him through Peel's saying that "England was governed by opinion." A few months later his diary notes that he is negotiating the purchase of the *Northern Star* for Ashurst; and two days after this he is offering to Thornton Hunt a little unstamped paper, the *Workshop,* owned by himself and Mr. Collet—who, curiously, makes no reference to it. A few weeks later he is offered an engagement on the *Daily News,* which began its career in 1846. Some time afterwards he is " invited to breakfast with Thornton Hunt to discuss Colonel Torrens' proposal re the *Globe. "* In a later year he speaks of "offering Hunt the *Melbourne Age."* I have seen

the minute and scrupulous accounts he kept of some of the papers he managed, and can understand that his judgment was of value. He was on the board of the *People's Journal* in 1856, and on the Metropolitan Press Committee in 1858. He speaks *(Sixty Years,* I, 301) of a wealthy gentleman who used to call at his office with money, and write in the *Reasoner,* whom he knew only as "Aliquis " (= Somebody) for ten years. This is not correct, however, as I find a letter from "Aliquis" to him in 1854, giving his name, George Gwynne. He was in Switzerland, and had to send a cheque instead of the usual note; but he directed Holyoake to "burn this leaf after copying the address "—a direction that seems to have been overlooked. Otherwise even in his private diary Holyoake never described him as other than "Aliquis." He lived at Ilfracombe. His descriptive reporting ranged from prize fights and cricket matches to public executions and royal ceremonies. But it is difficult to discover the extent of work that was generally anonymous. Letters from the editor of the *Morning and Evening Star,* one of the new papers brought out after the abolition of the stamp, show that he was writing leaders in 1856 for Mr. Hamilton, who signs himself his "good-natured brother in humanity." Another friend of his, Mr. J. Baxter Langley, edited it in 1857. In 1858 Mr. Langley (then editing the *People's Paper* and the *London News)* offers him the editorship of one of the two, but he declines. In 1859 he reports G. Stephenson's funeral for the *Newcastle Chronicle,* and engages to supply a weekly letter for that journal. Langley wrote him:

"You need not be too sensitive on my account about it being known that we are friends. I should not consent to pass you in the street without speaking, or do any such gross act of servility to the cant or convention of the place or time. "

A little later, when Holyoake fell ill, Mr. Langley wrote:

"I cannot tell how it is, but in all sincerity my attachment to you has become so strong that the knowledge of your sufferings has disturbed me much."

Other friendly letters show that he wrote in 1860 for the *Manchester Examiner and Times,* the *Daily Review,* and other journals.

His relations with the *Leader* deserve special notice. They were more chequered than one would imagine from his chapter on that journal. The *Leader* was started in 1850 with Holyoake as manager, and occupying a minor place on the brilliant staff. The publication of "Ion" letters and leaders, and the opening, under his control, of a Co-operative section, gave him more importance. There are cordial letters to him from the chief proprietor, Mr. E. Pigott, in 1852, though he shows a suspicion of petulance at Holyoake's failure to borrow money for him and secure more subscribers. The need for economy then led to a drastic curtailment of the staff, and Holyoake was asked to write little. A letter of Pigott's to him on May 31st, 1854, prevents us from misinterpreting this:

"My Dear Holyoake,

"It was a true pleasure to me to get a letter in your handwriting again this morning. It seems a century since we met or corresponded, and, I deeply regret to add, since ' Ion ' has appeared in the *Leader.* You know very well what my feelings are towards *you,* both personally as a friend and officially as editor of the *Leader,* and that it is neither my fault nor my purpose that you should have been so long absent from our pages. You know that, differing as I do conscientiously from you on the great subject of belief, I am with you heart and soul in the one great cause of freethought—absolute liberty of conscience...."

Thornton Hunt had disappeared, in the curtailment of expenses, with other of Holyoake's friends. In 1855, moreover, the *Leader* spoke with so little of its old radicalism on the American slavery-question that Newman, Miss Martineau, and others, dropped it in disdain. Miss Collet wrote that its tone was "unspeakably disgraceful " and " unblushingly impudent." He criticised it in his *Reasoner,* and Pigott seems to have

complained bitterly; Holyoake had to remind him of his services and sacrifices for the paper. Pigott had some notion of shifting the appeal of the paper to a more respectable audience, but he failed; and in a few years (1857) wrote letters of exaggerated cordiality to Holyoake, begging him to induce "the freethought party" to rally to his journal.

Holyoake continued to write on it until 1859, when Mr. Pigott passed from the editorial chair, on good terms with Holyoake. It is amusing to read in his letter that Holyoake is pleased with the new editor, Mr. Whitty, and to find a letter in which Whitty begs Holyoake to "regard the *Leader* precisely as before. " When we turn to the chapter on the *Leader* in *Sixty Years* (ch. xliv) we learn that Mr. Whitty was a Roman Catholic, and "sentiments appeared in it which made its friends wish that it had ceased to exist earlier." It did cease to exist shortly afterwards. With Thornton Hunt (now working on the *Globe* and the *Spectator)* Holyoake continued to be on terms of intimate friendship.

CHAPTER XIII POLITICAL AND SOCIAL ACTIVITY (1850-1860)

For the convenience of study I have now considered separately the chief interests that engaged Holyoake's attention from 1848 to 1860—the early struggles of the Co-operative Movement, the establishment of Secularism, the continental reaction, and the liberation of the press— and we may now retrace our steps a little, and follow the progress of his career year by year. We have found him working with such vigour in these movements that there would seem to be little of his time left. In point of fact, the whole decade is filled with a nervous energy that finds expression in a hundred tasks. The cares of the *Reasoner* and the "Fleet Street House," the constant exactions of the growing Secularist body—made painful and more exhausting by attacks from jealous colleagues—and the heavy pressure of lecturing, writing, and committee-work for half a dozen organisations, do not cover nearly the whole of his work in the fifties. Several times he wore himself down to a dangerous

point. Few movements in the civic life of London, or the political life of the nation, failed to put fresh burdens on him; and, to judge from the bundles of letters lying before me, or mentioned in the *Reasoner,* his correspondence was voluminous.

One is apt to forget, in studying his share in the great movements of the time, or reading the warm phrases of judicious correspondents, that he was still in his early thirties, and had worked in a foundry until his twenty-second year. His circle of friends was enviable. Amongst the visitors to his little house at 1 Woburn Buildings I find Robert Owen, Herbert Spencer, Sir Joshua Walmsley, the Rev. Brooke Herford, Francis Pulzsky (the Hungarian ex-Prime Minister), and others, forming a very varied and interesting group. But his friends generally knew the limit of his means and home, and preferred to entertain him, or to drop in at 147 Fleet Street. He seems to have been a frequent visitor at Lewes's, Hunt's, Stansfeld's, Allsop's, Ashurst's, Mazzini's, Pulzsky's, Newman's, and Crawford's; and wherever he went he found hosts in the provinces. Mrs. Holyoake was clearly liked by his friends, and tended the growing family—a fourth youngster arriving in 1855. The only shadow that fell on his family life at this time was when his second boy, Maximilian Robespierre, was run over and died in 1857. His uncalculating labours, genial manner, and virile character outweighed the unpopularity of his views on religion, which few of his friends entirely shared. Four times in a few years his portrait was painted—by Merritt, Robinson, Hahn, and Mrs. Hawkes— and tributes in the press began to multiply. The attacks that were made on him always evoked fresh expressions of esteem that healed the pain. Linton's attack drew a fine tribute from Miss Martineau, as we saw, Miss Collet, Ashurst, and others. Another attack in 1856 induced Thornton Hunt to offer his services, and say: "No public consideration could make me wish to throw the slightest veil over a friendship which does me honour." Golding Penrose wrote him that a friend of his had heard a minister at a Wesleyan Tract Society meeting " confess that one great need of Christian propagandism in these times was that of men like Mr. Holyoake in candour, cautiousness of statement, and love of the right." The *Nonconformist* described him (in January 1853) as "one of the most popular and learned of the apostles of unbelief," and "an author of no mean ability," whose "sympathies were on the side of virtue and truth." But we shall see plenty of this as we proceed. I will only add here an unpublished letter that Carlyle wrote him in 1854. He never met Carlyle, and that stern idealist detested his philosophy, but the note is not unfriendly:

"Dear S1r, Thanks for your civility and punctuality. The letter is for me, the second I have got under the same address—unhappily only from a dark remote blockhead, of the sturdy-beggar description, whom I am bound to make a strict point of not answering.

"I remain,

"Yours sincerely,

"T. Carlyle."

On one occasion Carlyle turned severely on some man who depreciated Holyoake at Lord Houghton's table. His relations with Mill, the other thinker in London at the time, were, as I said, more cordial. In 1856 Mill and a friend lent him 70 when he had put his name to some bills of a friend (Le Blond, I believe, who fell into drink and penury) and incurred a liability of 70 beyond his means. Holyoake repaid the money, but the friend made him a present of his £3$.

To have attained this position in so short a time, and with such disadvantages, was some recompense for the work we have described and the spirit in which it was done. The same spirit and energy are found in the rest of his occupations in the fifties. We have seen little up to the present of what is called political life in the more technical sense. The House of Commons lay generally outside the range of his vision until middle age. He had, it is true, listened to its debates with young eagerness when

he first came to the metropolis, under the shadow of a charge of blasphemy: he had looked to the Whigs in their new power in the Reformed Parliament with the same hope as most other Radicals; and he had followed the debates on the taxes on knowledge with keen interest. Generally, however, up to the end of his thirties he conceived the House in a Chartist or a Carlylean mood. It was a "talking-shop." Until an educated and fully enfranchised people brought it to face social maladies more boldly he had little expectation from it. His work on the *Leader* and his new association with middle-class reformers gradually drew it into his sphere of real interest, and it became a centre of his political eagerness. I find that as early as 1852 he was on the Council of the National Parliamentary and Financial Reform Association, and his relations with Milner Gibson, Fox, Cobden, and Bright increased his parliamentary interest.

The outbreak of the Crimean War in 1855 was little noticed by him. He got Collet to write on the Eastern question in the *Reasoner,* and he published a map for his readers; but one does not find any condemnation of it. Russia had long incurred his hostility for its treatment of Poland and its general despotism. Indeed, he confesses that he followed the war with a good deal of undiscriminating patriotism. At intervals he thought of arbitration, but habitually he was for "the success of England, right or wrong. " When the peace was declared, however, he refused to illuminate in Fleet Street, and put up a large placard bearing Eliz. Browning's verses on the plight of Poland, Italy, and Hungary. On the other hand, he wrote frequently— and with much dissatisfaction to both sides— on the question of American slavery. That he condemned every trace of slavery goes without saying, but he fell short of most of his friends in vehemence, and for a time was regarded with suspicion by Lloyd Garrison. In 1853 he wrote an "Address of the Democrats of England to the Democrats of America." Its moderation of tone offended many of his friends. T. Cooper refused to sign it, and Linton and Har-

ney scorned it. In America some of the chief abolitionists received it with respect. Horace Greely inserted it twice in the *New York Tribune,* and "earnestly commended it to the grave and candid consideration" of his readers. Wendell Phillips, who became a warm friend, told him it was the only English article on the subject that he cared to reply to. The moderation of his tone had another ground besides his general regard for that virtue. Our political relations with America had to be considered, and there were judicious politicians who thought that the language of the extreme English abolitionists endangered them. There is a very long and serious letter to Holyoake from Hunt on the subject in 1855, and the sober tone of the *Reasoner* must be considered in the light of their apprehensions; if sobriety needs any apology.

In 1857 he came within the penumbra of parliamentary life, when he offered himself as candidate at the Tower Hamlets. His chief object in seeking a seat was to press more effectively for the substitution of an affirmation for the oath, where there were scruples; but he issued a very full electoral programme. The chief points in it were: triennial Parliaments, the ballot, and equal electoral districts; home colonisation on wastelands; the abolition of Church rates; security to married women's property; and the opening of museums on Sundays. His chances of election were slight, but a committee was formed, and a subscription-list drawn up. J. S. Mill sent him 10, but he did not care to compromise Mill by publishing his name. On March 27th, however, Holyoake received a letter from Mr. Baxter Langley begging him to retire from his candidature, and he decided to do so. He found that Mr. Ayrton, a strong Liberal (afterwards Commissioner of Works) and a valuable worker for the abolition of the press-stamp, was offering himself for election, and he withdrew and gave his services to Mr. Ayrton. His letter was cordially acknowledged by Mr. Ayrton, who was "much gratified"; though he discreetly declined to have Holyoake's name in any prominence in his candidature. He was returned—and at once turned his back on the " infidel." Holyoake was on the platform when the result was announced, and part of the crowd clamoured for a speech from him. Mr. Ayrton was asked by the returning officer to get a hearing for Holyoake, as the religious opposition was turbulent, but he refused.

Two of the items in the electoral programme we have summarised enter for the first time in our story—the Sunday question and the Woman question. The idea of securing some recreation for the masses on Sunday was at this time beginning to assume the shape of a definite reform, and it naturally appealed to Secularists. There are few now who fail to see the evil of opening only two public doors—that of the church and that of the publichouse—to the workers on Sundays, but the early agitation in favour of opening the museums and arranging excursions met with the most violent opposition. An old bill I have tells of a modest excursion that the Secularists of Newcastle arranged. As soon as it was announced, a neighbouring preacher put up a huge poster to say— with all the embroidery of the time— that he would preach on this "Trip to Hell." The Secularists retorted, after their return, with a poster announcing the results of their exploration. In many other places a spirited war was going on over the new practice. The London Secularists were very active in the cause of "the Free and Rational use of the Sunday "; and their religious neighbours just as naturally resisted their efforts. The facilities that have been won for recreation on Sunday have done more than heretical propaganda to deplete the churches.

On Whit Sunday in 1856 Holyoake organised an excursion to Rye House for the members of the London Secular Society. He took his wife and two children with him, and addressed the excursionists on the "Right use of the Sunday." From that time onward he worked constantly in the new movement. His journal was one of the best organs in London of the newly-founded Sunday League. He attended the meetings of the

League, and the great demonstrations in the parks (in May and June) to protest against the removal of the bands. The cry of the "French Sunday" was met by him in several lectures in 1856. In the course of time he formulated a curious theory (described in *Bygones,* II, 205-7) that there ought to be two Sundays in each week. The present Sunday " would be left undisturbed, devoted to repose, to piety, contemplation, and improvement of the mind," and the other would be a day of universal and organised recreation—a sort of weekly "Bank Holiday." He does not mention any friend, or any section of his supporters, who favoured his theory.

The other reform which he inserted in his programme was a measure of justice to women. "First among social improvements," he said, "is the measure introduced by Sir Erskine Perry for giving, under just conditions, married women an independent right to their property." His interest in the cause of women was one of his legacies from the old Owenite movement, and a tradition almost confined to heretics at that time. Acquaintance with John Stuart Mill and Harriet Martineau confirmed his feeling, and he became one of the first parliamentary candidates to give a prominent position to the woman-question in his manifesto. Ten years previously (1847) he had written an article on the subject in the *Free Press,* and suggested a programme for them which even his womenfriends deemed wildly visionary, but which the women of the next generation almost fully realised. He urged that they should "take their own affairs into their own hands," and form a "fifth estate" in the kingdom. They should hold women-meetings with women-speakers—a thing abhorred at the time—"draw up a list of their legal disabilities, and take the usual constitutional modes of obtaining redress," and run a *Womaris Journal* with a purely feminine staff. It is singular that, while men so often resist women's demands on the ground that they are so largely conservative and subject to clerical dictation, the heresiarchs of the early half of the nineteenth century were their best

advocates. Godwin, Owen, Holyoake, and Mill pleaded for them, when to do so was a ready invitation of ridicule. Mary Wollstonecraft, Frances Wright, Harriet Martineau, Emma Martin, and Harriet Law were heretics, and had the co-operation of heretics alone.

He reprinted his "Letter to Lord Palmerston" on the Sunday question in a pamphlet entitled *The Rich Maris Six and the Poor Maris On Day,* in 1856.

But by 1857 Holyoake saw some movement in the direction he had indicated, and he took an active interest in it. When Miss Martineau's *Household Education* was published, he engaged his wife to review it in the *Reasoner,* in accordance with his principles. He himself wrote and lectured frequently on behalf of the movement. He reprinted—unfortunately without permission, which drew a philosophic rebuke from Mill— Mrs. Mill's article: "Are Women fit for Politics? Are Politics fit for Women?" and sold many thousand copies. He corresponded with a large circle of able women—Miss Martineau, Mme. Venturi, Mme. Mario, Miss Collet, Miss Barbara L. Smith (Mme. Bodichon), Miss Bessie R. Parkes (Mme. Belloc), Mrs. Crawford, Mrs. Stansfeld, etc.— and urged them to co-operate. Miss B. Rayner Parkes (a descendant of Priestley, mother of Mr. Hilaire Belloc) greatly appreciated his help, writing constantly to him and sending him pamphlets by herself and Miss Leigh Smith to distribute at his lectures—" which (allow me to say) God speed!" she observes. Miss Parkes edited the *Woman's Journal* (suggested by him in 1847) which was started in 1857, and bought large numbers of his *Reasoner* for distribution. "Please to send me 12 Reasoners. ... A thousand thanks for your valiant defence "; and again: "I have to acknowledge the safe receipt of several *Reasoners,* which gave great pleasure. " Miss Parkes was liberal in her religious views, and in 1858 she sent for insertion in the *Reasoner* (asking that her name be "carefully suppressed") a translation of "a curious controversy between Proudhon and one of the new light ladies of France," as she described it. Several pamphlets by her and Miss Smith were published by him.

Holyoake's correspondence with Mrs. Hawkes (afterwards Mme. Venturi—a daughter of Ashurst's) had more personal cordiality, but concerned the cause of Italy rather than of woman. In 1857 Mrs. Hawkes, who was separated from her husband, proposed that she should share a house with him and his family, but the proposal came to nothing. Her father died in 1855, and she expresses gratitude in every letter for the help Holyoake gave her in finding customers for pictures, etc. "I cannot say how very grateful I am to your friends for their kindness to me; it is doubly welcome as being shown for your sake." But Mrs. Hawkes was mainly interested in Italian matters. She clearly thought as little of bombs for Napoleon as Allsop did. When Percy Greg wrote his poem "The Peace of Napoleon," and Holyoake reviewed it, she wrote him that his "habitual benevolence" had "misled his judgment." Holyoake had merely trusted that the Empress would be exempt from any fate that might befall her husband! Of Greg's poem she said it had "rather a gas and orange peel effect, coming from the pen of one who has generally used your pages to proclaim his atheism." As it was stated at the time that the journal was written mainly by men, I may note that she assures Holyoake in a letter that every article not signed by a male writer (and they were few) is by a lady. Miss Isa Craig, Miss Blackwell ("Paris Gossip"), Miss Blagden, Miss Merryweather, and Miss Parkes wrote the first number, with one male contributor.

That Miss Martineau came nearer to Holyoake in sentiment than any other of his lady correspondents goes without saying, but the terms in which she at times expresses her admiration are unexpected. In a letter to him on May 31st, 1851, she says:

"I always read the *Reasoner*—every line of it. You must allow me to thank you, in the name of everything that is wise and good, for the glorious temper you manifest, without break or flattering, towards foe and friend. Great as is

your ability, one almost loses sight of it in the charm of your temper. You do not need to be told, as a general truth, that such a tone as I mean is the best service that can be rendered to a good cause; but you may need to be told that your readers gratefully recognise such a temper in you. I do long at times to put in my word, and try to help you in those pages. If I possibly could, I would. But my work is very heavy for one who is growing old."

The one point on which she differed strongly from Holyoake was, strangely enough, in his estimate of Mazzini. A letter of December 28th, 1857, runs:

"Dear Mr. Holyoake,

"I do not see what I can do, in replying to your letter, but speak the full truth. I am sorry to have to refuse any request of yours and to hurt anybody's feelings; but, in reply to a direct inquiry, I must say that I can do nothing in favour of Mazzini's policy. No one appreciates more heartily than I do the disinterestedness and devotedness of his character; but I disapprove of his cause so entirely that I would do anything in my power to check and counteract it. Of the many and mournful obstacles to human progress, Mazzini's life and action seem to me to be the most painful and discouraging. I disapprove both his objects and his methods as thoroughly as possible.

"I am, very truly yours,

"H. Martineau."

In 1855 Miss Martineau introduced him to her friend and collaborator, Mr. Atkinson, and sent him on his first visit to France. "Sure I am that you will never know a better or a wiser man," she wrote. Atkinson, whose correspondence with Miss Martineau in 1851 formed the work *Man's Nature and Development,* which her brother, Dr. Martineau, scornfully treated as "mesmeric atheism" (it was rather pantheistic), lived at Boulogne. He was a man of means, and a keen student of philosophy, with a cultured circle of friends. In August 1856 Holyoake crossed over, and spent two days with him at Boulogne. He had invited Holyoake to come and "dine together and catch a mermaid out of the

sea—chat and gossip, and gossip and chat—sipping sparkling bordeaux," and the bait was taken. He afterwards corresponded at length with Holyoake on philosophical subjects related to religious thought. His attitude was not distinctly "atheistic," as nearly all the reviewers pronounced it, but it tended to materialism.

A more interesting author with whom Holyoake was Vol. 1. u brought into relations at this time was Walter Savage Landor. A refined epicurean, of exquisite culture and complete dislike of the concrete mob, Landor had professed republicanism at Oxford, and advocated tyrannicide in his eightieth year. He had lost his fortune, and retired to Italy, when, in his eighty-fourth year, he asked Holyoake to publish a dangerous pamphlet for him. The circumstances that led to the publication are told with impenetrable discretion even in Forster's life of Landor, and Landor's letters to Holyoake (published in *Sixty Years,* II, 11-14) have been treated with still more discreet curtailment. The originals are no longer available. Landor had quarrelled with a lady at Bath, and lost a lawsuit she brought against him. Aged and ailing as he was, his customary passionateness was inflamed, and he wrote a pamphlet in his defence. Owing to the scandal and the loss of his means, his friends had sent him to Florence, and from there he directed Holyoake to publish and distribute his libel. Holyoake was careful to have the manuscript copied in his own house, so that no one else saw it. A reward of 200 was offered for the name of the printer, but the secret was kept for twelve years.

The correspondence with Landor was in 1859, but there are earlier episodes that must not be overlooked. In 1857 Holyoake was sent into Cornwall by the London Secularists to investigate the case of a poor well-sinker who had been condemned to twenty-one months' imprisonment for writing blasphemous phrases on a gate. The mission of Holyoake brought to light a terrible case of injustice, and led to Pooley's acquittal. Holyoake found it undisputed locally that the man was exceptionally sober and industrious, but very eccentric and very heretical in his confused way. He was a good husband, and would weep for hours over his child's grave. He never drank or swore. But his eccentricity had brought him more than once into collision with the magistrates, and when offensive phrases were discovered in chalk on gates in the district the writing was easily traced to him. Of two witnesses—one a carpenter and one a clergyman—the layman swore that the more offensive words detailed by the clergyman were not on the gate at all. However, Pooley was convicted, and Sir John Coleridge sentenced him to one year and nine months in prison. Buckle wrote afterwards with great severity on the judge and on his son, Mr. J. D. Coleridge, who was prosecuting counsel. Only one London paper, the *Spectator,* had any report of the extraordinary trial, and it passed heavy censure on the judge for "treating stark folly with a tragic retribution." When the judge pronounced his sentence Pooley told him to "put his black cap on and have done with it." "If this had been done," said the *Spectator, "*the ineptness of the sentence would only have been more signally exposed." Holyoake's full report in the *Reasoner* (afterwards published in his *Case of Thomas Pooley)* drew attention to the tragedy, and Pooley was released after a few weeks. The incident led a little later to some acquaintance of Holyoake with the historian Buckle, who made a drastic attack on Coleridge. To Holyoake he wrote: "I shall always entertain unfeigned respect for one who has not only fearlessly advocated his views, but has shown himself ready to suffer for them."

In 1857 Holyoake gave a great impulse to the Cooperative movement by writing the *History of the Rochdale Pioneers.* He began it as a series of articles in the *Daily News,* but the outbreak of the Indian Mutiny made great demands on their columns, and it appeared in book form. No other of his small works has had a tithe of the effect, and none of his works has had the remarkable popularity, of this historical sketch. It has been translated into Span-ish, French, Italian, German, and Hungarian, and has taken a Co-operative inspiration all over the civilised world. In England Co-operative Societies multiplied very significantly after its appearance. Authors and magazines that shrank nervously from the name of the writer borrowed it, or parts of it. He tells how, in 1863, a *Quarterly* reviewer included it in the list of works he put at the head of an article on Co-operation. The editor cut out Holyoake's name, which he thought " offensive to pious ears." When the writer pointed out that it would be odd to cut out the name of the writer of *one* of the books referred to, the editor expunged all the authors' names from that particular essay, rather than have Holyoake's odious name in the *Quarterly Review.*

The little work brought Holyoake his last message from the great inspirer of the movement, Robert Owen. Since 1853 Owen had been in friendly correspondence with Holyoake. To the last the aged reformer was framing plans for the regeneration of humanity on a grand scale. He wrote from Sevenoaks in 1856:

"My Dear Holyoake,

"You will see by the *Millennial Gazette,* Nos. 1 and 2, that a new movement of reform, which will include all other reforms, is about to take place, and it is proposed that negotiations should be formed to extend the movement at home and abroad, so as to make it universal, and thus to influence all governments through public opinion to take a right course for the interest and happiness of all.

"Your Secular Societies will do well to merge into this movement, as should all the societies of the working classes, because all their objects will be obtained by the New Reform of Nations, which will be advocated at the approaching congress of the reformers of the world.

"A mere Secular Society cannot be much longer supported. It is now too limited in its objects, and progress now requires much more from advanced minds. You and Robert Cooper require a much wider field of action, and should go forth as apostles of the only system which can ever become universal, or be of permanent practical benefit to the human race...."

Holyoake was now almost the only one of his old workers to whom he looked with hope, and his last letter to Holyoake, written shortly before his death, is a final effort to direct his energies into millennial work:

"My Dear S1r,

"I have to thank you for sending me the copy of the history of Co-operation in Rochdale, which I shall read with much interest. And I have to request you to tender my thanks to the Directors of the Pioneers' Society for their kindness in not forgetting me.

"Next week I hope to send you a pamphlet to which I wish to direct your particular attention, because I am very desirous to give your useful active powers a wider and far more valuable direction for yourself and for the public. The rights of Secularism are now fairly established, and, far more, the rights of all humanity to universal advocation, unexclusive and practical, and to universal, permanent occupation, beneficial for the individual and for the public.

"The subjects of the British Empire ought now to unite to obtain these for themselves and children as their national birthright. You should commence this agitation. With them, everything would be gained: without them, nothing worth having. Think of this.

"Yours affectionately,

"Robert Owen."

Holyoake gently ignored the too vague visions of the master. Owenism was dead; and Owen was too old to see that its finest thoughts were finding more victorious embodiment in the great young movements of the second half of the century. He died in his native Wales a few months afterwards (November 17th, 1858), after a last effort to win public interest at a great meeting in Liverpool. On the 21st Holyoake and one or two others took the night train to Shrewsbury, and the early morning coach to Newtown. Allsop, Ashurst, and a few other friends walked with Holyoake behind the coffin. Some of them were angry that the great heretic was buried with Church-service, but the rector had refused to allow lay speeches in his cemetery. "Better ten popes officiated at his funeral than disturb it with a broil," Holyoake said.

Rigby remained by the grave while Holyoake went home, and wrote his report and dined. Then Holyoake came back to watch by it until late in the night. Rigby had a curious reason for this, though Holyoake only took part in it to gratify him. Julian Hibbert had, years before, left his head for scientific investigation, and, though his relatives took extreme precautions, the head was secured for science. Baume, a phrenological Owenite and extremely eccentric man, had disguised himself as a mute, and got access to the body. Baume now lived in quaint circumstances in the Isle of Man, but Rigby dreaded a stealthy descent upon Newtown in his zeal for phrenology. He had the grave stuffed with furze-bushes, and induced Holyoake to watch with him beside it. Robert Dale Owen gave Holyoake a book of his father's, autographed for presentation to him. It was stolen immediately; and he was astonished to receive it from a Newtown pawnbroker forty-four years afterwards, when he spoke at the unveiling of the Owen monument. He returned to London with his and Owen's old friends, W. Pare and T. Allsop, and after a few weeks issued a grateful and reverent appreciation of his dead master.

Owen's life was written very shortly afterwards by an author who stood entirely outside the school, but wrote with sympathy, W. L. Sargant. Holyoake praised the work, to Sargant's extreme gratification. But it is only in recent years that the true significance of the great Welsh reformer is being recognised. There has been too obstinate a practice of regarding him as a man of action. In that character he was a brilliant failure. Apart from his splendid success at New Lanark, he touched little that did not collapse. His enduring importance was as the disseminator of principles that would provoke more

practical men to act. The spirit he brought into social service at the beginning of the nineteenth century was invaluable. It begot such attention to material and economic conditions as had never before been given; and few particular social problems arose on which he did not anticipate the later generation of reformers. As a theoretical student of social matters he had less limitations than most of his distinguished contemporaries. The course of this story amply shows how he sowed the seed of the successful reforms of the second half of the century. Owen had spoken of the Secular Societies as too narrow in their aim. I have already suggested that they were, on the contrary, too broad and diffused, and Holyoake was at this very time discovering the weakness of his organisation. Only a few months before Owen's last letter reached him he received one from Atkinson to this effect. "By trying to include too much within your walls," he wrote, "you are risking the whole slipping from your grasp: you seem to desire to make Secularism so elastic as to include everybody and everything—you conquer worlds and seek other worlds to conquer, and all by the force of a term." Atkinson thought that his party "was breaking up." He urged Holyoake to amend his formula, and make open profession that his aim was negative and destructive, but only because destruction was a necessary preliminary to any new construction. "Asa John in the wilderness your mission has been to make way for science and to make silence for philosophy." *Life and Last Day; of Robert Owen,* price fourpence. Rosamond Dale Owen (Mrs. Oliphant) wrote that she found it "very beautiful," and J. S. Mill and Lord Brougham spoke in high terms of it.

Within five years the weakness of his scheme had disclosed itself. It was an amiable and a characteristic weakness. By temperament and policy Holyoake, though a fighter of skill and competence, sought everywhere the principles and feelings that united people rather than the oppositions that divided them. His weakness was similar to that of Positivism, and his system was really Pos-

itivist in temper, without the encumbrance of ritual and without Positivist science. The Secular Societies were to foster intelligent interest in the problems of this world; even people who believed in a world to come might, he trusted, unite with atheists on this ground. But, besides the impracticable vagueness and largeness of the ideal, it was in itself more or less of a reproach to current ideas of the importance of another world, and from the first the Secular Societies had a predilection for addresses on theological subjects. Christians could *not* belong to them. Even Pantheists like F. Newman and Miss Collet lingered sympathetically in the courtyard. They strongly approved his educative and social lectures, which were still more numerous than the others, but he himself was compelled to maintain on his list lectures in criticism of theology. He admitted that this was his chief distinction from the Positivists, whose name he frequently substituted for Secularist; and we may remember that the atheist was still an outlaw in English courts of justice, and that people were as much interested in theology as in any other subject.

His ability and his impressive personality had for some years silenced opposition, and the movement seemed to be making rapid progress on the lines he indicated for it, In 1857, however, the malcontents found spokesmen, and a struggle began that was to last throughout his life. His chief opponent in 1857 was Robert Cooper. Lloyd Jones now moved in the small world of the Christian Socialists. Thomas Cooper stood aloof in his mystic views, and was personally friendly. But Robert Cooper was jealous of the younger man, and gathered the new critics about him. Most of these have passed into utter obscurity, and we need not notice them, except to glance for a moment at their personal charges. One of them, however, became a power in England, and will cross the line of our study many times in the years to come.

Before we consider the beginning of the relations between Charles Bradlaugh and Holyoake, it will be useful to glance at the position of the movement. We saw that the word Secularist was unknown until 1851, and there were very few freethinking centres, and no freethinking organisation whatever, until 1853. By the end of 1855 there were eight societies, with weekly lectures, in the metropolis, and there were Secular Societies at Liverpool, Birmingham, Manchester, Bradford, Dudley, Stalybridge, Leeds, Burnley, Bolton, Sheffield, Newcastle, Glasgow, Hyde, Huddersfield, Halifax, Stockport, and Oldham. In the following year there were thirteen London centres, and new Secular Societies were founded at Edinburgh, Northampton, Sunderland, Rochdale, Devonport, and Doncaster. Some thirty-five Societies seem to have been founded between 1853 and 1857; and to these we must add the many further centres where Holyoake had permanent groups of friends who organised lectures for him every year. In December 1855 he lectured at Swindon, Bristol, Exeter, Plymouth, Newcastle, Blaydon, Middlesborough, Hartlepool, Glasgow (six lectures), Paisley, Ashton, Rochdale, Todmorden, Mottram, Hyde, Halifax, and Bradford. Most of these places, and many others, were visited periodically, and were preparing to form societies. All this had been done in five years; and as the number of provincial Secular Societies stood only at 61 in 1880—36 being added in twenty-three years to the 25 Societies he had founded in four years— we can easily test the allegation of remissness or failure on Holyoake's part. The *Reasoner,* the weekly journal of the movement, had a circulation equal to that of the *Spectator,* and we have seen that it gained a respect that was not usually accorded to a freethinking journal. Even the *Saturday Review,* contrasting it with one of the chief Protestant organs, said (April 5th, 1856): "The *Record* is bitter, false, and malignant: the *Reasoner* is not by any means taxable with these faults— it is written with calmness, and admits contradiction with candour." Considering Holyoake's exertions in so many other reforms, he had made remarkable progress with his Secularist organisa-

tion in the first four years, when the opposition came to a head. Robert Cooper, an old Owenite, watched Holyoake's progress with unfriendly interest. He was editing the *Investigator,* a small atheistic journal, and in October (1855) he gave free expression to his feeling. He petulantly urged a claim to "co-paternity" of the new movement, and attacked Holyoake's " pretensions " and "personal rule," as well as his secular principle. It was a piece of obvious and natural jealousy on the part of the older man. Holyoake made a very temperate reply, pointing out that he had actually urged Cooper's appointment as President of the London Secular Society. He continued to receive subscriptions in the *Reasoner* for a testimonial that was being raised for Cooper, who shortly afterwards retired from active work. The *Investigator* passed to "Anthony Collins" (W. H. Johnson), one of Holyoake's bitterest opponents, in 1857, and then on in 1858 to " Iconoclast" (C. Bradlaugh).

The lad of seventeen, for whom Holyoake had taken the chair in 1850, had returned to London, after three years' service in the dragoons, in 1853. Under the name of " Iconoclast" he soon resumed his atheistic lecturing. His first lecture is announced in 1855, but it is not until the autumn of 1856 that he lectures with any regularity in the London halls—and then generally at the East London Society's Hall. By the middle of 1857 it is apparent that he is opposing Holyoake's broad scheme of Secularism, and trying to narrow the movement to atheistic work. In July a bill announces that Holyoake will lecture on the subject at the East London Society, and "Iconoclast will attend and reply to the lecturer." In the summer of 1857 Holyoake begins to publish for him, in serial parts, a work called *The Bible,* which was to be "an examination thereof from Genesis to Revelations," and was afterwards issued by Mr. Bradlaugh in a complete volume. After the third part had been issued it was transferred to the publisher Truelove. The reason for Holyoake's abandonment of it is not obscure: it was given to the public by Bradlaugh himself. "My original pub-

lishers," he wrote in the later issues, "more moral than the Queen's printers, decline to print or publish any comment upon, or any quotations from, the obscene parts of this chapter (Genesis xix)." When Bradlaugh went on to publish the comments that Holyoake objected to, Holyoake requested him to remove the name "Holyoake and Co." from the work; and Bradlaugh issued a complaining circular amongst the London Secularists and others.

One is not surprised to find Mr. Bradlaugh soon afterwards in companionship with Holyoake's more pronounced critics in the movement. The Secularist body had now come to occupy a position almost as prominent in public notice as that of the Owenite body a decade earlier. Within a few weeks in 1857 we find Holyoake lecturing to crowded audiences—often on the Rochdale Co-operators—at Plymouth, Bristol, Exeter, Glasgow (where he was offered 150 a year to remain as resident lecturer to the Eclectic Society), Paisley, Newcastle, Bolton, Blackburn, Todmorden, and other towns. In the summer of 1858 the Lancashire Secularists mustered to the number of 4,000 for an excursion to Hollingworth Lake, and Holyoake joined the formidable picnic and addressed the great gathering. Another address was delivered by "Anthony Collins," who was sowing dissension among the northern Societies.

In the south Holyoake's cause was making proportionate progress, and the same inevitable seeds of dissension were beginning to germinate. The chief dissentient was a Mr. Maughan, of the London Secular Society, and with this critic Mr. Bradlaugh soon began to co-operate, as well as with "Anthony Collins" in the north. The only point that concerns us is that Maughan and Bradlaugh gave legal and other assistance to a discharged employee of Holyoake's, a Mr. Wilks, who caused him very serious trouble. He had carried off with him the books of the Holyoake firm, attempted to collect the debts due to the firm, and professed to offer for sale his "share in the business." The incident is a peculiar reminder that Holyoake was from the first an ardent profit-sharer. The state of the law in regard to co-operation was then so unsatisfactory that Wilks based his exorbitant claims on Holyoake's vague assurance that he was a " profit-sharing employee." As he owed money to the firm, and declared himself insolvent, Austin Holyoake presented himself in court with a barrister. The Chief Commissioner declared that " a more false and fraudulent schedule had never been brought before the court " than that of Wilks. He gave Austin Holyoake an assurance, under the seal of the court, that the debts must be paid to the firm, and peremptorily ordered the return of the books.

In March (1858) Johnson made an attack on him in the *Investigator,* in which Holyoake found "thirty-eight direct statements utterly untrue." Most of the points were frivolous: as, that the *Reasoner* was pledged *not* to advocate atheism (which one or other contributor to it advocated every week), that it refused articles by Southwell, and so on. The sincerest grievance was, probably, the charge that Holyoake did not use the funds of the Fleet Street House to pay other lecturers besides himself. We saw that Holyoake was actually making over the profit of his lectures to the House; and when we learn further that this Mr. Johnson had printed funeral cards of his own death in 1856, and had imposed on the clergy an account of his own deathbed conversion, we can hardly be surprised at Holyoake's neglect of his genius. The article in which he attacked Holyoake had first been sent by him to an American paper, and was inserted in the *Investigator* as a reprint from that journal. Bradlaugh wrote in the *Investigator,* and after a time became its editor. In April, moreover, he was elected President (in the place of Holyoake) of the London Secular Society, of which Maughan was the leading spirit.

Wilks apparently relied on G. J. Holyoake's unwillingness to take an oath, and actually appealed for the quashing of the case on the ground that Holyoake would not come into court.

Austin Holyoake did not share his brother's view of the oath—he was not clearly an atheist at the time; and as he was joint-proprietor, and could sue on his own account, he had no hesitation in meeting such repellent knavery with recourse to law. Wilks refused extra-legal arbitration. This is the case on which Holyoake's critics rely when they say that, though G. J. Holyoake would never take an oath, his brother was convenient for that purpose when the business required it. They are careful to omit the details of the one case where this was done. At other times Holyoake suffered serious losses through his refusal to take an oath. In 1860 the printing business became Austin's exclusive property; and in 1861 the publishing business. He could defend it as he liked. In fact, he kept his views to himself, and is said to have been then a Theist.

For our purpose it is enough to note that Holyoake bore himself with unfailing dignity, and that the movement at large made him ample recompense for the pain inflicted on him. Mr. James Robertson (of Manchester) wrote a fiery reply to his critics, and was presented by his colleagues with a gift and address, which deplored "the outrageous defamation of a gentleman whom it is their pride and privilege to hail as leader." The Manchester Society passed, and sent to Holyoake, the following resolutions:

"Resolved, that the Manchester Secular Society, having carefully reviewed the recent allegations in relation to Fleet Street House, hereby express their unaltered conviction of the high personal honour of its Director, and of the great value of the services that House has rendered to English Freethought"

"It was further resolved that this Society considers the conduct of the managers of the *Investigator,* in making and reiterating charges of the grossest description without proof against Mr. G. J. Holyoake, alike unjust and ungentlemanly, and calculated to bring the Secular movement into contempt."

Similar resolutions came to him from the West Riding Secular Alliance, and from many of the branches. The chief

supporters of the movement expressed great sympathy with him. Trevelyan wrote: "I have a thorough belief in your integrity and judgment." But the general feeling of the best part of the movement sought a more emphatic expression. In August 1858 a sum of 642 was presented to Holyoake, in the name of the whole movement, to pay off the debts of the Fleet Street House. Subscriptions came from all parts of the country, and all classes—even, in several instances, from clergymen. At *Secularists and their Slanderers.* the soiree at which the presentation was made a letter was read from Thornton Hunt, which was taken as expressing the feeling of the subscribers. Hunt gave four curt reasons why he wished to attend:

"1. I do not know any other man who so consistently vindicates the right of every opinion to its own free utterance.

"2. I do not know any other man who is so unswervingly firm in paying a candid, courteous, and painstaking attention to the statement of opinions opposed to his own.

"3. I do not know anywhere a more dauntlessly faithful friend.

"4. And you have been assailed."

In October Mr. Bradlaugh began to edit the *Investigator.* Holyoake made courteous reference to the change —the " rivalry in usefulness "—and said he trusted the two journals would co-operate in freethought matters. Bradlaugh, in his first editorial, said: "If we find a rock in our path, we will break it; but we will not quarrel with our brother who deems his proper work to be that of polishing the fragments." Holyoake sold the paper in his shop. Ten months later it came to an end—a sufficient proof of the real size of the new party— and the editor found himself loaded with a heavy debt. The Secular body in the north started a subscription to assist him in discharging it, and at London Holyoake opened his columns for subscriptions to pay off " Iconoclast's printing debts." During the following year he freely inserted in his paper complimentary notices of Bradlaugh's lectures, and remained silent when, in April 1860, Bradlaugh (with the co-operation of Joseph Barker) started the *National Reformer,* and had remarkable experiences from his co-editor. It was not until the spring of 1861, when Bradlaugh offered to take the customary oath in a Wigan court, that Holyoake wrote severely of him. There were differences of opinionamongst the Secularists as to the taking of the oath, but Holyoake held the rigid view as to its impropriety, and suffered much injustice rather than do it. He felt it essential to the character of the movement to resist the injustice of the compulsory oath, and protested that no leader amongst them ought to repeat it.

A few further details will enable us to finish this unfortunate episode. One of the personal charges against Holyoake was that he retained an institution and journal that he had originally promised to make the property of the organisation. The presentation in 1858 shows how frivolous the best men in the movement considered this and the other charges, but there were other reasons than the absence of any other man of like experience and ability. We saw that the initial outlay was very great, and the expected income seriously short of the estimate. As a result Holyoake found himself struggling with heavy debts, and felt bound to clear these before he handed over the Fleet Street House. We can imagine what would have been the cry of his young critics if he had quitted it with a debt of,£1,000 on it. The fund subscribed in 1858 and a further,£500 subscribed in May 1860 enabled him to clear the institution and paper of debt, and he at once begged the party to make it a limited-company concern. The only outcome was the failure of the *Reasoner* (the last issue was on June 30th, 1861) and of the Fleet Street Institution. Holyoake's wealthier friends were merely anxious to see him set free from what had become a grievous burden, and had no Of the works published by him to make his position clear at this time we may note particularly his *Trial of Theism,* his largest Secularist work. A sub-title indicated that he mainly censured Theism "as obstructing secular life." intention of encouraging Secular-

ism in any other form than the one he had advocated. They thought the new school ought to call itself candidly Atheistic, instead of

Secularistic, and wrote strong letters about its more active representatives.

Worn with anxiety, vexation, and many labours,

Holyoake had a serious collapse in 1859. He was ill throughout most of the year, and was badly disfigured with acute eczema. He spent a few weeks at Carshalton in April with Dr. Shorthouse (editor of the *Sporting Times),* and then three weeks at Paris, as the guest of

Horatio Prater. Allsop had great hope of the gaieties and wines of Paris, but the trip does not seem to have done him much good. On his return he became worse, and Mr. Joseph Cowen, with whom he had been in cordial relations since 1851, took him to Newcastle and then to Silloth (on the Solway), where he remained four months. Percy Greg (writing as "Lionel Holdreth ") edited the *Reasoner* during his illness, but quitted the movement—on good terms with Holyoake, but very bad terms with the movement—immediately afterwards. At the same time he heard of the death of the optician, Mr.

Ross—" one of my best friends," he writes in his diary.

He returned to work early in 1860, not wholly recovered, and it was then that the second presentation (of 500) was made to him. Mr. J. G. Crawford was the most active in appealing for subscriptions, and with his were associated the names of Mr. Trevelyan, Col.

Clinton, Mr. J. Cowen, and Mr. Shaen. The extreme generosity and tenderness of his cultivated friends, and the wide response of the Secularist body to their appeal, tempered the pain of seeing a few young men make so unfortunate a use of the organisation he had laboured fifteen years to construct. During the earlier part of 1860 he worked with difficulty, and made frequent use of Vol. 1. x

Turkish baths—a new importation, which he did much to popularise. His interest in Co-operation was rapidly increasing, when he saw the effect of his

Rochdale history. He lectured on the subject everywhere, and had a special section of his journal headed "Co-operative News." The questions of temperance, education, and Sunday recreation also furnished the subjects of a large number of his lectures, and occupied much of the *Reasoner.* His political work continued, and the substitution of an affirmation for an oath began to call for practical work. These things we will resume later. In the early summer of 1860 Italian affairs once more entered on a phase of absorbing interest, and the second half of the year brought him a remarkable and interesting task.

CHAPTER XIV THE GARIBALDI LEGION

In an earlier chapter we saw how the Roman Republic of Mazzini was brought to the dust by the troops of Napoleon III, and Italy fell back into its old position of a mere "geographical expression." The Austrians in the northeast, the papal power in the centre, and the Bourbons at Naples, resumed their sway over the ignorant and distressed peasantry, and sought to extinguish every flicker of manly thought. Garibaldi wandered over the globe; Mazzini grew graver and paler in his cheerless London home. But by the time when Garibaldi returned to Italy from America a new power had arisen in the country. The diplomacy of Cavour had won sympathy and credit for the government of Victor Emmanuel. A small Italian army fought with the French and English troops in the Crimea, and Piedmont was represented at the Peace Congress that closed the war. When an alliance followed between their families, Napoleon III concluded a military alliance with Victor Emmanuel, and in 1859 the war was renewed with Austria.

Garibaldi was summoned by Cavour, and directed to raise a force of volunteers. Piqued at Mazzini's blunders at Rome, and discovering a guarantee of a speedier and more stable unity under the crown of Victor Emmanuel, he fell in with their plans, and led his 3,000 volunteers with brilliant success against the Austrians, in spite of all intrigue and all Cavour's efforts to keep his utility 307 within bounds. But Napoleon III had no idea of seeing an Italian kingdom take its place among the powers of Europe, and a premature peace was concluded. Austria retained Venice; the papal power and the Neapolitan despotism were untouched. Suddenly, while Garibaldi fretted in his home at Caprera, there came the news of rebellion in Sicily. Mazzini's agents had fomented the discontent of the Sicilians, and Neapolitan troops were pouring into the island to suppress the small and scattered bands of insurgents. With the hesitating assistance of Cavour, Garibaldi shipped a thousand of his volunteers at Genoa, and landed in Sicily on May nth to face the Neapolitan army. Within twenty days he had driven it out of the island, and, in spite of the prohibition of Victor Emmanuel, he crossed to the mainland on August 20th, and moved northward toward Naples, his little army swelling every day with local insurgents and volunteers from all parts of Europe. It was in this campaign in Southern Italy that the British Legion intended to take part; and his share in the creation and dispatch of the Legion forms one of the most adventurous of Holyoake's experiences.

In September 1856 the *Reasoner* published the fact that a fund was being gathered at Genoa for the purpose of buying 10,000 rifles for the first Italian province that should rise against its rulers. Holyoake offered to receive subscriptions. There is little more about Italian matters until June 1860, when the news of Garibaldi's campaign in Sicily reaches England, and fresh appeals are made for subscriptions. In August he announces that a Garibaldian officer, Captain Styles, has reached London to raise men and money, and he urges suitable men to volunteer, and offers his shop as a recruiting-room. By the beginning of September a committee of the " Garibaldi Fund" is announced, with Holyoake as secretary; and in the heart of London, in spite of Foreign Enlistment Acts, a group of business men with military advice organise a regiment for Garibaldi, equip it, and send it out in two vessels to Sicily. With all the documents before me, and after some

research, I am able to tell the interesting story of this British Legion in full for the first time.

There were Englishmen fighting under Garibaldi in the campaign of 1859. Mr. Peard, a Cornish gentleman of Italian sympathies, was made a colonel by him, and was long known as " Garibaldi's Englishman." Others joined him in Sicily. Colonel Dunne commanded a regiment of Palermitans, and Major Wyndham, Colonel Forbes, and other officers had commissions. Garibaldi felt himself to have the sympathies of England in a remarkable degree. The echoes of Gladstone's terrible impeachment of the King of the Sicilies still lingered in the country. Lord John Russell favoured Garibaldi's raid; and when his soldiers were landing at Marsala, and often afterwards when they marched near the coast, English warships lazily sailed between them and the guns of the Neapolitan cruisers. English captains freely gave their men leave to spend a few hours ashore, and refrained from seeing the wounds that they brought back with them to the ship. Garibaldi gratefully calls himself " the Benjamin of these lords of the ocean." He needed little pressure to authorise the raising of a special brigade in England. Colonel Forbes speaks of pointing out to him on July 28th the moral and material support such an addition to his troops would mean, but Garibaldi had already, on July 26th, sent one of his English officers to England with this note in his pocket:

"I give my authorisation to collect volunteers to come out to fight for the liberties of this people. The noble and courageous bearing shown by the Englishmen who shared with us the dangers and the glories of this campaign induce me to this resolution."

Garibaldi was then, just after the battle of Melazzo, in the early stress of his campaign, and seems merely to have meant that he would like the officer to induce many more English volunteers to make their way out, as Peard and Wyndham had done. He certainly did not foresee that his hastily-scribbled note would cost him 10,000. But he had made a serious blunder in his choice of

a representative, and that blunder trails over the whole story of the British Legion.

On August nth a young, bronzed, soldierly-looking man presented himself at Holyoake's shop, handed a letter of introduction from Captain de Rohan (one of Garibaldi's aides-de-camp, and known to Holyoake), and showed his note of authorisation. Holyoake had met Garibaldi in London in 1854, at a dinner at Stansfeld's, and was now following his expedition with the warmest interest. He at once took the young officer across the street to the editor of the *Daily News,* and his mission and purpose were announced on the following day and copied into the provincial papers. The magic of Garibaldi's name drew hundreds of volunteers, and the mere prospect of an adventurous time in Italy brought many hundred more reckless and courageous young men from all parts of the country. Holyoake was just starting on a provincial tour. He offered the use of his premises to the recruiter, and flung himself into the work of inspiring enthusiasm. When he returned he found his shop crowded with young men, and a "Captain Minchin" installed in the Political Exchange above the shop to examine candidates. Fleet Street looked on in amazement at this open violation of the Foreign Enlistment Act, but Holyoake had little alarm. His brother had written to him in the provinces:

"Styles leaves London for Sicily himself in the morning. He was with Lord John Russell this morning, and has a special message to the General. Sir Charles Napier took him. On Thursday I wrote to Sir Charles, making an appointment for Friday. Captain Styles saw him, and important results are likely to follow."

Further, in reply to questions in the House—for the London friends of Austria and Naples were not blind —Lord Palmerston had replied that the Government had no power to prevent a party of English gentlemen, however numerous, from going to witness the performances of Mount Etna.

But the energetic "Captain Styles

"was already in deeper water than was suitable for him. The history of Garibaldi's emissary would be interesting, if it were available. He bore as many names as he did medals, and they proved in time to be equally genuine. He appeared in different places as Edward Styles, Edward Steigel, Charles Smith, and Hugo de Bartholdy. The last was probably nearest to the mark, as he confessed under trial at Naples that he was a Dane, and his experience had been obtained in a large grocer's shop in the Borough! It was enough for Garibaldi that he was a good fighter, and, in fact, he was gazetted with especial distinction afterwards by Colonel Peard. But his business instincts revived in his new employment. Within the first week of his arrival he made contracts for arms and equipment to the extent of 4,000, deducting remarkable sums for himself, and sold commissions in the forming regiment to a number of officers, or would-be officers. As the English fund in the charge of Mr. Ashurst only amounted to a few hundreds—nearly three thousand pounds having been sent on to Genoa— the situation was critical. Captain Styles had, therefore, gone to receive instructions from Garibaldi.

Thus Holyoake found his premises inundated with volunteers and a fine chance of aiding Garibaldi about to be thrown away. He summoned his friends to counsel, and found a number of them equally disposed to help. As Styles wired from Messina that he had seen Garibaldi, and it was "all right," they concluded that the expenses would be guaranteed from Italy, and they formed a "Garibaldi Fund Committee." Mr. Crawford, M.P., was chairman, Mr. Ashurst (solicitor to the Post Office) treasurer, and Mr. Leverson, Captain de Carteret, and other experienced business or military men joined it; while Holyoake was engaged as secretary at a salary of five guineas a week—a fee that was amply earned. One interesting member of the Committee was a pale and handsome young man who gave the name of "Captain Sarsfield "—a name they were destined to hear much of in the months to come. He was Lord Seymour, son of the Duchess of Somerset.

The only business the Committee professed to undertake was that of raising funds in support of Garibaldi's military workers, but they found that they had to go beyond this sphere, if any expedition was to start at all. Not only did suspicions reach them in regard to "Captain Styles," but the "Captain Minchin"— military titles sprang up like mushrooms amongst the Garibaldians abroad—he had left as his deputy was little better. A pathetic letter came to them from Clonmel, from a lady who wanted to know if they had "anney news of her cruell husband," and they had to pension Mrs. Minchin. The husband was eventually found to have made handsome profits out of his work. There were now hundreds of applicants for places in the contingent, and Styles had promised most of them immediate dispatch, and a wage of at least a shilling a day (Garibaldi's troops were getting a few centesimi a day).

The Committee was therefore forced into some share in the military arrangements. Holyoake drew up a number of blood-red tickets, written in the spirit of Palmerston's remark, and scattered them broadcast. One of them runs:

"GARIBALDI EXCURSION TO SOUTH ITALY.

"A select party of English Excursionists intends to visit South Italy. As the country is somewhat unsettled, the Excursionists will be furnished with means of selfdefence, and, with a view of recognising each other, will be attired in a picturesque and uniform costume. General Garibaldi has liberally granted the Excursionists a free passage to Sicily and Italy, and they will be supplied with refreshments and attire suitable for the climate. Information to be obtained at Captain Edward Styles's offices, 8 Salisbury Street, Strand, W.C."

They had installed the recruiters in Salisbury Street, where the police genially overlooked the troops of athletic excursionists and ex-Crimean soldiers who crowded there. About a thousand were selected from the 1,500 applicants—the number could easily have been doubled or trebled—and

Holyoake's work became heavy. Applications from volunteers, applications from volunteers' friends for help or information, notes and bills of contractors, etc., came in showers; but all this was nothing to the angry correspondence that was soon opened with Naples, and the mass of work entailed by the return of the volunteers. As he wrote freely in his own journal of the purpose of the expedition, he says that there was some threat of a prosecution. In other journals he usually wrote of the " Excursion " under the name of " Landor Praed." "Landor" was a tribute to the aged poet, W. S. Landor, who was in friendly correspondence with him at the time. "I'raed" was taken casually from a Praed Street bus. A sonnet that Landor wrote for him on the struggle must be reproduced here:

The two chief reasons that moderated the first enthusiasm of the Italians for the British contingent were the delay in sending it and its enormous expense. All else was sheer calumny, and was put right after painful struggles. But the London Committee could not be held responsible for either the delay or the expense. Probably military authorities will allow that it was no small thing for such a Committee in such circumstances to form a corps of "800 picked men, magnificently equipped," as the Italians described them, in less than a month. Had ships been available, they would have been in Italy before the end of September. As to the cost, Holyoake was told afterwards that our own military authorities could not have done the work for so little. Some of the contractors, whom Styles had engaged, tried to impose on the Committee. At one meeting a Mr. Bate presented certificates of the efficiency of weapons supplied, when Mr. Crawford detected that they were forged, and snatched them from him. A struggle ensued, but the man knew they dare not bring in the police. All the arms, etc., were ordered of the finest quality. Styles had contracted for 600, and the Committee had to provide a corresponding outfit for the remainder. The shipowners, seeing that the payment was to be by drafts on

Garibaldi, demanded a sum proportionate to the risk. The men grew restive in London, and many were forced to seek employment. Nearly 300 of the applicants joined the British army, and 200 more had to be maintained in London by the Committee. In the end the "Emperor" had only 550 to convey, yet had to be paid for the 800 who had been enrolled. Thus the cost was unavoidably increased, and as the Committee dare not appeal too openly, and the time was short, they could raise only about .ooo. The chartering of steamers was a work of difficulty and delicacy for such an "excursion." Fortunately, as the Committee thought, another Garibaldian officer now arrived from Italy, as well as Styles. "Captain de Rohan " was another of the melodramatic characters in the play. I find him described in a letter to Garibaldi as the General's " naval aide-de-camp"—a quaint phrase —and within a few weeks he transformed himself into "Rear-admiral de Rohan" (possibly because he was believed to be the illegitimate son of Admiral Dalgren). He was a man of fiery energy, his American-skipper habits of bluff and audacity touched with the sun of Sicily and a genuine zeal for the cause. Within a week he had 260 men shipped on the "Melazzo " and out at sea. Holyoake witnessed their departure, and announced it in the *Daily News.* A larger steamer was chartered for the remaining 800, but as the " Emperor" was still at sea, and was delayed by an accident to its machinery, the 800 thinned to 550 before she was ready for them. There was no cowardice and no lack of fine men, but they were chiefly men who lived from hand to mouth, and many had to seek employment. At last, towards the close of September, Holyoake and a few others witnessed the departure of the last 550 at Shoreditch station. The Committee chose the quiet station and the early hour (5 a.m.) in order to spare the feelings of the Government and police, but the gay De Rohan strutted boldly about the platforms in a gorgeous admiral's uniform, trailing a long and ponderous admiral's sword behind him.

"S1car1a.
"Again her brow Sicaria rears
Above the tombs. Two thousand years
Have smitten sore her beauteous breast,
And war forbidden her to rest.

Yet war at last becomes her friend,
And shouts aloud
`Thy grief shall end.
Sicaria! hear me! Rise again!
A homeless hero breaks thy chain.'"
I repeat this with hesitation. The entire expense, including money appropriate-cf, seems to have been nearly £15,000. The chief item was the transport. They had to pay for the conveyance of 1,050 men (for a reason we shall see afterwards) and four Whitworth guns (presented by a group of Manchester men), at from five to six pounds a head. Then there were uniforms and equipment for 850 men, and rifles and revolvers, etc., for 600. All equipment was of the finest quality obtainable, supplied by the London Armoury and other firms.
Mr. Ashurst had sent £2,750 to Genoa before Styles came, and a further thousand was collected later. The total sum collected and paid by Mr. Ashurst in connection with this campaign was— I have his MS. balance sheet—£5,614 *1s.* cjrf. Mr. Hodge lent the Committee £1,000 for immediate purposes.
One last accident—one that was to have serious consequences—occurred at Harwich. The Committee had summoned one of Styles's officers, " Major Beach Hicks," to account for sums of money entrusted to him, and his explanation was "so unsatisfactory and marked with so much prevarication " that they decided to dismiss him. De Rohan explained the situation to the officers, when all were on board at Harwich, and they all signed a demand for his expulsion. He was removed with difficulty—with force, in fact—and he at once denounced the "excursion" to the local magistrates and to the officers of the "Pembroke," which lay off Harwich. But British officers in those days were familiar with Nelson's trick at Copenhagen. The "Emperor" steamed off on September 30th, and a telegram was sent to Colonel Peard to say that a man was coming with "complete evi-

dence that Hicks is a swindler." Finding little opportunity for mischief at Harwich, Hicks went straight to Sicily, and started the complaints and calumnies about the British contingent that have so much obscured its brief history. In this he had a willing auxiliary in Lord Seymour. "Captain Sarsfield" also had gone to Sicily, and from there he wrote letters of so haughty and impertinent a character to the Committee that they struck his name off their books. He remained in Italy, and helped to mislead the English press and the Italians in regard to the expedition.
The "Emperor" picked up the "Melazzo" at Cagliari, and both proceeded to Palermo, and on to Naples. Garibaldi had taken Naples on September 7th, and put an end to the reign of the Bourbons. But Francis II mustered his army once more at Gaeta, and marched southward with 30,000 men. Garibaldi had now 15,000 men, his red-shirted northerners being lost in a motley army of blue-bloused Neapolitans and English sailors (on leave or desertion—"desertion has become epidemic," the London papers announced), and volunteers from all lands, with General Heber's Hungarian brigade. The chief army lay before Capua, which was held by the Neapolitan and Papal troops, when Colonel Peard and the "British Legion " landed at Naples, and marched up the town amidst a shower of flowers and through brilliant lines of bunting. They "fairly astonished the Italians, who were not used to such giants," said the correspondent of the *Daily News.* "Ottocenti Inglesi, scelti uomini, tutti stupendamente equipaggiati, sono arrivati a Napoli" (Eight hundred English, picked men, all magnificently equipped, have reached Naples) was wired to Garibaldi at Caserta, and he ordered their immediate advance to the front.
The actual service of the British Legion, as it was called the moment it was clear of the English coast, does not properly concern us, but I may tell of their "firebaptism," and dismiss the rest in a line. They reached Naples on October 16th. On the afternoon of the 17th they marched into the lines before Ca-

pua, amidst great enthusiasm. Garibaldi, telling them "it was the proudest moment of his life that he had under him a Legion of the free children of England," gave them a position in the advance line on the extreme left, close to Capua, and within an hour of their arrival in camp they were in action. A Neapolitan brigade swooped on them at once from Capua. With a ringing cheer they spread out to receive them, and poured in so effective a fire— two or three companies charging with the bayonet—that the Neapolitans turned and fled. Ensign Tucker, an English artist who had joined them at Naples, fell dead at their head, and two privates were killed and eight severely wounded. The Neapolitan artillery then turned on them, and Colonel Peard drew them under cover. But the engagement lasted some five hours, and the Neapolitan brigade was driven back into the town. Colonel Peard reported to Garibaldi that every man fought with the most remarkable coolness and bravery, and it was only with hesitation that he singled out for special mention—the young grocer from the Borough I

The war-correspondents, English and French, are quite agreed that the Legion fought with the utmost bravery and effectiveness. The only defects of the men were the carelessness with which they exposed themselves and the difficulty of restraining them when restraint was advisable. A Parisian correspondent wrote to his paper that they had "thrashed the Royalists so soundly that they would never forget the Enfield bayonets." A regiment of Bersaglieri— the Piedmontese troops were now taking over the war—fought near the Legion, but those fine and seasoned companies did not eclipse them. Garibaldi addressed them with enthusiasm. He was genuinely astonished to see a regiment of young men, most of whom had never seen the muzzle of a rifle pointed at them before, behave so splendidly. In thanking Mr. Ashurst afterwards, he wrote:

"They came late. But they made ample amends for this defect, not their own, by the brilliant courage they dis-

played in the slight engagements they shared with us near the Volturno, which enabled me to judge how precious an assistance they would have rendered us had the war of liberation remained longer in my hands. In every way the English volunteers were a proof of the goodwill borne by your noble nation towards the liberty and independence of Italy."

And in his memoirs he says of them:

"The coming of the English contingent, which, though late in arriving, gave excellent proof of its mettle in the last actions on the plains of Capua, was greatly due to his exertions. If Bonaparte and the Sardinian monarchy had not prohibited our march on Rome after the battle of the Volturno, the English contingent, whose numbers increased every day, would have greatly helped us in winning the immortal capital of Italy. "

It is more than probable that, if Garibaldi had been permitted to fight his way to Rome, we should have to write a long and honourable chronicle of the British Legion, and the lateness of its arrival and cost of its equipment would have been forgotten in Italy. But the engagements on the Volturno were the last of the war. While all Europe watched with astonishment Garibaldi's progress through a country long cowed into servility, where every priest was still a spy of the Bourbons, there were three men who followed it with a peculiar interest. Napoleon III knew that Rome was his objective, and dare not, if he would, withdraw his protection of the Papacy. Cavour was bound to wait on the policy of France, and was equally determined to secure Garibaldi's conquests for the Sardinian monarchy. To him Garibaldi was "the revolution personified," and his Dictatorship in the south must not last long. The third man, Mazzini, looked to Garibaldi for a chance of erecting in Sicily what the General called his "mystic Utopia." The situation was brought to a close in November, when Garibaldi, having taken a plebiscite in the province he ruled as Dictator, handed over the power to Victor Emmanuel, and departed, heavy

with sorrow, for his island-home at Caprera. There were those who recalled Napoleon's abandonment of his army in Egypt, but retreat was Garibaldi's only possible course. Yet it was the close of the brilliant phase of his career; and it left the British Legion in a position that exposed it lamentably to ridicule and calumny.

He refers to Col. Peard—a quite unmerited compliment to that brave soldier. But to appreciate fully this second stage of the troubles of the London Committee we must retrace our steps a little. The very night before the "Emperor" sailed from Harwich, Holyoake received a disquieting letter from Colonel Peard. It hinted at the sale of commissions and expressed surprise at the enormous expense that had been incurred. Lord Seymour was by this time in Naples, and was acting as secretary to Peard. Holyoake had to dissociate the Committee from Styles, and disavow all knowledge of military appointments. In a few days an impertinent letter reached the Committee from Lord Seymour, and he was struck off the books. There was clearly trouble at Naples. Very soon it was learned that "Major Hicks" was busy in that town, and Peard's tone became stiffer. A contractor, who had presented a draft on Garibaldi for.£5,000, and got it signed by the General, was refused payment. Further letters stated that Lord Seymour had reviewed the men on their arrival, and addressed to them '' the most foul and unwarrantable aspersions " on the character of De Rohan. Styles was under arrest, and was to be court-martialled. Even De Rohan was put under arrest, but was quickly released. "We have been jockeyed by Hicks after all," Mr. Crawford wrote to Holyoake. When, on November 1st, the *Daily News* inserted a paragraph from Colonel Peard to the effect that the affairs of the Committee were to be strictly investigated, their indignation was very great.

It fell to Holyoake again to expose the intrigues and to disentangle the affairs of the Legion, though Mr. Crawford was now equally active. They relied on De Rohan to moderate the trouble at Naples, where "everybody was challenging everybody to a duel," one correspondent says, and the common talk at a *table-d'hote* was "honour and pistols." De Rohan, after narrowly escaping arrest in France, reached Naples on October 19th. He found Hicks, whom he had had thrown out of the ship at Harwich three weeks before, "cutting a swell in uniform as Lieut.-Colonel," Seymour denouncing him (De Rohan) as "a swindler and impostor," and, as his drafts were dishonoured, a responsibility for £10,000 hanging over him. Colonel Peard was entirely in the hands of the critics, and Garibaldi's Italian ministers were only too willing to believe stories that tended to relieve them from such heavy payments. The English quarters now presented a livelier spectacle than ever, and Garibaldi's ears were wearied with their explanations. "He seems much older, and is growing grey fast," said De Rohan. "Poor fellow, he ate no breakfast this morning... he seems broken-hearted." A few days later he wrote: "As for the General, he is no longer the same man. Vol. 1. Y

He refuses to see Mazzini, or Crispi, or any one, or to read any letters, or to go into any business whatever. In fact, Cavour has triumphed, and G. G. falls."

When De Rohan offered Garibaldi his heap of justificatory documents, he wearily said: "I cannot— I am worn out. Take Vecchi, and settle with him." He handed Major Vecchi his credential, and the Italian told him it was a worthless bit of paper. Who *was* this Ashurst, etc.? Vecchi had information that the London Committee had received £30,000 from Glasgow alone! "Major Styles" (at liberty once more), "Lt.Col. Hicks," and "Captain Sarsfield" were in high favour. They had at one time sixteen officers of the Legion under arrest. These were the men who supplied the reports about the Legion to the British correspondents at the time. Poor De Rohan—adventurer enough, certainly, but apparently honest, and devoted to Garibaldi —protests that he has to keep his room all day lest he murder one of them. Mazzini was disposed to help, but he was "living four-stair up in a miser-

able street, and dare not go out by daylight." Peard—"a Cornish attorney, two years in an asylum," De Rohan says— who was certainly brave on the field, cut a sorry figure off it; his mismanagement and excessive eagerness to obtain command of the Legion were responsible for most of the trouble.

I will not follow the Neapolitan farce through all its acts, but will be content to quote the last scene from De Rohan's nervous script (December 15th):

"Yesterday, at 3 p.m., the gallant Peard, surrounded by his staff, conspicuous among whom stood the 'Countess della Torre' (or Whorre, as Dowling calls her), with as sweet a collection of quidnuncs, little souls, runaway debtors, would-be-somebodies, and dandily-dressed but most useless officers—together with one or two sympathising friends of the 'late' Lord St. Maur Seymour, alias Sarsfield—such as Danby Seymour, M.P., and his brother, Sir Geo. L'Estrange, and Major the honourable Stuart Wortley—led 230 or 250, no one knoweth which, on board the 'Melazzo'—Lieutenants Drury, Walker, and Chippendale in command. I was advised not to go on board, but they know me not. So, dragging Hodge along, I tumbled like a bomb down into the cabin, to the amazement of Peard and Co., roared out for the steward, and eat a hearty lunch. At 5 p.m., seeing it was getting late, and that paying the men would occupy five or six hours (for the gallant Peard would not trust them with money ashore), I took command *plump,* and steered the little screw around the English fleet; and as I rounded to under the stern successively of the 'Renown,' 'Hannibal,' ' Queen,' and 'Cressy,' stopped her, and with a 'Now, boys, three cheers for old England,' made the whole harbour and woods ring again, to which all the fleet responded by dipping their ensigns, a rare honour. I then turned her head back toward the mole, and, as night had set in, shook hands with nearly all the men, took their letters, and bade them 'God-speed' for a freer land and happier hearths. As I shoved off with Hodge, the good lads, which they are, set up a cheer which did

not die away till I was out of sight."

It is unfortunate that the volatile De Rohan describes them a fortnight later as "the most complete set of scoundrels that ever went unhung." Hodge also wrote that in Naples one heard references sometimes to "the Brutish Legion." But Hodge loved spicy gossip, and had some anxiety about his thousand pounds. An adventurous trip of the kind they had embarked on would be sure to attract a few whose courage was greater than their sobriety. However, Cavour had rung down the curtain on the Neapolitan comedy. The men were giyejj.160 francs each (six months' pay) and sent home at the expense of his Government. Hodge received his thousand pounds. De Rohan followed Garibaldi, who evidently liked him, to Turin, and got his drafts signed by the General and paid by the Government. Garibaldi, infinitely weary, retired to Caprera, and for two years tried to forget Italy, Cavour, Mazzini, and everybody. But he sent Holyoake an autographed portrait with the following note:

"Caprera, 7 January, 1861. "sir,

"I fulfil with pleasure the duty of thanking you for all that you have generously done for the Italian cause, and at the same time beg you to believe me with all esteem, yours,

"G. Garibaldi."

The last act in the life of the " Garibaldi Fund Committee " opened on January 14th, 1861, when a troop of the Legionists landed in London, mostly penniless, scantily clothed, and irritable with cold and poor feeding. They naturally laid siege to 147 Fleet Street. Their clothes had been left on the " Melazzo " on changing steamers; their money either spent before they started, or exhausted in buying additional food on board. Many wanted arrears of pay, and most of them wanted their train-fare home. Holyoake pointed out that the Sardinian Government had assumed responsibility for this, in taking the victory out of Garibaldi's hands. The siege was transferred to the houses of the Sardinian minister and consul, and Cavour telegraphed instructions to pay them.

But for months afterwards Holyoake was engaged in correspondence about the Legion. He has given in *Sixty Years* (ch. lxxvi) a discreet account of his trouble with "a strange treasurer of Garibaldi." The banker whom he there calls Mr. Marvell was Mr. Durnton Lupton, of Leeds. There is no evidence of improper intent on his part. He had received upwards of 400 towards the Garibaldi Fund, and was very unwilling to hand it over to Ashurst, the central treasurer, who applied for it. Mr. Crawford also fruitlessly applied for it, and Mr. Lupton still refused when an explicit instruction was sent him from Garibaldi, who was then back at Caprera. Holyoake went to Leeds, industriously spread the news of the detention of the money amongst the subscribers in the town, and then called on Mr. Lupton. A cheque for 411 went to Ashurst at once. Ashurst suggests that Lupton "has been bitten by Urquhart or Ironsides, and believes that all moneys collected for Garibaldi are handed over to Lord Palmerston for Russian purposes. " There were treasurers who believed this.

His growing dislike of Mazzini gave concern in England. The press had published in 1859 a letter in which he called Mazzini "a coward," and said that Kossuth was "bought by the tyrants." De Rohan asked him in Caprera, at Holyoake's request, if it was genuine. Holyoake did not publish the reply, which was: "Yes, I did write it, and I think as I wrote."

Another source of trouble was that sixty of the volunteers were left at Gibraltar by the steamer that should have brought them home. They were eventually conveyed to England by the home Government. The affairs of the first Committee ended with a last pyrotechnic correspondence from De Rohan, who threatened to "expose everything" because Ashurst hesitated to pay some bill of his. But in October 1861 Holyoake announced a "new Italian committee" in his new paper, the *Counsellor.* The "Garibaldi Italian Unity Committee " included many well-known names (Cowen, Page Hopps, Trevelyan, Stansfeld, Beales, Dr. Epps, Shaen, etc.) besides some of the old ones; but it was content to gather funds, and Holyoake had no conspicuous part in it.

It may be accounted a triumph that only some 20 out of the 800 wrote letters of complaint in the press. I have many letters asking for a place in a second enrolment.

To conclude his relations with Garibaldi we must pass on to the General's visit to England in 1864. The visit was suggested to Garibaldi in 1861, and had attraction for him; but Holyoake and others represented it as inadvisable at that time. One of the obituary notices of Garibaldi (written, I think, by Holyoake) describes him as "a lion in the field, but a *bambino* in politics." However, Garibaldi made a fresh raid in South Italy in 1862, with Rome as his objective. This time his progress was arrested by Victor Emmanuel's army, and he himself received a bullet from a Piedmontese rifle. This did not improve the political situation, but friends continued to press him, and he started for England. The splendour and enthusiasm of the reception accorded to him have become historic, and need not be described in detail. From the moment he landed at Southampton he was greeted with ovations that befitted an English conqueror, and the whole country showered invitations on him. There are only two episodes of the time that call for notice here: an unfortunate experience of Holyoake's in connection with the visit, and the cause of its sudden termination, which is still somewhat of a mystery.

It need hardly be said that Garibaldi landed into a network of jealousies and intrigues at Southampton. The numerous "friends of Italy" in this country had the disadvantage of not being friends of each other. One party, headed by Colonel Chambers, boarded his vessel below the Needles, and tried to capture him, but were shaken off; though Colonel Chambers became, in some unexplained way, his "secretary," and dealt discreetly with all letters (including Holyoake's) addressed to him. Nearer shore Mr. Seely, M.P., was ready to board his vessel; and the Southampton Corporation had a third claim. He decided to enjoy the honours of the Corporation and the hospitality of Mr. Seely; while he found himself under the tutelage of gentlemen from London whose names and efforts had not hitherto reached him.

Holyoake went down to Southampton with various credentials. He went as a press-representative *(Leader, Morning Star,* and *Newcastle Chronicle)* ; he was deputed by the Society of the Friends of Italy to bring about an interview between Mazzini and Garibaldi, and supply information to the General; he had important letters from old friends to Garibaldi, and many invitations to press upon him; and he was personally acquainted, as few were, with the General, and had done such service for him as still fewer had done. Garibaldi himself said to Mr. Stansfeld that Holyoake was "the person he was most interested in seeing in England." But the "infidel " was not welcome to many of those crowding about Garibaldi, and there were unpleasant efforts made to keep him aloof. Mr. Seely invited him to dine at Brooke House (Isle of Wight) on the night of Garibaldi's arrival there from Southampton, and he had many hours with the General during the week. But the optician, Mr. Negretti, who was prominent amongst the committee sent by the Italians living in London, made an extraordinary attack on Holyoake, partly on account of his heresies and partly because he was a warm Mazzinian. He persuaded Mr. Seely that the company of the heretic would compromise Garibaldi in the metropolis, and obtained from him authority to remove Holyoake from the London train, in the press-carriage of which This remarkable tribute was only told to Holyoake in 1896, by Professor Masson, who heard it. See *Bygones,* I, 231.

Holyoake naturally had a place. He entrusted this work to the station-master at Micheldever station, who very zealously carried it out. Mr. Forster, who had twice previously entertained Holyoake, was on the platform, but he turned away when Holyoake asked him to interfere. Negretti, who was urging the station-master to act, declared in a passion that his chief reason was that Holyoake had sent word to the papers about the friendly meeting between Mazzini and Garibaldi *Leader,* August 13th, 1864). Holyoake was permitted to resume his seat on promising to leave the train privately at Nine Elms. In point of fact, the police would not allow him to leave the station at Nine Elms, where the General detrained, by any other than the main entrance, and he was forced after all into the procession of carriages, and shared the five-hours' triumphal march.

An indignant correspondence followed, which we need not linger over. Mazzini begged him to overlook the matter on the ground that "Negretti is, in intellect, tendencies, and manners, belonging to that class of men whom I call' irresponsible.'" Several papers commented severely on it, and Washington Wilks (of the *Daily News)* attacked Mr. Forster with warmth at the House. Mr. Forster wrote to Holyoake a feeble and evasive note, pleading that he knew only that there was a dispute between him and Mr. Negretti "as to railway arrangements," and had " no power to interfere." It was many years before Holyoake could overlook his conduct entirely, though after a time Forster apologised. Negretti took the bold line (to Mr. Seely) that he "was determined to prevent such a man as Mr. Holyoake from taking the General in hand," but he found occasion to leave the country when the Garibaldi Reception Committee called upon him for an explanation. Garibaldi's son, Menotti, was very indignant, and took the first opportunity of publicly associating with Holyoake. A short time afterwards Major Woolf wrote to Holyoake:

"Mr. Negretti got a rebuke from Menotti Garibaldi because he had the impudence to speak not respectfully of you under the pretence that you are an atheist. I had not yet the opportunity of speaking to the General of Mr. Negretti's shameful behaviour to you, but I shall take the first I can find. I already told the story to Menotti, who was highly indignant at it."

We may conclude with Holyoake's view of the cause of Garibaldi's sudden withdrawal from England. The procession from Nine Elms to the Duke of Sutherland's house passed between princely hedges of enthusiasts. In the rooms at Stafford House crowds of people, from every section of society, jostled each other in their eagerness to greet the revolutionary soldier, in his blood-red shirt and crimson silk scarf. Nearly every large town in the kingdom begged the honour of a visit from him. In the midst of all the excitement a physician, Mr. Ferguson, published a letter that questioned, with apparent gravity, whether Garibaldi's health would be equal to the exactions of the formidable programme of receptions and dinners that was being written for him. Mr. Gladstone, then Chancellor of the Exchequer, had a private conversation with the General. At once the whole programme was cancelled, and Garibaldi returned to Caprera. Nor did he ever care afterwards to dwell on his visit to England.

The known facts fitted so easily into a theory that the Government had asked Garibaldi to leave, that some of the Tory newspapers on the one hand, and many radicals on the other, were not slow to inform the working men of London that the Government had "truckled to the French Emperor." Other writers held, and still hold, that Garibaldi personally shrank from the ordeal of honour that awaited him. Holyoake has written *(Bygones,* I, 241) that he asked Sir James Stansfeld, who was in the intimacy of Garibaldi and of Gladstone at the time, about it, and Sir James (a warm friend of Holyoake's) said "that no foreign suggestion had been made, and that nothing whatever had been said to Garibaldi." Holyoake adds, however, that on reading Mr. Morley's account of the matter, in his *Life of Gladstone,* one would be inclined to think "that Garibaldi did not require much imagination to see that he was not wanted to stay in England." The papers he has left on the subject, though they contain no revelation, make this apparent.

I have related in a previous chapter how, on one occasion, Garibaldi described himself as "an atheist." He probably had no rigid convictions on the matter, and wavered. His proclamations in 1860 use religious language. Mr. Morley says that Gladstone was much troubled about his unbelief.

That Garibaldi should tell an Italian friend, as the manuscript notes say, that he left because he thought fit to do so, without instigation, proves nothing in regard to a diplomatic episode. It is known that Mr. Gladstone received a deputation on the subject from the working men of the metropolis. He explained to them that, when the physician's letter appeared, he had a consultation on the matter with the Duke of Sutherland, the Earl of Shaftesbury, Colonel Peard, General Eber, Mr. Seely, Mr. Negretti, and Mr. Stansfeld. They decided that Garibaldi's programme ought to be limited, in the interest of his health. Gladstone begged that the decision should be conveyed to him by personal friends, but they returned to say that the General wished to see Gladstone. He accordingly went to see Garibaldi, and merely expressed to him the solicitude of them all for his health in view of the heavy list of engagements before him.

Mr. Joseph Cowen gives a different version of this meeting, and declares that he had it from Garibaldi, with whom he was intimate. I will copy his version from a manuscript in Holyoake's writing (which does not seem to have been published at the time):

"Mr. Cowen was asked by the Working Men's Garibaldi Committee at London to give an account of his interview with the General on the matter of his departure. Mr. Cowen wrote from Stella House, Blaydon on Tyne, saying: 'What I understand passed between Mr. Gladstone and Garibaldi was this. Mr. Gladstone said: "If the same kind of demonstrations are repeated in the provinces that have taken place in London, they may damage the effect of your visit and lead to unpleasant complications." Garibaldi said: "Then I understand that you wish me to leave?" Mr. Gladstone said: " Yes." The General said: "Then I give you my word and that? I will go."

"'I Cowen said there was a general impression abroad that the request for him to leave came from the Government, and that it was the popular belief that the " complications" referred to were political. He said he knew that such was the belief that was generally entertained. He thought it was correct, that the Government did wish him to leave, and that as they (the Government) had received and treated him with so much kindness, he could not remain to be a source of inconvenience.

"' The conversation was in English, which the General does not speak very fluently. But if I have not reported the exact words that were used, I am quite certain I have reported the sense.'"

Holyoakethen wrote to draw Mr. Gladstone's attention to Cowen's statements. His secretary replied:

"s1r,

"The Chancellor of the Exchequer desires me to acknowledge the receipt of your letter of May 26th, and to thank you for the expression of your trust in his word.

"He adheres in full to his statements. No such word as complications was ever used by him. Nor did General Garibaldi ever ask Mr. Gladstone if he wished him to leave; nor did he allude in the faintest manner to his leaving, nor was there any allusion to the Government throughout the conversation.

"I am, Sir,

"Your obedient servant,

"C. L. Ryan."

The word "complications" may be sacrificed. It has many diplomatic equivalents. The only formal contradiction is in the statement that Gladstone made no allusion whatever to Garibaldi's departure. But this is a formidable contradiction. Mr. Morley has quoted a private letter of Mr. Gladstone's to Lord Clarendon, which strongly confirms his own judgment that nothing was said. In that letter Mr. Gladstone expresses concern that Garibaldi should have put the interpretation he did on his words, and not have openly told it to him. As Mr. Morley seems to know the other version

of their conversation only as a statement made by an anonymous lady, it is quite natural for him to regard it as unworthy of serious consideration.

Cowen's precise and repeated statement reopens the matter, and, I fear, will leave it open. Cowen was a zealous, a fiery politician, it is true, but a man of rigid veracity and honour, and Garibaldi's best friend in England. He described the conversation to Holyoake only a few days after he heard it from Garibaldi, and in a second letter to Holyoake (on May 31st), which he marks "Private," he insists that he has correctly reported Garibaldi's words to him. He speaks of a manuscript pamphlet by Mr. P. A. Taylor, M.P., in which his version is incorporated, and says that Mr. Shaen has the same account of the conversation. But Cowen is "heartily sick of the entire business," and wants the pamphlet suppressed, as it seems to have been.

There is thus no serious ground to doubt that Garibaldi told Cowen, his intimate friend, that Gladstone expressed a wish for his departure. The terms of the conversation he might forget, but such a man as Cowen could not forget or alter the important substance of it within a week. Holyoake does not help us to reconcile the contradiction. One note he has left stresses the fact that Gladstone was a man of honour; but another note insists that Garibaldi met all his honours with perfect composure, and seems to mean that there was no ground whatever for anxiety about his health; and a third note observes that more courts in Europe than those of Paris and Rome were "mad" at Garibaldi's triumph. On the other hand, we do not know that Gladstone read his secretary's letter and endorsed its terms. However, the contradiction is irreconcilable, and I leave it to the reader. He may prefer to strike a balance of statements. Certainly, Gladstone would not speak as an envoy of the Cabinet, and certainly he would not talk boldly of "complications." But Garibaldi's account of what he did say, told immediately afterwards to an experienced man of business and politics, is a much

greater mystery than his departure, if there is no truth in it. Shortly after Garibaldi's departure Holyoake began to issue the *English Leader.* In the first three issues he deals with this question. In these articles he insists emphatically that Garibaldi was in excellent health, and was assured by two physicians whom he consulted that there was no ground for anxiety. Negretti—whom he describes as "alleged to be an agent of the Turin Government to spoil the effect of the visit"— and others were propagating the fiction of illness. Holyoake insists that "any gentleman would have done as Garibaldi did" after receiving a hint from Gladstone that "a sojourn in the provinces might weaken the effect of his visit." CHAPTER XV SECULARIST VICISSITUDES AND CO-OPERATIVE PROGRESS

It is hardly necessary to observe that, while Holyoake willingly assisted revolutionary action on the Continent, he fully recognised the duty of constitutional procedure in the freer province of home politics. But before we trace his increasing interest in parliamentary work, it will be well to glance at the changing fortunes of the two great social movements he had done so much to establish. The middle term of his career brought him heavy disappointment with regard to the system of Secularism to which he had long devoted the greater part of his energy and hope. It passed largely into the hands of others, who did not share his broad social ideal of its work, and seemed to him to be in danger of falling away into mere Southwellism. On the other hand, the Co-operative Movement advanced with the stride of the young giant it was, and soon displaced Secularism as the central interest of his life.

In spite of the growing unpleasantness in the Secularist body, and the constant, silent pressure of nearly the whole of his cultivated friends, Holyoake would not desist from critical work. Press cuttings, of which bundles remain, were sent to him weekly, telling of the incredibly harsh treatment men still endured for not sharing the prevalent religious views; and the growth of a hostile scientific culture on the one hand and a Broad Church of strange elasticity on the other deepened his feeling for consistency. One incident of the early sixties has been described at some length by him in *Sixty Years,* and some details of it may be recounted now with more candour. This was the suicide of Gunner Scott, of the Royal Artillery, at Aldershot. On the 12th of August, 1860, he received a letter from Scott, complaining that he had entered the army on the word of the recruiting authorities that he would receive the pay of a bombardier from the first. The promise was at once ruled "unauthoritative," and he was ranked as a gunner. He had some education, and was employed as schoolmaster. He worked to the rank of bombardier, and was at last allowed to present himself for an examination for the Military Asylum at Chelsea, which he passed. But he was discovered to have works by Holyoake and other freethinkers in his kit, and, after a kind of trial before the colonel and officers, " on the charge of being an atheist," he was sent back amongst the gunners (7th Battery), and served through the Indian Mutiny.

Holyoake could do nothing for him, and he sought an interview with his colonel (Fitzmayer). The colonel said that "so long as he held those horrible opinions of atheism he would never allow him to hold any rank or appointment in the Royal Artillery." When Scott persisted (not too politely) he was hurried to the guardroom, and charged with "insubordination." A refusal to go to church brought a second charge of insubordination. The court-martial that followed was one-sided, and he was condemned with perfect technical correctness. His health gave way in prison, and he was sent to hospital, where surgeons, ladies, and chaplains tried to convert him. At last, despairing of getting release from the army or peace in it, he committed suicide. A comrade informed Holyoake that Scott had left all his small possessions to Holyoake, but the authorities sent nothing to him.

The courts of justice were still equally inclement to extreme heretics in most parts of the country, and in the professional or the political world one had carefully to conceal one's views. At the same time the new scientific culture was beginning to stand in menacing contrast to the religious views of the early part of the century. Lyell had published his *Principles of Geology* in 1830, and in 1859 Darwin issued his *Origin of Species.* In 1863 came Huxley's *Mans Place in Nature,* and the historic struggle was fairly opened. Holyoake followed the new culture with interest. He obtained journalistic appointments to attend the meetings of the British Association, and endeavoured to popularise their work. The success of this branch of his journalistic work can be seen from an early letter of Professor Tyndall to him in 1861:

"My Dear S1r,

"I did not think I could be caused to read any more than I have already done regarding the Dundee meeting. But you have fairly carried me along with you. I have rarely seen a pleasanter account of a scientific meeting, and I think this judgment is independent of the many kind things you say of me. "Believe me,

"Yours very truly,

"john Tyndall."

The Newcastle meeting in 1863 he reported in the *Morning Star.* With Herbert Spencer, a frequent visitor to his house, Holyoake had long been intimate, and I find a friendly letter from Professor L. Buchner, during a visit to England. Of his constant correspondence with students like Francis Newman I have already spoken.

Curiously, in the same year (1862) Holyoake had a second "bequest of a suicide." A Pole, Theophilus Jurecki, who had had kind words from Holyoake about some wonderful philosophy he had framed, was forced by poverty to take his life, and left the system and his box of clothes to Holyoake.

It will be opportune to insert a word here about the third brother of the Newman family, who corresponded industriously with Holyoake in 1861 and 1862. Charles Newman was an Agnostic, but it is not the unpopularity of his opinions that has condemned him to obscurity/

He had not only inferior ability, but was liable to mental trouble. In sending copy for the *Reasoner* he would sometimes warn Holyoake that his mind was failing, as it often did. His abler brothers had largely to maintain him, and the Cardinal has written in high terms of the purity of his character. His long, closely-written letters show wide philosophical and historical reading, but an inevitable failure of judgment. He speaks freely of having a " mental infirmity of a chronic character," from infancy upwards. One of his sanest letters is on his ailment, which he attributes to enteric trouble that was neglected in his boyhood. At times he writes with ability on philosophical subjects, though he says Holyoake only prints one-fourth of what he writes. His metaphysical tendency is, in the circumstances, remarkable. But the friendship was short-lived. In 1862 he collected (at Tenby, where he lived) five pennies for the anti-oath agitation, and added two shillings of his own. He professed to discover that it was applied to some other purpose, and concluded his correspondence with several quires of closely-written argument and censure.

This agitation to substitute an affirmation for an oath in all courts occupied much of Holyoake's time in 1861 and 1862, when Sir John Trelawny introduced a Bill to that purport. As early as 1858 a circular was issued to all the clergy urging them to use every effort to prevent "the abolition of Christian government," by permitting any such measure to pass. But the injustice suffered by conscientious objectors in all parts, and the gross treatment of them by many magistrates, inclined many Vol. 1. z politicians to grant relief. A letter to Holyoake, undated and unsigned (but with the initials ofW. Coningham, M.P. , I think), says that the writer expressed a hope to Lord Russell that oaths would soon be abolished, and the Premier replied: "I should not be sorry." Sir John Trelawny, after some correspondence with Holyoake, took charge of a Bill, and between February and June (1862) a hundred petitions (many very small) were presented to Parliament in its favour. But the Bill failed, and the agitation had to be carried on for many years more.

Amongst the contributors to Holyoake's Affirmation fund was Mr. John Stuart Mill, who had been friendly for some years. In 1859 he sent Holyoake a copy of his essay *On Liberty,* asking him not to review it until the other reviewers had done so. "It is likely enough to be called an infidel book in any case; but I would rather that people were not *prompted* to call it so." He said shortly afterwards that there had been "an amount of response to it far beyond what he expected." In 1861 he sent ten pounds towards the fund in support of Sir J. Trelawny's Bill, and he made further contributions afterwards. He differed from Holyoake as to the actual taking of an oath. Though he agreed that prominent freethinkers who had expressed public dissent from its terms ought not to take it, he maintained that for ordinary freethinkers it was a legitimate way of obtaining justice. The point offered a nice problem in utilitarian morality, and Holyoake differed strongly from his master. Mill's conclusion was:

"I conceive that when a bad law has made that a condition to the performance of a public duty, it may be taken without dishonesty by a person who acknowledges no binding force in the religious part of the formality; unless, as in your case, he has made it the special and particular work of his life to testify against such formalities, and against the beliefs with which they are associated."

Another letter of Mill's to Holyoake contains an interesting passage:

"The root of my difference with you is that you appear to accept the present constitution of the family and the whole of the priestly morality founded on and connected with it—which morality, in my opinion, thoroughly deserves the epithets of' intolerant, slavish, and selfish.'"

The letter, however, seems to belong to an earlier date (1848), and we may postpone discussion of it until we have occasion to touch on Mill's ethical development, in a later chapter.

The authority of Mill, who often made public his regard for Holyoake, and the rise of a formidable scientific opposition to current theology, gave great force to the popular attack conducted by the Secularists. In a different way the growth of the Broad Church favoured them. It could easily be described as a homage wrung perforce from theologians to the new culture. Holyoake pointed out the significance of the liberal theologians with his usual temperateness, and won the respect of many of them. Dr. Temple made pleasant reference to him in a letter to the *Times.* Canon Kingsley came in time to write him the following letter:

"My Dear Sir,

"I have just read your manly and sensible letter in the *National Reformer* on workers and their Unions. I agree with it thoroughly.... It is a bad business, and society owes much to a man in your peculiar position who will have the courage to take the tone, and to do the work, about it, which Mr. Hughes and Mr. Ludlow tell me you have done.

"Much as we disagree, and must, I fear, on many very important and solemn matters, your conduct in this has made me sincerely respect you, independently of, and indeed long before, the kind expressions, etc., from you in your letter about a book of mine with much of which you must utterly disagree.

"Believe me,

"My dear Sir,

"Yours sincerely,

"C. Kingsley."

We shall see that Professor Maurice and Judge Hughes came to adopt a similar tone.

One episode in the liberal theological movement of the time had an especial effect on the popular mind, and more closely interests us. This was the widespread agitation in regard to the biblical heresies of Bishop Colenso. It is not yet entirely known—it would possibly pain many people to know—how much Colenso owed to freethinkers. Some ten years ago an aged solicitor (Mr. Domville) showed me a list he had compiled in the sixties of many hundreds of agnostics. The sole purpose of compil-

ing it was to obtain subscriptions from them in aid of the Bishop of Natal's cause. Holyoake has given an interesting account of his connection with the bishop's heresies, and left papers and letters concerning it.

The carpenter who taught heresy to the Zulus who —popular legend had it—taught it to the Bishop of Natal, was a Secularist follower of Holyoake's. He took a Secularist library with him to Natal, where he worked for Colenso, and the bishop borrowed Holyoake's writings from him. It is not improbable that Ryder lent him also Lecount's *Hunt after the Devil,* which contained a number of the arithmetical criticisms of the Pentateuch that Colenso afterwards popularised. In 1858 he sent an account of the liberal bishop to the *Reasoner,* and, although Holyoake suppressed all names of persons and localities, it reached the eye of a rival Dissenting missionary, and led to trouble. The clergyman based on it an article, published in the *Natal Mercury,* on "Atheistic Socialism in Natal." Colenso dismissed his carpenter, but retained respect for Holyoake. In an earlier year Holyoake had found that the bishop was advertised to lecture at the Secularist Hall of Science in City Road. He at once wrote to him and pointed out the danger he incurred amongst his colleagues from the character of the place, and Colenso took the hint. When his friend Mr. Thomas Scott spoke to him disparagingly of Holyoake, Colenso told him to call at Fleet Street, and he "would find the devil not so black as he was painted." Scott became a life-long friend of Holyoake.

When (in 1863) Holyoake contributed to the controversy his little pamphlet, *Cumming wrong, Colenso right,* the bishop ordered two dozen copies of the publishers, and wrote as follows to Holyoake:

"The Bishop of Natal is much obliged to Mr. Holyoake for a copy of his reply to Dr. Cumming's publication on the Pentateuch.

"As so much has been said by Dr. Cumming and others—totally ignorant of the subject which they are discussing—of ' the want of scholarship,' 'ignorance of Hebrew criticism,' etc., which is exhibited in the Bishop's books, and as even Matthew Arnold has allowed himself to speak of it in *Macmillaris Magazine* as 'going forth amidst the titters of educated Europe'— a phrase which he seems to have borrowed from Mr. McCaul of the *Record,* who has been so smartly handled in the last number of 'Evangelical Christendom,' a journal in the service of his friends—the Bishop thinks it right to forward for Mr. Holyoake's perusal two or three letters which he has received from scholars of high character and European reputation...."

The letters were from Kalisch, Huffeld, and Kuenen. A passage from Holyoake's reply shows the temper in which he corresponded with many of the clergy at the time:

"My own views on many points are such as your Lordship would deeply dissent from. My very praise would be perilous to your Lordship, yet I cannot refrain from expressing how much I honour the Christian chivalry displayed in your works. I can reverence forms of faith not my own, and I can feel that the human spirit of Christianity, set free from Mosaical fetters, would be a ministration of mercy in Englisl1 homes as well as Kafflr kraals. I cannot but regard your Lordship's courageous efforts as adding new dignity to the English Church and race."

The correspondence afterwards became less formal, but has no particular interest. Colenso sent him a subscription for the fund for abolishing the oath. In a long letter he describes it as " demoralising," "superstitious" (" as it implies that the Divine Judge will be more present when appealed to by an oath, than when a deliberate lie is told in ordinary circumstances"), "illiberal," "unjust," and "impolitic." He said that "the best comment on the practical value of the system of taking oaths " was found in the statement of Baron Martin that "the offence of perjury was becoming exceedingly common: he did not believe there was a single day in which perjury was not committed in Courts of Justice." He thought the oath should be abolished altogether.

These different tendencies in the thought of the time gave opportunities for popular criticism of theology that had never existed before, and the audiences at Secularist meetings greatly increased. But the rift within the Secularist body that we considered in an earlier chapter now grew wider. In June 1861 the *Reasoner* was brought to a close, partly owing to Holyoake's illness and partly (I assume) to lack of support. It is difficult to understand on what grounds he started an entirely similar paper (but monthly) in August with the name of the *Counsellor.* There were only five issues of it. Mr. Bradlaugh was in the meantime having unpleasant experience with the *National Reformer* which he had begun in April 1860. He had as coeditor a freethinking lecturer of great popularity, Joseph Barker, who had just returned from America. Rumours of Barker's conversion to theistic views had preceded him, and were openly discussed in the *Reasoner;* but he seems to have evaded inquiries, if not equivocated, and he readily entered into editorial partnership with Bradlaugh, the most explicit atheist in the country. Before long the two halves of the paper presented a most grotesque spectacle of contradiction, and Mr. Bradlaugh rightly sought relief from the shareholders, who dismissed Barker.

This was in August 1861, the month in which Holyoake began to issue his *Counsellor.* It appears that the northern Secularists were now eager to bring about a co-operation of the two leaders, and very shortly afterwards Holyoake received an invitation from Mr. Bradlaugh to merge his *Counsellor* in the *Reformer,* and assist him in the production of the paper. What the precise terms of the co-operation were to be is a matter of dispute, and gave serious trouble afterwards. Bradlaugh contended that he invited Holyoake to take the position of " chief contributor," and Holyoake maintained that he was engaged as joint editor of the *Reformer.* The draft of agreement that Holyoake drew up, with an eye to possible differences, was not discoverable when such differences actually arose. It was at all events agreed that Holyoake should supply three pages of uncontrolled copy each week, and for this Bradlaugh would pay him two pounds out of the five allotted to him by the company.

Holyoake was eager to restore unity in the movement, but he consulted first a number of his more judicious friends at London. As far as the letters remain, they made an effort to dissuade him from abandoning his paper and joining the *Reformer.* Mr. Crawford, a well-known barrister (one of the prosecuting counsel to the Mint), and chairman of the Garibaldi Committee, wrote an insistent letter to turn him from his proposal. He reminded him, in strong terms, of the Wilks episode of four years previously (see p. 300), and urged that he had no security against the recurrence of some such unpleasantness. Others, observing the vagueness of the terms of the engagement, represented to him that, if he accepted the post of a mere contributor, he would "lower himself in the eyes of his friends" by occupying a position lower than the one Barker had held on the paper. This difficulty seems (from letters I find in Holyoake's papers, written to him by shareholders in the company) to have been removed by a definite offer of dual editorship of the journal.

Holyoake disregarded the advice of his friends. He closed the *Counsellor,* and in January 1862 began to work on the *National Reformer.* "One Paper and One Party" was the attractive message he gave out to his followers in the last issue of the *Counsellor* (December 1861). The circulation of the paper at once arose to 8,000, with prospect of increase. But Crawford was right. In less than three months Bradlaugh represented to a meeting of the shareholders that the arrangement he had made had miscarried, and the schism reopened. Bradlaugh was confirmed in his editorial capacity, and he asked Holyoake to write two columns each week, instead of supplying and controlling three pages, at the same salary as before. Holyoake naturally resented the change as lowering his position, and maintained that he had been engaged for twelve months on the original basis. He claimed the balance of the salary due to him on their first contract—a sum of 81 18j. *od.* They agreed to settle the dispute by arbitration, if possible; but as Bradlaugh appointed W. J. Linton, who had neither legal training nor an impartial feeling to Holyoake (the reader will remember his vicious attack in the *Liberator),* and Holyoake appointed Mr. Crawford, whose feeling towards Bradlaugh I have indicated, an agreement was impossible. For the delicate office of umpire they chose Mr. Shaen, a distinguished solicitor of progressive sympathies, whose character and friendship for Holyoake were well known to both. His rigid feeling of justice and his legal skill were unquestioned—before the verdict was given, at all events. The only comment on the result that Holyoake has left is one line in his diary (July 31st, 1863): "Arbitration awarded to me," and we may leave the matter there.

The *Secular World and Social Economist* had been projected by Holyoake in 1861, and was started by him as soon as he quitted the *Reformer.* It went entirely on the lines of the *Reasoner,* except, perhaps, that it gave even more attention to politics and to Co-operative matters. He was at once assured of considerable support. His older friends, Mr. Gwynne, Mr. Trevelyan, etc., generously contributed. The Yorkshire Secular Societies, the strongest branch of the movement, held a conference, and unanimously resolved to support Holyoake's paper. The Sheffield delegates were especially indignant with Mr. Bradlaugh because he had, they alleged, suppressed the report of a meeting of Sheffield shareholders in his paper. But the scission seems to have weakened the movement generally. In August the *Secular World* was reduced to a monthly issue, and in January 1865 it was renamed the *Reasoner* (as a monthly organ). On the other hand, Mr. Bradlaugh abandoned the *Reformer* in February 1863, the company that owned it being liquidated some months previously.

From the middle of the sixties Brad-laugh had the greater influence over the Secular movement as a whole. In a popular movement the powerful physique, sonorous voice, and real gift of oratory that Bradlaugh possessed were decisive advantages. The fact, too, that religious interest of a critical character was exceptionally inflamed at that time by the tendencies of culture that I have noted favoured Bradlaugh's programme. Holyoake was not willing, as his critics said, to dissemble his views on religion; his position in the press and political life was one of constant sacrifice because he would not do this. His position was that he "would not make atheism the badge of the party." In truth, however, he wanted criticism to be so subordinated to positive culture that theists might join them. His ideal was an impossible one. In spite of all their respect for him, the Secularists felt that their *distinctive* work was criticism of theology, and Bradlaugh's plan suited them. Not, indeed, that Holyoake ceased to be one of their chief lecturers. His provincial tours continued year after year, though there was less adventure in them now that his manner was mature. The *Yarmouth Independent,* to quote one of many provincial notices, spoke of him in 1862 as "a gentleman whose courtesy in debate, sincerity, eloquence, and intrepidity have won him the respect of many eminent Christians." His subjects were "secular" in his broad sense of the word, and many a clergyman took the chair for him, or entertained him. At London his detractors were silenced, and he lectured regularly. There is a letter written by one of them in 1863— the end is unfortunately missing, but it seems to be from Maughan—expressing sorrow. "Misled in some particulars," the writer says, "I wrote of Mr. Holyoake with more impetuosity and firmness than I should in my calmer moments have done.... Let me say distinctly that any imputation on Mr. Holyoake's personal honour I never intended to cast.... Mr. Holyoake has, for a long series of years, advocated Freethought with rare tact, ability, and courtesy. While some have gloried in edifying a mob with fustian and advo-

cating infidelity with the same brutal ferocity that characterises the converted costermonger, he has invariably aimed at something higher." One by one the frivolous calumnies were disposed of. With the co-operation of a London barrister, Mr. J. Clark, Holyoake founded a new centre in Fitzroy Square (the "Metropolitan Institute"), and here and at other metropolitan centres continued to "aim at something higher." 1 The Unitarian *Inquirer* made friendly reference to the *Secular World,* as the *Saturday Review* had done to the *Reasoner.* In 1864 Holyoake simultaneously conducted the *English Leader,* of which we shall see a little in the next chapter. He was, of course, writing for half a dozen ordinary journals all these years.

From his wearying experience with the Secularist body Holyoake turned with relief to the consistent growth of the Co-operative Movement. In the early sixties the northern Co-operative Societies were hampered by the generally disastrous effect of the American War and the Cotton Famine, but it was noticed that their members suffered less than improvident neighbours. The story of Rochdale, told in attractive manner by Holyoake in 1857 (and before that in the *Leader),* was slowly moving over the country, and indeed the Continent. His friend Talandier translated the Rochdale history into French. Several inquirers wrote to him from Italy in 1861. The editor of the *Popolo d'Italia* asked him for further information about the "Pionieri di Rochdale," and Dominico Longo wrote from Sicily. Longo seems to have thought it was quite sufficient to put on his envelope,

"Au tres Illustre Philosophe,
Monsieur Holyoake,
Londres," and our admirable postal servants discovered the "illustrious philosopher." A few years later Luigi Cossa (Professor of Political Economy at the Pavia University) sought Co-operative information of him.

In this country he was recognised as the chief writer and propagandist of Co-operative principles. The Paddington Equitable Society asked him to be one of its arbitrators in 1860, and we find him in constant touch with Societies throughout the sixties. At the Social Science Congress in London in 1862 he read a paper on "The Moral Mistakes of Co-operators," which the section (including the Rev. W. Molesworth) begged him to publish. In 1863 he took a more important step. There were at that time some 20 or 30—no one was quite sure—Co-operative Societies in the metropolis, out of about 460 in the country at large. The Christian Socialist organisation had long since disappeared, and these stores fell into individual ways, which were often peculiar. Organisation was urgently needed, and Holyoake took the initiative. For more than ten years he had been almost the one journalistic link of the English Societies. The Lancashire and Yorkshire Societies were represented in a little weekly *Co-operator,* of private ownership, after 1860, but the real chronicle of the progress of the Co-operative Movement from 1850 to 1868 is to be found in Holyoake's columns in the *Reasoner, Leader,* and *Secular World.* The *Secular World* made a special feature of its Co-operative section, and this was edited by a Secularist friend of Holyoake's named Edger.

It appeared, in less drastic form, as a penny pamphlet entitled *Moral Errors which Endanger the Permanence of Co-operative Societies.*

The two now joined in an attempt to unite the stores that were scattered over London, and a meeting of secretaries was convened at a coffee-house in Theobald's Road, kept by a Co-operator and Secularist with the Dickensonian name of Jaggers. Eleven secretaries attended, and presently they started a "London Association for the Promotion of Co-operation," with Francis Newman, J. S. Mill, and E. Vansittart Neale as honorary members. From the coffee-house the Association found it possible to pass to the Whittington Club (in the Strand) for its meetings, and J. S. Mill was induced by Holyoake to deliver to the members there his first public speech.

But at this juncture Holyoake met a man whose association with him in the Co-operative Movement has become historic. His diary notes that in the spring of 1863 he "first met Mr. E. O. Greening" at Manchester. Holyoake was lecturing at Manchester, and staying at the house of a wealthy young German, Max Kyllman, who had taken the house built for himself by the architect Waterhouse on Oxford Road. Kyllman was interested in Co-operative matters, and Greening was then editing a small Co-operative journal, the *Industrial Partnerships Record.* Both Greening and Holyoake held firmly to what one may call apostolic Co-operation—the sharing of profits with employees and care for education —and they at once entered upon their life-long and cordial friendship. Events were then occurring in the Lancashire Co-operative world that drew closer together all men with these ideas.

Mr. Greening tells me that he had certainly seen Holyoake, and they had probably met, before 1863: chiefly at the Socialist or Secularist Hall, where Mr. Greening was, I fancy, a polite young opponent.

I have previously related how the Rochdale Pioneers had applied their surplus capital to productive enterprise. In the mills they erected they adhered to the original principle of profit-sharing. The mills had a period of great prosperity, with the result that workers in it—sharing all the profits between them after five per cent, had been paid on capital—found themselves in a singularly fortunate position. The mill could have paid 25 or 30 per cent, on the quarter of a million capital sunk in it. The capitalists were, of course, to a great extent the workers of Rochdale, and they soon came to reflect uneasily on the large sums that went to the minority of them who could be employed in their own mill. An agitation against the original basis of profit-distribution was started, and after a fierce struggle it was abolished. The decision has affected the whole history of the Cooperative Movement. The "practical men," as the victors at Rochdale styled themselves, obtained control of the movement, and the "theorists"—who fought for the original

idea of sharing profits among the employees after paying a moderate interest on capital—were kept in a critical minority. We shall see how their doctrine afterwards found embodiment in a separate Co-Partnership movement. It is even claimed by them that the fatal decision at Rochdale led to a rapid growth of modern Socialism. Certainly F. Lasalle in Germany used it as a powerful argument in persuading the workers that Co-operation was only a slightly modified form of capitalism, and that they must turn to industrial Collectivism. Holyoake and Greening were prominent amongst the idealists. Their first answer to the Rochdale decision Molesworth says that during the cotton-famine many had sold their shares to people who had not the Co-operative ideal at heart, and that these mere speculators were responsible for the change. —*Hist. Engl.,* Ill, 214.

was to establish a mill at Manchester on the original basis of profit-sharing. Holyoake could have little to do with this remote experiment, but Mr. Greening was deeply interested in it, and Kyllman provided the capital. Unfortunately, the tide of 1 prosperity had by this time turned, and their undertaking struggled in shallow water, and shortly failed. The failure was wholly due to extrinsic causes, but it naturally strengthened their opponents. The Wholesale Department, which began in 1864, fell under their influence, and its vast organisation—its profits grew from £267 to,£19,963 in the first ten years (and to more than three millions in 1904)—is framed on their principle.

Holyoake and Greening now united their forces in the presentment of the original Co-operative doctrine. In 1868 they brought out together the first national organ of the Co-operative societies, the *Social Economist.* Mr. Walter Morrison promised the small capital required *(£300),* and Mr. Greening merged his journal in the *Economist.* He stipulated that Holyoake should be "editor, conductor, and manager," and he himself would take care of the accounts; though I find him also doing valuable work in promoting the circulation. "In truth," he wrote to Holyoake, "I feel as regards the paper that it is the only concern I have to do with, or have had to do with for some time, in which I have a strong man to lean upon, and you must not take it ill if I leave you pretty much alone in the management." The paper proved of great value to the movement, which was now spreading rapidly. "A good, respectable-looking paper is of some benefit to the Co-operative cause, like living in a decent house is good for self-respect," Morrison wrote. Mill wrote to him: "I always look through the *Social Economist,* and have been struck with the great improvement in its quality."

Mr. Greening was convinced that a closer co-operation amongst the idealists of the south and the business men of the north was desirable, and in the later sixties he removed to London. He had seen the modern movement in Manchester arise from the fusion of the Owenite Socialist and Christian Socialist workers, and he exerted himself to effect a similar junction at London. With the help of W. Morrison, Thomas Hughes, Cowper-Temple, and others he started, in 1867, the Agricultural and Horticultural Association in Long Acre, on a labour co-partnership basis, of which he is still the presiding genius. In the first ten years its membership rose from 174 to 1,113. Finally, in 1869 was celebrated the first of the series of Congresses of the modern Co-operative movement, and it was attended by the Comte de Paris, the Earl of Lichfield, the Hon. E. Lyulph Stanley, Mr. Fawcett, and many other distinguished social students. Holyoake was made a member of the first Central Board.

Thus there was on the Co-operative side some compensation for the distress experienced in other sections of Holyoake's work. Indeed, his position had now so greatly improved that in his fiftieth year (1867) he must have looked back with genial pride on the strenuous exertions of the preceding thirty years. He had begun his public career, little more than twenty years before, in such obscurity that he could be described in an official document as "a labourer "

and treated with the brutality that it is customary to show to hardened felons. From the shadow of the jail he had come, penniless, to try his fortune in the life of the metropolis. By conviction and sympathy he was detained amongst the most derided and despised bodies in the country, and was forced to associate with social outcasts, poor workers, and, too often, vulgar adventurers. But in those ranks of ungentle warriors, superciliously dismissed by cultivated journals as "familiar with every jail in the country," he had found inspiring examples of self-sacrifice and moral heroism.

Their phrases struck stridently on the ears of the wealthy and the politician, but he knew well the pervading misery and injustice that had given edge to them. Melodious periods would not form in that world of moral and social discord. It was his distinction that he learned to utter the warmest sympathy with "the people" in terms that the middle and the wealthier class could entertain, and to move with respect amongst deeply religious men and women while he maintained an unflinching protest against what he thought to be false in their beliefs.

So much of the labour we have considered was so illpaid, or wholly unpaid, that his income was still poor, and his bank empty. One grows accustomed to reading in his diary such lines as: "The past two years have been eleemosynary, propagandic, and precarious, to terminate early, I trust, in their unsatisfactory respects." As long as he retained his strength those features never did fall from his years. With his journalistic skill, which was well appreciated in his fiftieth year, he might have earned much, but he chose to keep his freedom to utter unwelcome truths. He was content to earn enough to support a bright little home and to educate his children; though in this friends were helpful. In the beginning of 1862 he had removed from Tavistock Square to a small villa in the Oval Road, Regent's Park. He wrote to J. S. Mill:

"I have a pleasant home here, surrounded by more than half an acre of

plantation. Mr. Das Haldar, a Bengal gentleman who visited me, called it a Bungalow.... In summer it is a Paradise. "

"Dymoke Lodge"—"the nunnery," his daughter called it—had many interesting visitors. Amongst them were so mixed a company as Karl Blind, W. Hale White,

Herbert Spencer, W. Coningham, F. Newman, T.

Cooper, Stopford Brooke, Somerset Beaumont, T. Allsop, Vol. 1. A A

J. G. Crawford, T. Hughes, Major Bell, Mr. Pulzsky, Col. Clinton, Dr. Shorthouse (editor of *Sporting Times),* Toulmin Smith, Cowen, Ashurst, Shaen, Sir J. Stansfeld, and others.

How he found time for social engagements it is difficult to see, but one is glad to find that he did. Mr. Ashurst had succeeded to his father's friendship as well as ability, and there was open house for Holyoake at Norfolk Crescent. Asking Holyoake to a New Year dinner in 1863, he invites him to bring his daughter, but warns: "We are frivolous—in our unguarded moments—and young ladies nowadays are not frivolous, but intellectual, d d intellectual, I think!"

Stopford Brooke was one of the clergymen with whom he formed a warm friendship, as his letters tell. He was brought to Dymoke Lodge by his brother-in-law, Somerset Beaumont, and both became very friendly. Toulmin Smith (son of his old Unitarian tutor, and an able barrister) writes to him:

"Be assured that henceforth you will be the one man in all London who will be most cordially welcome at my house, and with whom I shall feel that I have the most genuine sympathies, present and past."

His old Chartist friend, T. Cooper, wrote warm letters: "Oh, that these things the Bradlaugh trouble might drive you to Christ. The whole Christian Church would welcome you and rejoice over you."

There was no lack of varied interest. One day it is an invitation to lunch with the engineer Mr. Francis Train, the inventor of the tram-car. Another day (or week) is spent with the sporting editor, Dr. Shorthouse, his neighbour in Fleet Street. Shorthouse hears that he has '' drawn Lord Lynn" in some handicap his neighbours have induced him to try, and says: "Don't be an ass, I'll give you ten pounds for it." At Mrs. P. A. Taylor's, where he is a constant visitor, he meets Bishop Colenso, and other religious and philosophical thinkers. Mr. Garth Wilkinson sends on Henry James to see him, and Moncure Conway writes: "In my own work far away in the west I have seen the good results of your labours as a thinker and a friend of man. Mr. W. Hale White ("Mark Rutherford") dedicates a pamphlet to him in 1866, and when Holyoake modestly protests, says: "You are all wrong as to the 'honour' done you. The honour is rather mine than yours." The eminent politician, Mr. Roebuck, writes: "Seeing your name, I read the article, to do which was contrary to my usual custom, as generally I read nothing respecting myself.... Your critique not only demands my warmest thanks, but excites my special wonderment." Charles Forster, the biographer of Landor and Dickens, wrote: "I beg you to believe that I shall at all times have an «««professional pleasure in seeing you here upon these subjects." At Woburn Buildings and for some years at Dymoke Lodge he had the artist Merritt living with them. Merritt, who was of a sensitive and irritable nature, left them in 1866, and, though I find friendly relations continued between them, it was suggested af-

ter Merritt's death that Holyoake had profited unduly by his lodging with them. This is very clearly the reverse of the truth, as the figures and entries in the diaries show.

The next chapter, on his political activity, will greatly enlarge the circle of those who esteemed him, when we shall find him in friendly correspondence with Lord Elcho, Lord Amberley, Lord Stanley, and others. In view of his earlier experiences and his actual views, expounded weekly in the press and on the platform, there is biographical significance in these letters. In 1867 Lady Strathmore wrote to thank him for some journalistic reference, and sent a portrait from her " little boy." In the following year the dowager Lady Buxton invited him to join a British Association party that was

'Holyoake's daughter Eveline was married to Mr. Praill by Dr. Conway in 1866, at South Place Chapel.

visiting her place at Northrepps. Sir Charles Buxton often wrote to him. In 1863, when he was on a lecturing tour in the north, he spent a day or two with Mr. and Lady Beaumont, and was taken by them down their lead mines. Lord and Lady Suffield, Sir John Shelley, and other guests, were staying at Allenheads at the time. I will conclude with the citation of a passage from the *Westminster Review* (January 1869), though it more properly belongs to the following chapter. It is taken from a comment on Holyoake's election manifesto at Birmingham in 1868. But it is more valuable

as an indication of the place that he had won in public regard, and may close the series that I have chosen from the many letters before me.

"We are glad to be able to take for our text so excellent a piece of true literature as the report of Mr. Holyoake's speech at Birmingham. He must be a very mean man or a very ignorant man who can read this speech without the sincerest admiration for the energy, the calmness, the penetrative sagacity, and yet withal the delicate appreciation of all that is not wholly bad in those he would oppose, evinced by the speaker."

With these many assurances ot success about him, and a long record of useful public service behind him, Holyoake entered on the period of mature manhood. He was very far yet from having reached the highest point of his career. More than half his public life, and the great bulk of his literary work, still lie before us. But it is clear that he had passed so far through struggles that test character no less than frame without falling from the high standard he had set up in obscure Halls of Science thirty years before.

Lightning Source UK Ltd.
Milton Keynes UK
UKOW06f1923041113

220437UK00007B/273/P